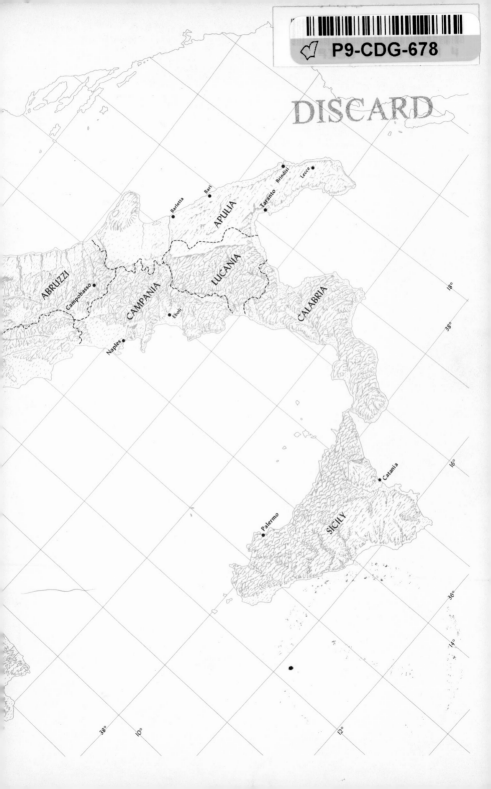

The United States and ITALY

THE AMERICAN FOREIGN POLICY LIBRARY

Crane Brinton, Editor

The United States and Britain
Revised edition. Crane Brinton

The United States and South America
The Northern Republics Arthur P. Whitaker

The United States and China
Revised and enlarged. John King Fairbank

The United States and Scandinavia Franklin D. Scott

The United States and Japan
Third edition. Edwin O. Reischauer

The United States and France Donald C. McKay

The United States and Turkey and Iran Lewis V. Thomas
and Richard N. Frye

The United States and Mexico
Revised edition, enlarged. Howard F. Cline

The United States and India and Pakistan
Revised and enlarged. W. Norman Brown

The United States and Italy
Revised edition. H. Stuart Hughes

The United States and Argentina Arthur P. Whitaker

The Balkans in Our Time Robert Lee Wolff

The United States and the Southwest Pacific C. Hartley Grattan

The United States and Israel Nadav Safran

The United States and North Africa
Morocco, Algeria, and Tunisia Charles F. Gallagher

The
United States
and
ITALY

REVISED EDITION

H. Stuart Hughes

Harvard University Press
Cambridge, Massachusetts
1965

Distributed in Great Britain by
OXFORD UNIVERSITY PRESS
LONDON

ENDPAPER MAPS BY R. L. WILLIAMS

LIBRARY OF CONGRESS CATALOG CARD NUMBER 65-13845

PRINTED IN THE UNITED STATES OF AMERICA

TO THE MEMORY
OF
MY MOTHER

Note on the Revised Edition

The present editor can claim no credit for this welcome revised edition of Professor Hughes's book. *The United States and Italy,* which has proved to be one of the most successful books in the Harvard Foreign Policy Library, was commissioned and appeared under the editorship of his predecessor. Professor Hughes has, most happily for the present editor, fully lived up to the intention of his original editor and teacher, the late Donald McKay, that a volume in this series be thoroughly revised at suitable intervals. For these books, though they are by no means concerned solely with current events, are meant to serve as guides toward an informed public opinion on American foreign policy. Clearly, in a world such as ours of rapid change, much of importance in Italy has happened since the original edition of this book in 1953. Professor Hughes has continued his special interest in Italian affairs, and gives us in this new edition the fruit of this unbroken first-hand study of that fascinating land, which is in many respects today singularly unlike what many generations of Americans have thought it to be.

CRANE BRINTON

February 1965
Cambridge, Massachusetts

Acknowledgments

While it is impossible to list all the people—Italian, American, and British—who have contributed to my understanding of contemporary Italy, I wish to acknowledge my particular debt to the following: Carlo Almagià, Vittorio Calef, Antonio Calvi, Mario Einaudi, Aldo Garosci, Felix Gilbert, Vittorio Ivella, Arturo Carlo Jemolo, Carlo Levi, Philip A. Mangano, Gabriele Morello, Ernesto Rossi, Gaetano Salvemini, Victor Sullam, and Cecil and Sylvia Sprigge.

I owe a more direct debt to Hollis Chenery, who read and criticized the sections of the book dealing with economic problems.

A special word of personal appreciation goes to Winston and Giorgina Burdett, who have taught me how to bridge the gap between the American and Italian traditions.

Finally, I should like to offer my homage to the memory of that devoted advocate of Italian-American understanding, Count Carlo Sforza, who in the last years of his life honored me with his friendship and encouragement.

June 25, 1953   H. S. H.

Preface to the Revised Edition

With the passage of twelve years in which so many things in Italy have changed so basically, it has proved necessary to make substantial alterations in the original text of this book. While the first six chapters have been only lightly revised, Chapters 7 and 8 (combining the previous Chapters 8 and 9) have undergone major surgery, and the final four consist almost entirely of new material. The appendixes have also been brought up to date. Parts of the new Chapters 9 and 12 have already been published in *The Virginia Quarterly Review* (Spring 1954 and Summer 1958) and in *Commentary* (October 1964).

In the same twelve years I have made many new friends in Italy whose conversation has substantially enriched my presentation. I think particularly of Mario Casalini, Renzo Conte, Cesare Mannucci, Guglielmo Negri, Rosario Romeo, Manlio Rossi-Doria, Giorgio Spini, Leo Valiani, Franco Venturi, and Paolo Vittorelli.

I am also grateful to my wife, Judy, for her unfailing encouragement. My secretary, Nanette Mengel, gave me constant help both in typing the manuscript and in protecting my working time. Dante Della Terza and Federico Mancini kindly read and criticized the newly-added chapters.

H. Stuart Hughes

February 1965
Cambridge, Massachusetts

Contents

1. Terra Incognita 3
   1. The Course of Italian-American Relations 3
   2. The Rediscovery of Italy 9

2. The Land and Its People 14
   1. North and South 16
   2. The Regions of Italy 22
   3. The Italian Population 28
   4. Social Characteristics 36

3. The Legacy of History 42
   1. Glory and Humiliation 42
   2. The Manner of Unification 46
   3. The Parliamentary Regime 50
   4. Prelude to a National Revival 55
   5. The Collapse of Italian Democracy 59

4. The Legacy of Fascism: The Corporate State 65
   1. The Theory and the Practice 68
   2. The Institutions of the Corporate State 74
   3. The Government and the Classes 83

5. The Legacy of Fascism: The Church and the Opposition 93
   1. The Reconciliation with the Church 93
   2. The Opposition 99
   3. The Reckoning 107

6. The Second World War 112
   1. The Fall of Mussolini 115
   2. The Forty-five Days and the Armistice 118
   3. The Governments of the South 123
   4. The Partisans in the North 127

7. De Gasperi and the Triumph of Christian Democracy 133
   1. The "Wind of the North" 134
   2. The Coming of De Gasperi 140

3. The Peace Treaty   148
4. The Institutional Solution   152
5. Christian Democracy in Power   156
6. The Disloyal Opposition   163

8. Economic Recovery and Land Reform   171
    1. The Structure of the Italian Economy   171
    2. The Stages of Economic Recovery   174
    3. Fiscal Reform and the Bureaucratic State   178
    4. The Standard of Living   181
    5. Population Pressure and Agrarian Tenure   183
    6. The Progress of Land Reform   190

9. The Heirs of De Gasperi and the "Opening to the Left" 196
    1. The Fall of De Gasperi   196
    2. The Search for a Political Formula   201
    3. The Election of 1958   205
    4. The Tambroni "Adventure"   211
    5. The "Opening to the Left"   215

10. Economic Expansion and Planning   219
    1. Planning and the Common Market   220
    2. The Role of Parastatal Enterprise   223
    3. Population Shifts and Social Stresses   227
    4. Unfinished Business   230

11. The Cultural "Renaissance"   236
    1. Post-Crocean Social Criticism   237
    2. The Universe of Neorealism   242
    3. From Fantasy to Psychology in Depth   246

12. Italy in the Western Community   251
    1. A European Foreign Policy   251
    2. The New Political Course   256
    3. The Ideological Alternatives   264

APPENDIX I: Charts and Statistics   269

APPENDIX II: Suggested Reading   276

Index   287

The United States and ITALY

1

Terra Incognita

1. THE COURSE OF ITALIAN-AMERICAN RELATIONS

AMERICAN relations with Italy today rest on a paradox—a paradox concealing a profound misunderstanding. For Americans, Italy is a land that seems greatly familiar: actually it is little known. Italy appears in many capacities in the present configuration of United States foreign policy: as one of the four great powers of Western Europe—an indispensable partner, first in the European Recovery Program, subsequently in the Atlantic Alliance; as a friend in one World War and an enemy in the next—forgiven and reaccepted into the democratic fraternity; as the territorial headquarters of the Catholic Church, the birthplace of modern fascism, and the home of the most important Communist party in the non-Communist world. In all these guises, Italy thrusts itself on the attention of the American newspaper reader. Yet in no one of them does it fix his attention for very long. Italy seems omnipresent—but never very important. From none of the major international groupings that link the Western world together is Italy absent; yet in none does she play the leading role. Only as the directors of world Catholicism can Italians claim an unquestioned pre-eminence.

This has been true ever since the unification of the peninsula in the decade between 1859 and 1870 made Italy the last of the great powers, both in date of formation and in physical power. And in general—despite epochs of frantic national aspiration—Italians have accepted with grace and good humor their country's modest position in the world. For Americans, however, this intermediate situation has given Italy a deceptive appearance of familiarity. The American tends to take Italy for granted and to assume that he knows more about it than he actually does. He visits it as a tourist and, having paid his respects to the art of Florence and the restaurants of Rome, comes away with the feeling that he understands Italy's present-day problems. He finds its language so easy that he does not bother to learn it. And he ascribes to native charm, dirt, or congenital incapacity, the distressing Italian tardiness in arriving at a social and political equilibrium.

This again is a long-standing situation: the mixture of familiarity and strangeness, of admiration and contempt, in the American attitude toward Italy, dates back to the earliest contacts between Americans and Italians. When the United States was founded—when no Italian nation as yet existed—Italians were already playing a not unimportant role in American life. It was Dr. Filippo Mazzei, a Tuscan friend of Jefferson and Madison, who supplied the former with at least one of the celebrated phrases he later used in the Declaration of Independence; it was Colonel Francesco Vigo who helped open the great Northwest, and Paolo Busti who founded the city of Buffalo. Yet these were simply individuals—casual Italian settlers or adventurers, frequently drawn from the wealthier and more educated classes of their own country, who had felt stifled by the atmosphere of petty despotism at home and had yearned for the personal freedom that the new nation offered them. They were a small selection of Italians, personally distinguished and hence unrepresentative. As opposed to the large number of Americans of British, Irish, Dutch, German—or even French—origin, there were few Italians in the United States until the last quarter of the nineteenth century.

Nor was there any one of the Italian states that became involved, in either a friendly or a hostile fashion, in regular and close relations with the government of the United States. Italy and America went their separate ways, with interests that seldom conflicted or coincided. A certain sentimental interest linked the two in the middle of the century—when the Italian struggle for the unity of the peninsula paralleled in time the American war to preserve a unity already attained. Throughout the period of the Risorgimento, Italian political refugees found a haven in the United States; in the year 1850–51 the great Garibaldi worked as a journeyman candlemaker on Staten

Island. But even this sort of contact was largely a question of personal sympathy between active minorities in both countries. Until well after the Civil War, American interest in Italy was virtually restricted to a vague friendliness borne across the sea by the sort of people who could afford to travel—a friendliness expressing itself in a vast and frequently quite uncritical admiration for Italian art and literature.

This is the first of the two main forms in which American contact with Italians has traditionally manifested itself. In the nineteenth century—and up to the First World War—Italy was familiar ground to cultivated Americans. The literary leaders of New England read Petrarch and Dante—Longfellow even translated *The Divine Comedy*—and on their trips to the peninsula they viewed with admiration the masterpieces of Renaissance art. It is not entirely clear whether they understood and approved all that they saw: Hawthorne's *The Marble Faun* reflects the disarray of nice New Englanders confronted with the unblushing sensuality of Rome. Yet properly imprisoned as plaster casts and faithfully executed copies, all but the most shocking of Italian works of art could be transported back across the Atlantic and in the chaster atmosphere of America become surprisingly demure. Thus suitably diluted, Italian art passed into the cultural equipment of the well-educated American. And similarly it was expected that the American of culture should possess at least a rudimentary knowledge of the Italian language. Nor was it too unlikely that he or she might contract an Italian marriage: like the sister of Henry Adams or a heroine out of Henry James, the sensitive American might find in Italy the sort of sympatheic life companion of which his own country seemed to be in such short supply.

These Italian-Americans by marriage looked and thought of themselves as virtually of another race from that newer type of Italian-American that began to pour off the immigrant ships in a steadily increasing stream beginning in the decade of the 1870's. Swarthy, ill-washed, uneducated, the peasant immigrant was something new to the American experience of things Italian. Even the language he spoke seemed to bear little resemblance to the language of Dante. Although he worked hard and usually led a life of austere self-denial, the Italian immigrant seldom succeeded in making a place for himself in American life. The older-established inhabitants looked on him with suspicion—sensing that here for the first time in American history there had appeared upon the scene a large national group that could not be fitted into the traditional American pattern. And the Italian immigrant seemed to confirm their fears by stubbornly clinging to his old ways and by his pathetic efforts to save money against the day when he might return across the sea to his native village. Thus the second of the characteristic forms of American contact with Italians very soon crystallized into hostility—occasionally mitigated by an amused tolerance spilling over into contempt.

It was no accident, then, that the first serious diplomatic incident between Italy and the United States—the "Mafia" incident—should have arisen out of the situation of these immigrants in their new country. The scene was New Orleans, where a large number of Sicilians had settled. On March 14, 1891, eleven of these Sicilians were lynched by an angry mob as suspects (although some of them had already been tried and acquitted) in the recent murder of the local chief of police. The result was an outburst of indignation both in Italy and among Italians in the United States. The Italian government—in line with the customary international procedure in such cases—demanded an indemnity. Secretary of State Blaine replied that under the American federal system Louisiana alone had jurisdiction over the case. This lesson in constitutional law the Italian Ambassador refused to accept, Blaine lost his temper, and the Ambassador was subsequently recalled to Rome—sped on his way by truculent and derisive comments from the American press. But there was no total rupture of relations: a chargé d'affaires remained in Washington, and the anger in Rome began to cool when it was discovered that only three of the murdered men were actually Italian subjects. Eventually the American government agreed to close the incident by paying "as a friendly act" the sum of $25,000.

From then until the First World War Italian-American relations remained untroubled. The United States took no official notice of Italy's one major foreign adventure—the seizure of Tripolitania and Cyrenaica from Turkey in 1911–12. And even the outbreak of general war in 1914 brought little change in the relations between the two countries; in this respect, the most important effect of the hostilities was to cut off the flow of Italian immigration that had reached its all-time high in the preceding decade. In 1917, however, the American declaration of war brought the United States and Italy into military alliance; both of them late arrivals on the side of the Entente powers, they now rather unexpectedly found themselves allies. Here again, Italy was present, but nearly forgotten: Americans might have strong emotional sympathy with the presumed struggle for democracy being waged by Britain and France —few of them thought of Italy's role in the conflict. And it was only a handful of Americans, like those ambulance drivers immortalized by Ernest Hemingway in his *A Farewell to Arms,* who actually saw service on the Italian front. Most Americans, if they thought of Italy's part in the alliance at all, reflected the widespread disappointment over the Italian contribution to the war effort: the Italians, they concluded, might be fine artists or stonemasons, but they made poor soldiers.

The threatened misunderstanding between the two allies-by-accident flared into open hostility at the Peace Conference of 1919. In January of that year President Wilson was greeted by deliriously enthusiastic crowds when he paid a visit to Italy just before the opening of the conference. Four months later he failed utterly in his attempt to appeal to the Italian people over the heads of their official delegates at Paris. What had happened in the meantime was that Wilson had shown an unwonted firmness in resisting the Italians' claim for the greater part of the territorial reward promised them in the secret treaties that had brought them into the war. It is true that the Italian negotiators had shown themselves inept—more particularly in adding to their other demands a claim for the port of Fiume, which had not been specified in the original treaties. At the same time there was merit in the Italian contention that Wilson had been accommodating so long as the claims of France, Britain, and the British dominions were under discussion, and had failed to take a stand on the purity of his principles until he came to the demands of the less influential Italians. The breach that had opened between Italy and the United States was never fully healed. Wilson held out to the last, and the Italians were left to settle their Adriatic frontier by separate negotiations with the new state of Yugoslavia.

The sense of hurt national pride left among the Italians by the disappointments they had sustained at the Peace Conference was a fateful legacy to the future. It had more than a little to do with the coming to power of Mussolini three years later. Few Americans, however, saw the connection, or their country's involvement in the tragic difficulties that led to the collapse of Italian democracy. Again, the American newspaper reader was reminded of Italy only rarely, and then usually in connection with some other more important power. When one scans the references to Italy in the chronicle of American foreign relations in the twenties and early thirties, one finds only two recurring problems—war debts and the reduction of naval armaments. In both these connections, Italy figured alongside France as a defaulting debtor and a power unaccountably intransigent in maintaining a navy far larger than it seemed able to afford.

Although Americans might not notice it at the time, the advent of Mussolini was to prove one of two key developments of the early twenties that would radically alter the character of the traditional relations between Italians and Americans. The first was the passage of the American quota laws of 1921 and 1924. By the terms of these sweeping measures, Italian immigration to the United States—which in 1913 had totaled nearly 300,000—was reduced to a trickle. The annual quota was set at 5800, but fewer than that number could actually comply with all the specified formalities. In the quarter century from 1925 to 1950 the total number of Italian immigrants that entered the United States was probably smaller than in the single prewar peak year. Demographers and sociologists have uniformly condemned the quota laws as hasty acts of legislation based on thinly veiled racial theories that could not fail to prove insulting to those peoples (like the Italians) whom they virtually excluded from the country. The best that can be said for these measures is that they gave the swollen Italian-American population of the United States a full generation in which to become absorbed into the life of their new country and so reduce that air of strangeness that had aroused the hostility of their fellow-citizens. But even this process had its limitations. If the average Italian-American applauded the provocative oratory of Mussolini, it was partly because the Duce's assertions of Italian supremacy offered compensation for the grievous psychological wounds that the quota laws had inflicted.*

The new restrictions on immigration and the advent of Musso-lini, then, interacted to some extent. If the first of these develop-

* Oscar Handlin, *The Uprooted* (Boston, 1951), pp. 292–293, 296.

ments drastically reduced the mass contact between Italians and Americans, the second had a similar effect in limiting that cultural contact that was the older form of Italian-American interchange. Not that Americans ceased to visit Italy. On the contrary, they went there in great numbers and usually enjoyed themselves thoroughly. But these new tourists were less discriminating than the more leisurely travelers of the nineteenth century. They seldom spoke Italian and they were unable to see below the surface of Italian life. Hence they easily succumbed to the official propaganda of the regime. The characteristic American tourist of the twenties and thirties returned home full of the praises of a Mussolini who had at last set the Italians on the path to order and cleanliness. It was only a rare scholar who by discreet listening and a painstaking gathering of scattered statistics was able to arrive at a fairly exact idea of what was actually going on.

So the American visitors continued to shuffle through the art galleries of Florence and the churches of Rome, and to ride gaily in the gondolas of Venice. But the leaders of American culture were no longer so closely attached to Italy as they had been in the past. A knowledge of Italian ceased to be one of the marks of the well-educated man. And the writers and artists, if they did not precisely shun Italy as they did Germany after 1933, found the atmosphere there less congenial than it had been before the war. Those who knew the distinguished anti-Fascist exiles who congregated in Paris, London, or New York realized very well why Italy had lost its charm. Others simply failed to form the habit of intimate contact with the country. Of course there were exceptions: George Santayana and Ezra Pound, the former with discretion, the latter with un-bridled enthusiasm, declared their admiration for the Fascist state. But both of these were carry-overs from the prewar era. For the younger men—whether of the flaming generation of the twenties or of the socially conscious age-group of the decade following—Italy never became a spiritual home.

2. THE REDISCOVERY OF ITALY

Hence when the United States once again found itself involved in a wartime relationship with Italy—this time as an enemy rather than an ally—the American government discovered to its surprise that few of its citizens possessed any expert knowledge of contemporary Italy. The British encountered no difficulty in staffing the wartime agencies that were to deal with things Italian: the Americans were at a loss for suitable talent. Actually it was easier to find qualified specialists on the Soviet Union or China—despite all the difficulties of language—than for such an apparently familiar country as Italy. And so for the work of military government and intelligence, the United States tended to turn to second generation Italian-Americans as the only large reservoir of people who spoke the language. The results were not always fortunate: with certain notable exceptions, Italian-Americans during the war adopted a superior attitude toward the inhabitants of the old country for which these latter could find no justification. For the American of Italian extraction usually spoke only a dialect of the language and had little knowledge of the cultural inheritance or political tradition of the land of his ancestors. Here again the circumstances of the earlier mass emigration offer some extenuation: for Americans whose parents had felt themselves literally pushed out of their homeland by poverty and heartless neglect, it was impossible to resist the temptation to show off their dramatic reversal of fortunes to the cousins who had remained behind.

Indeed, like the American-Italian alliance of the First World War, the fact that the two nations were on opposing sides in the Second War had something accidental about it. Mussolini's foreign adventures had never aroused as strong feelings of hostility in America as Hitler's had, and it was not until the invasion of Albania on Good Friday, 1939, that Secretary of State Hull forthrightly denounced the Duce for this "additional threat to the peace." And when on the outbreak of war five months later, Italy decided to remain a nonbelligerent, the earlier American attitude of restraint appeared justified. All this was changed the following June. Italy's intervention in the war just in time to share in the destruction of France shocked Americans nearly as much as the original German attack on Poland. At Charlottesville, Virginia, President Roosevelt voiced the sentiments of millions of his fellow-countrymen—and deeply offended many Italian-Americans—in the now-celebrated reference to Mussolini he inserted in his prepared address: "On this tenth day of June, 1940, the hand that held the dagger has struck it into the back of its neighbor." During the year 1941 there followed a number of official acts that brought the United States closer to war with Italy—the seizure of Italian ships in American ports, the freezing of Italian assets, and the closing down of Italian consulates. But all these actions were simply parallel measures supplementing those taken against the major potential enemy, Hitler's Reich. Once again, Italy was appearing in the familiar role of junior partner to a greater power more deeply involved with the United States. And it was in this fashion that war eventually came. Four days after Pearl Harbor, Italy, like Germany, declared that a state of war existed with the United States—a declaration promptly reciprocated by the American Congress. In the general relief that the German initiative had spared the United States the dangers of a debate over entering the European war, the parallel Italian action passed virtually unnoticed.

Actually the period in which Italian and American troops faced each other in battle was mercifully brief—the five months in which the last Axis stand in North Africa was liquidated and Sicily conquered. With the fall of Mussolini and the Armistice of September 8, 1943, Italy changed sides. Hence it was not as enemies but as forces of occupation and liberation that American troops landed on the Italian peninsula.*

The slow, disheartening campaign that the Allied armies waged for the liberation of Italy—a campaign twice stalled for a whole winter, once between Naples and Rome, once just north of Florence —left an indelible mark on relations between Americans and Italians. Here the decisive fact was that the peninsula was liberated from the south rather than by the more familiar northern invasion route. It was from the impoverished, backward South rather than from the more prosperous and progressive North that the American troops derived their first—and most lasting— impressions of Italy. These impressions, added to the mediocre record of the Italian armed forces, seemed to confirm the prejudices that Americans already entertained: that the Italians were a dark, dirty, and ignorant people, corrupt, thieving, and cowardly. And so the American soldiers usually behaved with arrogance and tactlessness—if not outright brutality—toward "Eyeties" they frankly considered their inferiors. It was only an occasional military government officer—

* See Chapter 6.

like the hero of John Hersey's *A Bell for Adano*— who conscientiously tried to understand and sympathize with the plight of the
people under his supervision. Readers who want a starker, but
substantially accurate, picture of the behavior of Americans in wartime Italy can find it in John Horne Burns's collection of sketches
and episodes entitled *The Gallery*. It is all here: the cynicism and
discouragement, the collusion in the black market, the high living
of rear-echelon officers, the heartless exploitation of half-starved
women. All this is perhaps no more than the customary behavior
of any army toward the civilian population among whom it is
quartered. But in southern Italy this familiar situation took on added
poignancy from the fact that the local population seemed both
close to America and very far away: they were the blood relatives
of the Italian-Americans and yet they did not fully belong, like the
British, the French, or the Germans, to the modern civilization of
the West; in some ways they appeared almost as alien as the Arabs
of North Africa.

Yet this relationship of scorn and grudging tolerance had its
compensations. It was not for nothing that thousands of Americans
of Italian origin found near relatives in the cities and villages of
Sicily and southern Italy—the part of the country from which the
bulk of the Italian-American population had originally come. These
soldiers with relatives in Italy—for all their bragging and obtuse-
ness—offered an initial bridge between the two worlds. The fact that
so many American soldiers spoke some variety of Italian gave a start
toward mutual sympathy. As opposed to the British, who remembered that they, unlike the Americans, had really been at war
with Italy and in general remained coolly aloof, the Americans
became deeply involved in Italian life. In their half-scornful, half-
affectionate fashion, they began to make friends. And the Italians
responded with their customary joyful warmth to the least sign of
human sympathy. Many American soldiers found a woman, or
even an entire family, who offered them a second home. Others
became engaged or married to "nice" girls whom their parents had
sedulously sheltered from the perils of the streets. This close, intense relationship between Americans and Italians has been faithfully reflected in such postwar Italian films as *Paisà* and *To Live in
Peace*. In the end a large number of Americans—like the author of

The Gallery himself—fell in love with the whole country. Not infrequently they would plan to return to Italy after the war—as students, writers, importers, or actors of English-language parts in the films. The net result was a mass rediscovery of Italy by Americans originally sent there against their will.

The liberation of Rome and later of the North intensified the process by at length exposing the liberating armies to the major centers of Italian cultural life and economic development. And after the war's end this rediscovery of Italy steadily gathered momentum. Rome and the islands of the Bay of Naples became headquarters for an influential wing of the cultural *avant-garde*. The postwar American programs of economic and military aid sent to the peninsula hundreds of United States citizens—economists, army and navy men, and agricultural specialists. The American motion picture industry experimented with making films in this land of low wages and reliable sunshine, and in their turn Italian pictures enjoyed a high prestige in the United States. Similarly, Italian luxury products found eager American buyers. Above all, the years after 1947 brought to Italy a flood of tourists that reached its height in the mass pilgrimages to Rome during the Holy Year of 1950.

Out of all this new interest in Italy, there has come a wide variety of books on Italian life and culture— first among them in merit Eleanor Clark's subtle evocation of the spirit of the Roman past and present in her *Rome and a Villa*. Most of these, however, have been more literary than political, more concerned with the atmosphere of Italy than with its economy and social structure. One has the impression that Americans have been so busy enjoying the country that they have not had time to think about its problems. Italy is certainly to be enjoyed. But it is not to be enjoyed with the guilelessness of those tourists who assume that all is well just because the shop fronts are shiny and the food in the restaurants is delectable—as their fathers assumed that all was in order because Mussolini had cleaned up Naples and made the trains run on time. To enjoy Italy and to love it is not enough. One must also see, in the words of one of its greatest contemporary students, that it is "a tragic country—with a smiling face."* The present volume will try to pierce behind this deceptively happy mask.

* Leonardo Olschki, *The Genius of Italy* (New York, 1949), p. 8.

2

The Land and Its People

THE MOST important thing for the foreigner to realize about Italy is that it is a poor country. Travelers and poets have written of it as a "garden"—and quite naturally have thought it such, since the most famous and attractive sections of the country have the look of a well-kept series of terraces and fruit groves. Actually, these favored districts form only a small fraction of Italy's surface. One third of Italy is mountains, another third is hills. And several of the plains and plateaus ostensibly best favored for agriculture have only recently been brought under adequate cultivation. One can get some idea of Italy's geographical limitations if one reflects that her total area is only a little more than half that of France, that her agricultural area is perhaps a quarter of the French, and that on this meager allotment of productive territory she must support a population larger than that of her more prosperous neighbor.

Italy almost totally lacks mineral resources. She must import nearly all her coal and her iron ore. Water power, however, is abundant, and after the Second World War large reserves of natural gas and smaller reserves of oil were discovered and exploited. Under these circumstances, Italians have managed by ingenuity and hard work to make their country an important industrial power, but they can never hope to make it a first-class one. It is as peasants and traders that Italians have left their characteristic mark on history.

A mere glance at Italy's situation on the map will show why the Italians have traditionally been famous as seafarers and traders. Italy is technically a peninsula, but it is at the same time practically an island. Ringed as it is on its one land frontier by the barrier of the Alps, Italy has almost perfect natural boundaries. Only in the area of the Brenner—the lowest of the great Alpine passes—and to the east, where the irregular Julian Alps and the rugged plateaus of the Carso offer no clear line of demarcation between Italians and Slavs, is it difficult to draw a logical frontier. This quasi-island, nearly cutting in two the Mediterranean sea, of which it forms the geographical center, early became the great market where the trade routes of Western Europe met those from Asia and the Levant. During the Middle Ages, the fleets of Amalfi and Pisa, and later of Genoa and Venice, carried the sea-borne commerce of Europe and transported the Crusaders to their destinations. This commercial primacy of Italy ended when the Portuguese and Spanish discoveries at the end of the fifteenth century opened up a new route to the East and turned the energies of Europeans across the Atlantic to the New World. And with the loss of trading supremacy began the 300-year decline in Italy's political importance. It is significant that the opening of the Suez Canal in 1869—which put Italy once again on the main route to India and the Far East—coincided with the unification of the peninsula that made possible the resumption of an aggressive commercial policy. Italy was again able to become a great maritime power—with a merchant fleet that in 1939 ranked sixth in the world.

Internally, the problem of Italian communications has always been more difficult. The spinal column of the peninsula, the Apennine chain, bisects the country not only north and south, but also east and west from Rimini to La Spezia. Indeed, the only places where communications are easy are in the great Po valley of the North, and along the Adriatic from the Foggia area south to the heel of Italy. Elsewhere not only the Apennines but a number of coastal ranges and isolated groups of broken hills cut up the country. Hence geography has contributed to the disunity of the peninsula—a disunity which may be politically a thing of the past but is still reflected in the multiplicity of Italian dialects. The founders of the Kingdom of Italy realized that political unity would mean little unless an economic knitting-together of the peninsula accompanied it. And so they gave first priority in expenditure—and in doing so grievously overburdened the new state with taxes—to the construction of a railway system. In the four decades from 1860 to 1900, when the net was virtually completed, Italian rail mileage grew eightfold. The result was a triumph of engineering: even the casual tourist notices that Italian trains always seem to be going either over a bridge or through a tunnel.

The peasant, however, has been the real maker of Italy—the peasant and the stonemason, the traditional type-figures of the Italian masses. The Italian countryside is his creation. Forced to earn his livelihood in a difficult land—where arid uplands alternated with malarial swamps—he has literally created the Italian landscape. The upper classes have frequently squandered Italy's resources. Deforestation—the curse of Mediterranean countries—while not so severe in Italy as in Greece or Palestine, has eaten away at the country's farmland as noble or bourgeois landholders have striven to make a quick profit; particularly after 1860, the indiscriminate lumbering on southern estates acquired from the sale of Church and domain lands became a national scandal. Meantime the peasant has done his best with what he had. He has terraced the hills and constructed the villages in so harmonious a fashion that it is sometimes difficult to tell where the work of man ends and the realm of nature begins. The Italian countryside is a living monument to the toil of unnumbered generations of peasants.

1. NORTH AND SOUTH

Italy is conventionally divided into a North, a Center, and a South. The North comprises the regions* of Piedmont, Liguria, Lombardy, Venetia, Trentino-Alto Adige (the South Tyrol), and Venezia Friuli (the area facing Yugoslavia, which was drastically reduced in size following the Second World War). The Center is made up roughly of what were formerly the States of the Church—the territorial domain of the Popes—and Tuscany, the lands once dominated by the great city-state of Florence. The South is the former Kingdom of Naples or the Two Sicilies—the whole peninsula south of Rome, including, as its name implies, the island of Sicily. The other major Italian island, Sardinia, is also usually bracketed with the South for purposes of sociological comparison.

* In Italy the regions are the large divisions of the country, corresponding roughly to French provinces. They are not units of local government, except in the case of five peripheral areas, which under a series of postwar autonomy statutes, have their own elected assemblies (see Chapter 7). The normal units of local government are the 90-odd provinces, corresponding to French departments.

This threefold division is by no means exact. Actually, most of Latium, the region surounding Rome, belongs more with the South than with the Center. In cultural terms, the South begins a few miles north of Rome: the motorist driving from Florence to the national capital can easily detect a rather sharp change in the character of the villages. Rome—like Washington—is a partly northern, partly southern city located just within the South. Moreover, between North and Center there is no clear cultural division. When Italians speak of the fatal cleavage that divides their country, they include the Center with the North as the area of economic progress and higher living standards. This twofold division rests on differences of climate, physical features, and long-standing cultural tradition.

North of the Apennines, Italy has a continental climate. While the summers in the Po valley are just as hot as in southern Italy, the winters are actually colder than those of Denmark. The rainfall is abundant and well distributed throughout the year. Although the total annual precipitation is not much greater than in the South, it is far more useful, since it reaches its maximum in the right seasons —spring and summer—to favor the cultivation of Italy's basic food crops: rice, corn, and, above all, wheat. This climate, in conjunction with a soil responsive to fertilizers and intensive cultivation, has made the Po basin Italy's foremost agricultural region.

Throughout the peninsula, the mountain areas offer similar extremes of hot and cold seasons—as American soldiers, accustomed to think of Italy as a land of warmth and sunshine, discovered with chagrin during the Second World War. In general, however, the Center, and more particularly the South, have a characteristically Mediterranean climate. The winters are wet and only moderately cold—although the cold has a peculiarly penetrating character, as any foreigner who has spent a winter in the chill, draughty dreariness of a South Italian *palazzo*, can well testify. The summers are hot and nearly without rain. Actually, the summer heat is no greater than that regularly endured by Americans throughout most of their country, and it is perhaps less oppressive, since it is drier. But it is more continuous. This continuous, dry heat of summer, coupled with certain peculiarities of southern soil and topography, has had a disastrous effect on the development of southern agriculture.

In northern Italy, 31 per cent of the land surface can be classified as plain: in the South the figure is only 14 per cent. And the mountain area, which in the North is fairly clearly delineated as the Apennine chain, begins to break up south of about Campobasso in Molise into a confused maze of uplands and valleys. Each group of mountains sends out its own series of watercourses, which pursue their separate ways to the sea without any visible system or reason. Moreover, most of them are steep and rapid. In the spring, they tumble down the hillsides as foaming torrents, brown with silt. By summer their beds are nearly dry—wastes of boulders traversed by a thin trickle of running water and marked at intervals by stagnant pools, once breeding grounds of malaria.

Through the centuries these torrential rivers have carried off to the sea the topsoil of the uplands, left unprotected by the ruthless deforestation. By now most of the mountain area of the South has been reduced to a bare and rocky desolation. In the arid hill country —more particularly in Lucania—landslides are a common occurrence. Despite all the efforts of the peasants to terrace and wall in their holdings, these slides have sometimes carried off whole stretches of agricultural land—on rare occasions, even an entire village. "It may come about that the proprietors of vineyards will suddenly awake as the possessors of olive groves, which during the night have slipped down from above, while their own vines have likewise been deposited downhill as flotsam at the feet of strangers."* These are the dramatic cases. More usually, a steady, implacable erosion has done its work of agricultural destruction.

The soil of the South lends itself to this process. As opposed to the North, where clay soils are relatively infrequent, vast stretches of the southern agricultural land are clay—in Sicily, as much as three-quarters of the total land surface. Here geographers have noted that the area of clay soil coincides closely with that of the *latifondo*— the traditionally backward, extensively cultivated great estate. Everywhere clay means poverty and a ceaseless struggle with natural obstacles. For soil and climate work together to produce a heartbreaking combination of unfavorable conditions.

The paradox of south Italian agriculture is that it suffers not so much from lack of water as from an excess of water at the wrong season of the year. Under the long rains of winter the surface soil

* Friedrich Vöchting, *Die italienische Südfrage* (Berlin, 1951), p. 20.

of clay becomes waterlogged and reduced to a kind of gelatinous muddy porridge—which, however, lets little water through to the layers of soil below. This "steppe-like" undersoil resists the efforts of the young plants to penetrate its hard surface. By summer, then, the new wheat or corn is inadequately rooted in the ground; it is ill-prepared to withstand the ravages of the hot season—the ceaseless beating of the sun and the winds that frequently tear up the parched growth. By the end of summer the soil may be reduced to dust or to a hard-baked surface, equally desolating to the peasants' eyes. It is little wonder that in Apulia cultivators of the soil reckon that an average decade will bring two total and two partial crop failures.

Of course, the whole South is not subject to this combination of difficulties. Where the soil is volcanic in origin—as around Naples or in the more favored parts of Sicily—a variety of crops flourish without difficulty. And in general it may be said that for fodder crops and tree crops, large areas of the South are well endowed: oranges, lemons, and olives have traditionally been its chief exports. Unfortunately the area under wheat is much too large. Since Roman times, wheat has been the staple crop of the *latifondo*. And this imbalance of southern agriculture was intensified during the 1920's and 1930's by the Fascist campaign for self-sufficiency in food. One of the most pressing problems of today is that of diversifying the crops grown in the South—and simultaneously introducing varieties of wheat that will withstand the rigors of its climate.

Historians and geographers have long puzzled over the reasons why southern Italy and Sicily, which in ancient times were in the forefront of civilization, are today in so depressed a state. These reasons are extremely complex: most of them go so deeply into the social structure and historical past of the country that they can best be discussed under these heads. Two, however, arise directly from the physical geography of the area. The first is deforestation. In Roman times, Sicily and the southern Apennine slopes were heavily wooded. Almost certainly the rainfall was heavier than it is today. Even in the last century, precipitation decreased. For the city of Lecce, in Apulia, the mean annual rainfall at the beginning of the century was 32 inches; towards the end of the century, it had sunk to 21 inches. The second reason is malaria—directly connected with the first, since it was deforestation that created the stagnant pools in which the anopheles mosquito bred. In ancient times, malaria was almost certainly less widespread than it became in the early modern era. Its greatest ravages were in the period 1860–1900. With the turn of the century, modern medical methods succeeded in radically reducing the malaria mortality rate. But the total number of malaria sufferers fell much more slowly. Until after the Second World War, Italy was the most malarial country of Europe. And within Italy it was the South—as well as southern Tuscany and Latium—that was chiefly affected. The corresponding scourge of the North—pellagra—by 1920 had practically disappeared.

The prevalence of malaria was also in part responsible for the nearly universal practice among the southern peasantry of living in compact towns or villages rather than in individual farmsteads on the land they cultivate. While in the North and Center— particularly in areas of share tenancy like Tuscany—farmhouses are the rule, in the South they are almost unknown, except in areas brought very recently under cultivation and those affected by the post-1950 land reform. The characteristic southern town is a tight knot of primitive, but essentially urban-type dwellings, perched on the slope or the summit of a hill. They are invariably of stone or plaster: as throughout the peninsula, wood construction is virtually nonexistent. But it was not only to escape the malarial lowlands that the southern peasants originally began to live in this fashion. They had other equally pressing reasons for doing so, and it is impossible to determine which one came first. In the early Middle Ages, there was the fear of pirates—later replaced by the fear of banditry. There are also long-standing habits of mutual solidarity and sociability. Still more important, the system of agrarian tenure in the South does not lend itself to living on the land. The average southern peasant—whether small-holder or tenant—does not culti- vate a single compact farm. He tills a number of tiny strips or plots, scattered over a wide area and sometimes changing from year to year. Hence he has no alternative but to live in a central location far from the land itself. This system, of course, is extremely wasteful of time and physical strength. The southern peasant must arise well before dawn to begin the long hike—sometimes taking two or three hours—to his place of work; at dusk he must wearily retrace the same road, this time uphill, back to his village. For those who work as seasonal or day laborers on the great estates, the journey may be even longer—with the ever-present possibility that all the jobs will be filled when they arrive, and the resultant pressure to get up and started on their way still earlier than their competitors. One can understand the attitude of the inhabitants of Viggiano, in Lucania, who a half century ago found it preferable to make the single terrible journey as emigrants across the Atlantic than the still more terrible daily journey to work at home.

Partly as a reason for living in compact settlements, partly as its consequence—but in any case reflecting the general poverty of the area—can be reckoned the lack of farm animals throughout the South and the islands. The cow and the horse are rare; the poor peasant owns only a couple of goats and a donkey—his greatest capital investment, his fellow-worker, and his friend. These animals, as in peasant communities in other Mediterranean countries, when they do not remain outdoors, share the family dwelling. The house of the southern peasant is usually an extremely simple affair, with perhaps two rooms and an earth floor and no heating or plumbing system. About the North it is more difficult to generalize: many of the houses are no better than those of the South, while the more prosperous peasants may possess spacious, agreeable dwellings. One can trace the difference in the housing statistics: a generation ago the dwellings of the South were 50 per cent more crowded than those in the North. And the proportion of dwellings consisting simply of caves, rush huts, and the like, which in the North was only .4 per cent, was 3.9 per cent for the South. Indeed, the occurrence of this type of housing was tragically frequent in the more backward areas like Lucania and Sardinia.

Other statistics reflect the same difference of living standards. In 1960 income per capita in the South was less than half what it was in the North. Figures for food consumption tell a similar story. Southern Italy and the islands are typical of any poor peasant area in that meat figures in the diet only as a luxury. Spaghetti, macaroni—all the numberless varieties of *pasta*—and vegetables are about the only foods that the southerner regularly consumes. The northerner also relies heavily on starches, but his diet is more abundant and varied and includes dairy products, which in the South are as rare as meat.

During the whole second half of the nineteenth century, the figures on literacy showed a similar gap. More recently, the gap has narrowed, as primary education has been extended to nearly the entire Italian population. But a qualitative difference in educational levels has remained. Indeed, in most respects the gap between North and South has widened rather than diminished in the past half century. The old generalization still holds true: if northern Italy unquestionably belongs to the advanced West European civilization typified by France, Britain, and Germany, the South is culturally closer to Spain, or even, perhaps, to the countries of North Africa.

2. THE REGIONS OF ITALY

Within the major contrast between North and South, even the casual traveler can detect a variety of strongly marked differences, roughly corresponding to the boundaries of the various regions. For Italy is a land of tenacious regionalism. Local consciousness and local pride offer a partial compensation for national disappointments as a great power. An Italian will commonly refer to himself as a Lombard or a Tuscan, or, even more proudly, as a son of his native city. In the countryside at least, most people speak some kind of dialect. While several of these are close to the literary language, others—like Piedmontese or Sicilian, to cite cases from the two extremities of Italy—are virtually separate languages and nearly incomprehensible to people from other parts of the country. Alongside the literature in "official" Italian, a vigorous dialect literature has traditionally pursued its separate course. The case is similar with the dialect theater. In the past quarter century this popular theater has been more alive and entertaining than the drama in literary Italian.

In the North, Piedmont and Lombardy are the key regions. Separated by contrasting histories, they are intimately related by geography and economic activities. The boundary between them is no more than a conventional dividing line and has frequently fluctuated in the past. Ringed on the north and west by the Alps, Piedmont and Lombardy are regions of gentle hills gradually descending to the broad valley of the Po. This great plain owes its position as the most highly developed agricultural area of Italy not only to its favorable climate but to a long tradition of intense, systematic cultivation, symbolized by the irrigation ditches and canals that divide the countryside into neat sections. In the more hilly areas, small farms are common, but in the plain the practice of scientific cultivation has favored the development of farms of 250 to 400 acres—large by Italian standards, if not so extensive as the great estates of the South. These large farms are generally directed by a professional manager, acting in the interests of a proprietor who is often an absentee.

Piedmont and Lombardy are also the headquarters of Italian industry—particularly the textile and metallurgical industries. Their chief cities, Turin and Milan respectively, rank as the great metallurgical and automotive centers and somewhat complacently regard themselves as the leaders in economic and cultural progress for the whole peninsula. The seaport for this industrial area is Genoa—a manufacturing city in its own right and the only one of the medieval maritime republics to continue into the present time as a major port. Genoa is the chief city of Liguria—more familiar to the tourist as the Italian Riviera. This narrow arc of rocky coast and dramatic scenery owes its comparatively temperate climate to the range of low mountains that separates it from Piedmont and protects it from the cold winds blowing off the Alps.

Piedmont, Lombardy, and Liguria comprise the Italian northwest —the original nucleus of modern Italy. To the east of them the lower stretches of the Po separate the regions of Venetia and Emilia. Here the land is flatter and the canals are wider than they are farther west. Much of the land in and near the Po delta was originally swamp and was reclaimed by elaborate drainage operations in the latter part of the nineteenth century. Some of it remains swamp to this day: the coast of Venetia ranks along with a number of southern areas as a major focus of land reform. At the same time, the flat, heavily watered character of the lower Po plain has enabled it to become an important producer of corn, rice, and dairy products.

Farther inland, Venetia changes into an area of hills and uplands gradually rising to the Alps. This territory, as its name implies, comprises the hinterland of the island city of Venice—a region of historic cities like Verona, Vicenza, and Padua that eventually fell under the rule of the great maritime republic. Its hill country is less prosperous than that of Lombardy or Piedmont; the area of the

Friuli, north of Udine, has long sent its surplus labor force to seek work abroad. Here in the northeast, the Alps cut farther south and rise more gently than they do in the west. These lower Alpine ranges offer a number of vacation resorts long frequented by prosperous Italians anxious to escape the heat of summer. The most famous of the mountain groups—the Dolomites—was formerly divided between Italy and Austria. In 1919, the Austrian Dolomites passed to Italy along with the rest of the Tyrol south of the Brenner. The lower part of this region, the Trentino, had long figured as a deep indentation within the cultural frontier of Italy and was overwhelmingly Italian in speech and sentiment. For the northern part, however, around Bolzano, the Italian case was far less clear. Its assignment to Italy could be justified only on strategic grounds and was carried out over the protests of the greater part of its population. Despite the excesses of forced Italianization perpetrated under Mussolini's regime, the region has remained preponderantly German in speech; even today its villages are virtually indistinguishable in architecture and customs from those of the Tyrol north of the Brenner.

Emilia is the transition area between the North and the Center. Its eastern half, traditionally known as the Romagna, belongs definitely with central Italy. In the Middle Ages, the Romagna was a land of tumultuous warring cities—Bologna, Ravenna, Imola, Rimini, Forlì. In the late nineteenth century it became the classic region of political quarrels: the rival sects of the Italian Left, the Republicans, loyal to the tradition of Mazzini, and the newer and more aggressive Socialists acquired the habit of fighting frequent and occasionally bloody political battles. It was the Romagna tradition of violent Socialism that fathered Mussolini—whose apostasy to Fascism was to give the region still another extreme political faith. Most recently, the Romagna has been a Communist stronghold. In seeking a reason for this apparently congenital effervescence, students of the area have drawn attention to the fluidity and contrasts in its rural society: to this relatively backward region, the late nineteenth century brought rapid and dramatic changes; alongside the traditional small farm operated on a *mezzadria,* or share tenancy, contract, the vast drainage operations installed a new type of large capitalistically operated enterprise, worked by a mass of landless laborers whose sufferings inclined them toward revolutionary courses.

South of the Romagna lie the favored areas of central Italy—Tuscany, Umbria, and the Marches. Here the *mezzadria* contract still predominates. Many of these contracts are very old: the scattered farmhouses and neatly terraced slopes reflect centuries of conscientious labor by peasants proud of a plot of land that has descended to them through many generations with as much continuity as though they were its legal owners. Tuscany and Umbria, by and large, give the impression of being Italy's happiest countryside: the hills, the vineyards, the farm buildings blend harmoniously into a gentle, tranquil perspective under a blue sky just tinged with haze toward the horizon. To those accustomed to the landscape backgrounds of Renaissance painting, this appears the classic, the typical Italian countryside. It is one of the many paradoxes of present-day Italy that this central belt of provinces should vote more heavily Communist than any other area of the peninsula.

The coast of southern Tuscany, known as the Maremma, is a low-lying stretch of territory that already begins to look like the South. And when one reaches the center of Latium, the Roman Campagna, one has definitely crossed the cultural dividing line. The approach to Rome has for centuries astounded tourists and pilgrims: until very recently the Italian capital was unique among European cities in the way it suddenly loomed up, without warning and almost without suburbs, from a desolate countryside. Up to sixty years ago, the Campagna was virtually uninhabited: its owners, the Roman nobility, left their estates simply as vast stretches of pasture alternating with wheat. All through the latter part of the nineteenth century, the owners waged a running fight with the peasants of the surrounding hills, who would try to establish squatters' rights on the neglected agricultural land. Here they would live a precarious existence in reed huts—popularly known as "Abyssinian villages." As late as the 1890's members of Parliament were voicing their indignation at these scandalous conditions so close to the national capital.*

In the present century, the Roman Campagna has come under

* Emilio Sereni, *Il capitalismo nelle campagne (1860–1900)* (Turin, 1947), pp. 201–202.

more systematic cultivation. It is still, however, amazingly empty for the surroundings of a great city. It is not until one reaches the Alban hills—the traditional center for Roman villa life and holiday-making—that one is again in an area of dense settlement. Beyond these hills lies the Pontine plain—familiar to Americans as the Anzio beachhead in the Second World War. The drainage and reclamation of this marshy area, which had long defied the efforts of earlier innovators, was one of Mussolini's most advertised achievements, and one of the few things he did that proved of permanent benefit to Italy. Here, as in so many areas of recent land improvement, the farmhouses are scattered at regular intervals over the countryside rather than grouped in villages in the traditional fashion.

The southern regions of the peninsula, while they do not have separate histories like those of the North, are also marked off from each other by clear divisions of topography and dialect. The most northerly is the rugged Abruzzo and Molise, collectively known as the Abruzzi—a region of hills and mountains inhabited by a tenacious breed of peasants whose struggles and sufferings have been chronicled by Ignazio Silone in his anti-Fascist novel *Fontamara*. Southwest of the Abruzzi lies Campania—the hinterland of Naples. The richest and most densely populated region of the South, Campania is the only one familiar to the average foreigner. Yet even here no more than the coastal area is really favored by nature; inland and upland the usual southern poverty resumes its grip.

The corresponding region on the Adriatic shore is Apulia—a long strip of plains and plateaus stretching from the ankle down through the heel of the Italian boot. With a climate more continental than that of the Bay of Naples, Apulia contains a variety of agricultural areas. The northernmost is the wheat-growing Tavoliere, or tableland —another center of land improvement. To the south, the coastal plain from Barletta through the seaports of Bari and Brindisi to Lecce produces a wide range of specialized crops—fruit, olives, wine, and tobacco. Farther inland the country again becomes rugged and poor, until one eventually reaches Lucania, the instep of Italy, which has ranked as the most depressed area of the entire peninsula. This region, earlier known as Basilicata, is the classic land of arid hills and clay soil, of hopelessness and desperate overpopulation, reaching an extreme of desolation in the wastes bordering the Ionian sea.

It was at Eboli, in Campania, that Carlo Levi's peasants declared that Christ had stopped: he had never gone on to Lucania.

Calabria, the toe of Italy, is a more attractive region, if only slightly less depressed. Much of its coastline is fertile and prosperous and its hillsides have not been totally ruined by deforestation; many are still heavily wooded. In its center lies the high plateau of the Sila—a wild, sparsely inhabited upland, where the post-war government made its initial experiment in land reform. This parceling out of some of the neglected *latifondi* of Calabria was the first sign of hope that had reached a southern peasantry long accustomed to seeing vast stretches of potentially productive land left neglected by their absentee owners.

The two main Italian islands belong geographically and culturally with the South. Of the two, Sicily is by far the more important. Although separated from Calabria only by the narrow straits of Messina, Sicily feels itself to be distinct in character and tradition from peninsular Italy. Its eccentric dialect and strongly marked customs reflect a long heritage of non-Italian influences—Greek, Arab, and Norman, to mention only the most important. This deeply rooted localism has found expression in a tradition of resistance to the regular agents of law and order and reliance in their stead on a code of violence and personal solidarity, of crude justice and honor, collectively grouped under the name *mafia*. Mussolini thought he had stamped out the *mafia*. Yet it revived during the Second World War, and it was only the postwar grant of regional autonomy that succeeded in reconciling Sicilians who had seriously talked of seceding from Italy and even of making their island the forty-ninth State of the American union.

Some areas of Sicily are extremely fertile. In the northwest, around the city of Palermo, the coastal strip known as the Golden Shell recalls the Neapolitan shore in its prosperous groves of oranges and lemons tended by small or medium proprietors; the eastern coast around Catania is similarly favored. The greater part of the island, however, is poor and arid—and dominated by the *latifondo*. Yet compared with Sardinia, Sicily is a land of plenty. Sardinia has been the most backward region of Italy—more backward even than Lucania. It is a land of bare mountains and desolate plains and valleys, sparsely populated and the victim of centuries of neglect.

Sardinia lies off the main path of commerce and travel, isolated from the rest of Italy. Not until the 1960's did it begin to benefit from government support for economic development.

3. THE ITALIAN POPULATION

The population that inhabits this peninsula and these islands can be considered either extremely homogeneous or extremely varied depending on the way one looks at it. In the sense of conscious nationality, Italy is one of the most homogeneous countries of Europe. True national minorities exist only on its Alpine frontier—a pocket of French in the Val d'Aosta in Piedmont, a few Slavs along the eastern frontier, and the one important minority, the German-speaking Tyrolese of the Alto Adige. In the South and in Sicily, one can find clusters of Greeks and Albanians, and scattered families whose names reveal their Greek or Albanian origin. But most of these people consider themselves Italian. Indeed, the vast majority of the population of the peninsula and the two islands think of themselves as Italian and speak some variety of the Italian language.

From the physical standpoint, however, the Italians are extremely diverse. "No country in Europe in which one language and one cultural tradition prevail shows a greater diversity of race between its southern and its northern extremities."* The northern population is almost impossible to classify: one finds Mediterranean, Dinaric, and Alpine elements all mixed up together, and even a certain number of recognizable Nordics. Northern Italy belongs to the vast racial conglomeration of Western and Central Europe: it is only by manner and gesture that one can distinguish its people from Frenchmen or Germans. In fact, there are probably as many blonds in northern Italy as in most parts of France and even certain regions of Germany; one would see no more fair complexions and light hair in Munich than on the streets of Milan.

This extreme diversity of physical type dates from long before the beginning of recorded history. It was presumably intensified by the mass levies of slaves that the Romans brought back to Italy from all parts of their empire. Many of them were dark-skinned, and of these the greater number seem to have been settled in the south-

* Carleton Stevens Coon, *The Races of Europe* (New York, 1939), p. 559.

ern part of the country. It is to this "oriental" admixture that some anthropologists have ascribed the prevailing brunet character of the southern Italian population. The theory is highly speculative. Yet it is unquestionable that out of their highly mixed ancestry, the southern Italians have evolved a physical type far more strongly marked than that of the North—and far more familiar to the average American.

In southern Italy and Sicily, the vast majority of the people have brown or black hair and eyes, and a dark or olive-colored skin. They vary from the usual Mediterranean type in their more abundant beards and body hair and heavier features. Medium to short in stature, they tend to corpulence in middle age, and, in the case of the women, as soon as their first youth is over. This distinctive, tenacious stock accounts for a good deal less than half the Italian population. Yet to most American it appears the characteristic, indeed the only, Italian physical type—and quite naturally so, since the great majority of Americans of Italian origin originally stemmed from Sicily and the South.

In a racial sense, then, the term "Latin country" as applied to Italy is meaningless. Culturally, however, the epithet is deserved and is a source of justified pride to the Italian people. Of all the long succession of conquerors and invaders who have ruled the peninsula, the Romans left the most lasting impression. They spread their language over the country—and no succeeding influence has been able to uproot it. Like the other Romance languages, Italian is simply an outgrowth of vulgar Latin, the colloquial speech of the later Roman Empire. Yet it is closer than the others to the classical language, close enough so that the words of the Roman Catholic Mass can carry nearly their full meaning to the average member of a church congregation. In Italy, as throughout the Catholic world, the clergy pronounces the language of the liturgy softly and musically as though it were Italian—not with the strange, harsh-sounding consonants that are taught to American schoolboys.

Next to the tradition implicit in a Latin language—a tradition of ordered concepts, of precise expression, and of universal interests —it is the Catholic Church that has given unity and meaning to the term "Italian." In the Church, the Roman tradition of universality has descended to the Italians in spiritual form. Through periods of national humiliation, the fact that their country provided the territorial headquarters of the Church and regularly supplied its spiritual ruler and chief officials has been to Italians a source of pride and consolation. A young Italian might never hope to play a great role in world politics—but he could always aspire to be Pope. Until the foundation of united Italy, the Church offered even to those who sought worldly success in administration or diplomacy by far the most promising career.

To Italians the Church is something very familiar—perhaps too familiar for their own religious development since they tend to take Catholicism for granted. In Italy nearly everybody is technically a Catholic. Yet among this overwhelming majority of Catholics a great number, particularly of the men, scarcely practice their religion. They are baptized, married, buried by the Church—little more. In politics, they frequently take an anti-clerical stand—in the sense that they object vociferously to Church intervention in political and social life. This phenomenon of nonpracticing Catholicism baffles the visiting American: he is used to the situation in his own country, where nearly all Catholics actively profess their religion. He forgets that in the United States the Catholics are a militant minority. In the majority faith—among Protestants—laxity in religious practice is probably just as common as among Italian Catholics.

Under the bright Mediterranean sun, and with the splendors of imperial Rome in their memories, the Italians tend to emphasize the formal, the ceremonial, the magnificent aspects of their religion. In the pomp of a canonization ceremony under the great baroque baldachin of St. Peter's, the regal element of Italian Catholicism reaches its triumphant expression. This also sometimes shocks Americans: they contrast it with their own Catholicism—the heir of the impoverished, hunted faith of a downtrodden Irish peasantry. At the same time they forget that there is another side to Italian Catholicism—that in isolated monasteries and rural parishes, the Italian clergy labor devotedly for the welfare of the faithful, and that Francis of Assisi, the gentlest and least pretentious of saints, was also an Italian.

The saving grace of this laxness, this formalism in religious practice, is the spirit of tolerance it fosters. Such a statement may surprise

Americans who have heard reports of popular outbreaks directed at Protestant missionaries from the United States. These reports are true and they are shocking—but they are explicable in terms of the recent history of Italian Protestantism. In Italy, there are only about 50,000 Protestants. Half of them are the descendants of the Waldensians of the Alpine valleys—the earliest European Protestants, whose profession of a personal religion antedates by three centuries the Lutheran and Calvinist Reformation. They constitute a long-established and respected element in Italian life. Most of the remaining Protestants, however, are more recent converts, the product of the proselyting activities of British and American missionaries. In the past century, such missionaries have carried on their propaganda with more zeal than discretion: they have frequently attacked the majority religion in scurrilous fashion and in times of stress they have resorted to financial inducements to win impoverished families for their missions. The scant success of these tactics is suggested by the modest total of conversions and by the high turnover of those passing through the mission experience. Moreover, the strenuous efforts of the Anglo-Saxon evangelical sects have boomeranged; they have ended up by creating an anti-Protestant feeling where virtually none existed before. Even the most tepid Italian Catholic may object to having his country—which he regards as the fountainhead of European civilization—treated as mission territory. To him, Catholicism is one of the normal institutions of his country, a part of its age-old culture, with which it would be folly to tamper. In a country where any form of excessive religious zeal appears suspect, the indiscreet activities of missionaries from Protestant lands make Italians feel that they are being put in the same category as African savages.

The reaction came in the illiberal and retrograde provisions on Protestantism embodied in the Concordat of 1929* This same Concordat grouped the religious Jews of Italy along with the Protestants as members of an "admitted cult." But the term "admitted cult"—with its implication of interior status—does not reflect the true position of the Jews in Italy. So far as popular attitudes go, Italy offers a model to the whole of the Western world. The Italian

---

* See further in Chapter 5. On this whole subject see D. A. Binchy, *Church and State in Fascist Italy* (London, 1941), chapter 20.

Jewish community is small—about the same size as the Protestant. Its Sephardic origin has meant that, unlike the Jewish communities of eastern Europe, it has never been separated by language, dress, or personal manners from the rest of the population. It was only in the period from the late sixteenth to the eighteenth century that regular ghettos existed. Since the early nineteenth century, the Jews have been fully assimilated in Italian life; particularly in intellectual fields they have played an extremely distinguished role. Today Italy is the least anti-Semitic country in Europe. Proof of this is the regularity with which Italians evaded and sabotaged Mussolini's anti-Semitic legislation in the years after 1938.

In general, Italians cannot be said to be racialist or even chauvinistic. Except when they have been systematically worked over by demagogues, they take a good-humored view of the outside world and are balanced and skeptical in assessing their own national claims to greatness. They customarily recognize with generosity the values of other countries; literature in translation—including a great deal of American literature—is their chief intellectual fare. Italy, after all, has been the center of two universal institutions: the Roman Empire and the Catholic Church. To concentrate the Italian tradition on a modern and exclusive national loyalty would be to diminish it, to limit the universality of its inheritance. This is the meaning of humanism as a popular way of life. In Italy the term signifies something more than the exercises of Renaissance scholars or the content of a nonscientific university curriculum: it is a deeply felt attitude, inculcated by more than two thousand years of civilization.

If the Italian, then, cultivates his role as a member of a wider humanity, he is also profoundly attached to his family, his home, his village. His feeling for his *paese,* for his wife and children, is close and intense. The idea of family "honor" carries a deep and tragic meaning. Americans are all too familiar with the excesses of blood vengeance to which this feeling can lead among the sons of illiterate Sicilian peasants. The family is the core of Italian life. The Italian mother is the revered symbol of gentle devotion and sacrifice: on formal occasions a husband of mature years will quite naturally give his mother precedence over his wife; even though widowed, she remains the center of the family. The same husband may deceive his wife with some regularity—but he will not break up the home. It is no accident that Italy has never had a law permitting divorce. Even legislators of strongly anticlerical views have hesitated to endorse a practice that seems to strike at the foundation of society.

Rooted as he is in his native place, in the affections of his family, the Italian is seldom a wanderer by inclination. It was only overwhelming necessity that started the great migrations to America. For Italians, the voyage across the Atlantic represented the most dreadful sort of rupture. Once abroad, however, whether in the United States or in a European country of settlement like France, they have shown a capacity to make the best of their new situation and to adjust with rapidity—considering the magnitude of the adjustment they have had to make. Within one generation, they have become devoted citizens of their new country.

Those who know the Italians at first hand agree in calling them good family men, sober, and hard-working. (The frequent American accusation of laziness is outrageously unjustified—except when applied to the leisure classes.) The Italians have had a long experience of privation, disappointment, and deceit. Knowing that life is hard, they think it wise to get enjoyment from it when and as best they can—to live as far as possible in the present. The practical wisdom of centuries has taught them to expect little either from the external world or from their fellow men, and in particular to be distrustful of fine words and large-sounding phrases. Their reputation as bad soldiers is not totally undeserved; they learned long ago that wars seldom accomplish very much. Nor do they feel it worth while to inquire too deeply into the ultimate problems of life. These they can safely leave to the Church—which can be relied on to give untroubling answers. It is significant that Italy has produced no regular philosophical tradition comparable to the English or the German, and that the rare philosophers of Italian birth have usually interested themselves in history and politics rather than in ethics or metaphysics.

As one sympathetic but penetrating critic of the Italian tradition has put it: "A faith without spiritual anxiety and a wisdom without philosophy [have] withheld from the Italians the tragic sense of life." The result is a widespread attitude of skepticism verging over toward indifference. To an American it may look like cynicism—in contrast to his own "idealism." But what the American calls idealism the Italian will suspect of being hypocrisy or at least a lack of sophistication. His own ideals he may cherish so deeply that he will hesitate to speak them; they will reveal themselves only in moments of sudden and unexpected enthusiasm.

In such moments, the Italian throws off his habitual air of patient acceptance and becomes a new man, vibrant with youth and energy. The change frequently takes the foreigner quite unaware, disclosing a second aspect of Italian behavior apparently in total contrast with the first. The same observer quoted a moment ago sees in this contrast a key to Italy's many paradoxes; he detects in the Italian masses "two lasting and characteristic attitudes . . . developed from the same sources of human experience . . . a patient fatalism derived from practical wisdom and moral indolence, and . . . an almost anarchical individualism . . . expressed in creative and adventurous outbursts of natural vitality."* If the former attitude seems to deny the possibility of any real change in the God-given circumstances of existence, the latter implies a taste for the process of living itself, and an emphasis on personal development, as the sole means of lifting one's life above the level of mere senseless repetition.

And so Italy, the land of mass resignation, is also a country in which personal prowess has always drawn applause. Discipline and regimentation are distasteful; the resistance the Italian offers to them may be merely passive, but it is extremely effective. The dramatic act, the colorful scene, the *bel gesto*—these are the sources of unfailing delight. In Italy, a drama may develop anywhere within a few seconds. A mere word, a gesture—and before the foreigner knows what has happened a crowd has collected, noisy, excited, electric with sympathetic participation. Gesticulations come naturally and gracefully: mere bystanders commenting on the event begin to look like apostles from Leonardo's *Last Supper*. Or—to change the artistic metaphor—the whole scene quite as though by design falls into the poses of a chorus from Verdi. The foreigner recoils in dismay: everyone seems so very angry; surely blood will be spilt. And then somebody makes a witty remark—people laugh, the drama is over, and the crowd disperses as quickly as it collected,

* Olschki, *The Genius of Italy*, pp. 243, 342.

leaving the foreigner more bewildered than ever and vainly inquiring what it was all about.

This love of the dramatic and this tendency toward indiscipline have been responsible for much of Italy's history of political misfortune. The communal rivalry of the Middle Ages, the bloody quarrels and private wars of Renaissance despots, have found their reflection in the violent factionalism of contemporary political life. In the sixties of the last century, Karl Marx struggled vainly against the Anarchist tendencies of the Italian wing of his First International. Today the Italian Socialist Party is split more grievously than any other in Europe. Under normal circumstances, Italian political parties seem to break up naturally into splinters and factions. Political differences that appear inexplicable on ideological grounds fall into focus when one understands the personal rivalries behind them.

All this ebullience may seem like so much waste motion until one realizes the reserves of vitality it betokens. If the Italian frequently strikes the American as prematurely old and wise, at other times he appears disarmingly youthful. He may weep unashamedly at misfortune, but he will rarely be discouraged for very long. American visitors who used to tax postwar Europeans with apathy and defeatism made an exception for the Italians. And those who knew the Italian people during the war itself have retained an impressive memory of physical endurance and cheerfulness in the face of disaster. The resilience of the populations of ruined villages was astounding. Hardly had the fighting ceased when they would come down from the bare hills in which they had taken refuge and begin to resume their former lives. Without waiting for government aid, they would simply rebuild their houses themselves. Within five years towns that were a pile of ruins at the war's end—like Cisterna on the road from Anzio to Rome—were nearly totally rebuilt, long before the corresponding cities in other countries.

Along with this restless vitality goes an admiration for its outstanding exponents—the individuals of great talent in all fields. At its worst, such a sentiment may lead to uncritical adulation of a demagogue like Mussolini. More usually, it expresses itself as reverence for creative genius—in art and music and also in science, a field in which the Italian contribution has been nearly as significant as in that of aesthetics. Individuals of great talent may be rarer in Italy than in some other countries. But when an Italian is good at something he seems to be supremely good. As though to compensate for the triviality and shallowness of others, he feels it incumbent on him to be even more serious in his endeavors than he would be if he lived in a less tolerant land. Customarily his personal habits will be ordered, self-disciplined, even austere. Surrounded by the esteem of his fellow-citizens, he will consider it quite natural that he should lead a life radically different from theirs.

And so Italian history has been peculiarly the history of elites. In a country in which illiteracy was long the norm and has not yet been totally wiped out, a country of extreme differences between rich and poor, it has appeared natural that a narrow segment of privileged or highly endowed individuals should alone play a role in history. From Machiavelli to Pareto, the great Italian political writers have uniformly stressed the dominance of elites. Until very recently, democracy in the American sense has been totally foreign to Italian society.

4. SOCIAL CHARACTERISTICS

Italy is a land of cities. The "hundred cities of Italy" have made its history and still dominate its society. In the early Middle Ages, two Italian societies existed side by side—the feudalism of the Germanic conquerors who ruled the countryside, and the society of the cities, maintaining under arduous conditions the vestiges of a Latin tradition. The eventual triumph of the Latin over the German—the fact that the Teutons left so small a trace on Italian life—forms part of a wider victory of the cities over the countryside. Only at the extremities of the peninsula, in the Kingdom of Naples and in the partly French territory of Piedmont, were feudal institutions able to maintain themselves.

The specifically Italian society that emerged in the later Middle Ages was a society grouped around city-states. As in ancient Greece, the city-state seemed to Italians the normal form of political organization. Its classic home was the north-central belt extending from Lombardy through Umbria, but everywhere the city marked the growth of a mercantile, cultivated society. Even today the administrative map of Italy gives the impression of a collection of city-states. The Italian province, unlike the French department, is no artificial territorial unit. It is the surrounding countryside of a historic city, which gives its name and its character to the province as a whole.

Nor is Italy dominated—as are France and England—by a single metropolis. Like Germany or the United States, Italy has a number of great cities, which vie with each other for pre-eminence. Rome, the capital, may have a historical tradition unparalleled in the Western world. But, as an *Italian* city, it is an upstart: in the fourteenth century, when Florence and Milan were leaders of trade and culture, Rome was a collection of squalid villages huddling amidst monumental ruins; its career as a metropolis dates only from 1870, and even today, like Washington, it is primarily a civil service and tourist city. A few decades ago both Naples and Milan were larger. The former is still the metropolis for the whole South and one of the peninsula's two major ports. The latter plays a similar metropolitan role for the North: the "moral capital of Italy," it has been headquarters for both Fascism and Socialism; it takes the lead in publishing, in intellectual life, in all forms of progressive activity. And then of course there is Florence—quiet, mellow, dignified, not unlike Boston in its position of a cultural capital long past its zenith.

The South does not share fully in this predominantly urban culture. Sicily contains a number of important cities, but on the southern mainland Bari, the next largest city after Naples, has only a quarter its population. The characteristic southern city is a large market town—provincial and miserable behind the pretentious architecture of its public buildings. Many of them are not really urban at all in the sense of housing a population engaged in industrial or commercial activities. Towns like Cerignola in the Tavoliere of Apulia are peasant slums, filled with unemployed or semi-employed agricultural laborers.

The agricultural classes, landowning peasants, tenants, and laborers, may be a third the population of the country—somewhat less than a third, in fact, get their living from the soil—but for the most part they have simply been passive spectators of its history. It is true of peasants everywhere that they should live without a history. But in a country so urban in its tradition as Italy—and at the same time so heavily rural—the misunderstanding and latent hostility between city and country have been peculiarly intense. The city-dweller has a more than customary scorn for the rustic, the *cafone* or *villano*—which the latter returns with a silent but profound distrust. To the Italian peasant, the man from the city may be an absentee landlord, a merchant, or a government official—in all cases, he is an exploiter. He appears infrequently and with only one purpose: to cheat the peasant of what he has earned through desperate and unending toil. The nation may be called his nation—but most of the time it forgets about him. He feels its presence only in the guise of the policeman and the tax collector, or when it takes away his sons to fight in some distant and incomprehensible war.

As late as 1880, the vast majority of the Italian peasants were illiterate and disenfranchised. They now read and they now vote—after their fashion—but they still lead their own life, closed in on itself and apart from that of the nation as a whole. This is particularly the case in the South. Here in the more backward areas the peasants carry on a mode of existence that has remained basically unchanged through thousands of years. Italian writers have called it pre-Christian, even pre-Roman. Technically, these peasants are Christians: in reality, their religion is a primitive nature-worship, inadequately clothed in Christian forms, in which the priest commands little respect except as a kind of earth-magician. The powers of nature are terrible and require propitiation. Each domestic animal has its patron saint. And these latter form a hierarchy of deities, culminating in the local saint—the lineal descendant of a pagan god —who has taken the village under his especial protection.

Through the centuries, the southern peasants have borne their lot with patience. Only very occasionally, when the measure of their sufferings has seemed to pass all human bearing, have they risen in desperate, inarticulate protest. Then for a few days or years their fury has known no limits as they have burned and murdered with the blind pent-up anger of centuries. The last and greatest of these outbreaks was the "Brigandage" of 1860–1865—a bewildered, hopeless uprising against the new masters who had descended from the North in what the official historians called the unification of the country. To old peasants in remote districts the "Brigandage" long remained "the war," the only one that had a real meaning for them

—much as in comparable districts of the American South old women used to speak of another sort of civil war that occurred at the very same time. This tradition of direct peasant action found a more peaceful echo in the autumn of 1949 when the Calabrian peasants of the Sila area staged their mass occupation of neglected land that was to galvanize a reluctant government into finally doing something about the problem of the great estates.

In the South, at least, the peasants' idea of the city-dweller as an exploiter is by no means inappropriate. The Italian South never possessed the sort of independent, responsible middle class that created the democratic governments of France, England, or the United States. Outside the major cities, the southern middle class for the most part has consisted of hangers-on, of the go-betweens who transmitted the orders of the great landowners to the peasants. These *galantuomini*—to use an over-flattering title—might be the renting agents, the lawyers, the notaries, and the pharmacists of the larger villages and market towns. As a class, they formed the least attractive element in Italian life. Brutal to those beneath them and servile to those above, they were characteristically mercenary, narrow-minded, lazy, and pliable. This latter quality is revealed in the instability of southern politics, which has been substantially under the domination of the local *galantuomini*. In the South, until very recently the only regularly organized political party was the Communist: the rest of the vote shifted from one party to another as the circumstances of the time appeared to dictate. From the First World War to the mid-century, the area witnessed no less than four of these mass shifts. It was the southern middle class that Carlo Levi had primarily in mind when in *The Watch* he wrote of his countrymen as being divided into two great groups—the *contadini* (literally "peasants"), who actually worked and produced, and the *luigini* (after Don Luigi Magalone, a southern local official), the appallingly numerous class of parasites who lived off the labor of the others.

In the North, society follows the more normal western European model. Businessmen and industrial and clerical workers form nearly as high a percentage of the population and perform roughly the same functions as in France or western Germany.* Yet even here, the middle classes have demonstrated a curious lack of self-confi-

* For a more detailed analysis of Italian social classes, see Chapters 8 and 10.

dence and faith in their own values. In manners and standards they have tended to take their cue from the aristocracy—a numerous and extremely heterogeneous class, with titles of the most varied origin, some old and highly honorable, some new, and some frankly spurious. In Italy titles do not mean very much. Nearly every educated person has some sort of title—knightly or academic as the case may be. Not only physicians and professors are addressed by their title, as in other western countries, but also lawyers and engineers. Under the Savoy monarchy, *cavalieri* and *commendatori* sprouted wholesale among civil servants and business leaders: as the good-humored King Victor Emmanuel II is reputed to have said, "A cigar and the cross of a *cavaliere* are things that you cannot refuse to any one." Today Italy is a republic—but the penchant for titles persists.

This exaggerated respect for rank and hierarchy is at variance with what is most vital in the Italian historical tradition. After all, it was the free tradesmen and artisans of the cities who founded the modern concept of the "Italian" by challenging the prerogatives of the local nobility. For three centuries, the merchant patrician was the type figure of the public-spirited Italian. Then in the mid-sixteenth century came the Counter Reformation and the Spanish domination of the country—and with them a stifling of intellectual life and a rigidifying of social forms. The two centuries of Spanish predominance have left permanent traces on the social behavior of the peninsula. From this period dates the usual form of polite address, the *lei* (literally "she")—an awkward locution, for which Mussolini tried in vain to substitute the more natural *voi*. Today Italian social life bewilders the American visitor by its combination of an inherited formalism and a spontaneous informality that makes him feel closer to home than in France, Germany or even Great Britain.

Such contrasts in social behavior bring one to the central paradox of contemporary Italian life. Italy is in name a democratic republic —yet at the same time it is a country in which class lines are still very much in evidence. It has never experienced the sort of classic, epoch-making revolution on which nations like France have founded their democratic tradition. Its modern, fluid, industrial society is a recent accretion superimposed on a hierarchical, unchanging, quasi-feudal society. Centuries apart in mentality, these two societies have somehow managed to coexist. Although the former may predominate in the cities of the North, and the latter in the back country of the South, in most parts of the peninsula they can be found side by side. And so the two great problems of contemporary Italy that have occupied us up to now—the problem of general poverty and the cultural cleavage between North and South—actually merge into a third problem that is the deepest of them all: how could a Western-type democracy evolve out of a society that remained basically conservative, stratified, and profoundly rooted in the manners of the pre-industrial age?

3

The Legacy of History

1. GLORY AND HUMILIATION

WHETHER or not they are consciously aware of it, a sense of history hangs over the Italian people. Italy has the longest continuous history of any great Western country. Throughout the peninsula, and even more strikingly in Sicily, the architectural monuments of twenty-five hundred years confront each other, disparate in style but somehow blended into harmony by the touch of the same bright sun and the softening influence of time. None of the successive epochs of Italian history has failed to leave its mark on the landscape. As opposed to a country like Greece, which lived for centuries in the backwaters of history, in Italy the record is continuous, the stream of civilized activity has never been interrupted.

Sometimes Italians feel crushed by the burden of their history. There is so much to remember, so much to live up to. At other times, they are perplexed by the ambiguity of their inheritance. For their memories are conflicting: memories of glory and memories of humiliation are equally obsessive. Italian history has offered first one and then the other in a regular succession of epochs varying in length from a few decades to a span of seven hundred years.

Few Italian memories go back before the era of Rome. Scholars may busy themselves with the Etruscans and with the Greek colonies of Sicily and the south Italian shores, but for the run of Italians their great history begins with the conquest of the peninsula by the city-state of Rome and the subsequent establishment of a universal empire over the whole Mediterranean basin. This, of course, is the greatest of Italian memories. Italy has never been so important since, nor can she hope to be. Hence the memory of Rome has doubtless done Italy more harm than good. Those who have tried to reawaken Italians to their "Roman" mission have generally proved to be mere demagogues and deceivers—like the visionary, unstable "tribune" Cola di Rienzo, whose proclamation of a restored Roman Republic bore little resemblance to the squalid realities of life in the eternal city of the fourteenth century, abandoned even by its popes, and like Mussolini, whose promises of Mediterranean dominion were only slightly less fantastic. Sensible Italians today tend to discount the Roman inheritance as a will-o'-the-wisp leading the country away from a realistic assessment of its potentialities in the twentieth-century world.

On the glory of Rome, there followed seven centuries of humiliation. When in the year 330 Constantine transferred the imperial capital to the Greek city of Byzantium, Italy ceased to be the center of the Empire. And with the territorial dismemberment of the whole western half of the Roman dominion, the peninsula and the islands fell prey to a bewildering succession of foreign invaders and over-lords—Vandals and Goths, Arabs and Byzantine Greeks, Normans and Lombards. Even the Papacy sank into miserable disrepute. And its restoration to a position of spiritual and moral prestige was again the work of foreigners: the German emperors from across the Alps.

In the eleventh century began the age of the communes—and with it the development of a specifically Italian consciousness. The communal assertion of urban independence could not give unity to the peninsula—quite the contrary—but it brought Italy again to the forefront of Western civilization. The next five centuries were to be another period of pride and self-confidence. Although most of the urban republics eventually fell under the control of unscrupulous and high-spirited despots, they continued to advance in practical endeavor and in the cultivation of the plastic arts. By the fifteenth century—the century of the so-called Renaissance—it was clear that the Italians were the cultural, if not the political, masters of Europe. Few saw the dangers to which their disunity and constant quarrels exposed them.

These dangers were suddenly revealed to an astonished world in 1494 when the French King Charles VIII inaugurated a new era of foreign invasions. The next four decades—the "High Renaissance"

—saw the culmination of Italy's artistic endeavors, but also the destruction of her liberties. There followed a second epoch of humiliation—the two centuries of Spanish domination which were to leave so strong an impress on Italian social life. It was in these centuries that Italians acquired their reputation for subservience and frivolity: by the eighteenth century, Venice, once the mistress of European commerce, had become little more than a shadow republic, the playground of dissolute foreigners. But the "decadence" of the period 1550–1750 has been greatly exaggerated. In different forms, perhaps, but with undiminished vigor, the Italian creative impulse continued to manifest itself. The sixteenth century was the great age of Italian science. The seventeenth saw the triumphs of baroque sculpture and architecture and the rebuilding of Rome as the predominantly baroque city that it has remained to this day. And in the late seventeenth and eighteenth centuries the Italian school of music produced a succession of masters—many of them recently rediscovered—who for sheer fecundity and verve of composition have never been surpassed.

Some time after the middle of the eighteenth century, Italians date the beginning of their "Risorgimento"—the epoch of national renewal, both cultural and political, that was to culminate a hundred years later in the unification of the country. Despite its slow beginnings, and the checks and disappointments to which it was subject, the Risorgimento clearly ranks in Italians' memories as one of the glorious epochs of their history. But the succeeding era, the first half century of united Italy's existence, has proved more puzzling. Was it a fall from glory or the prelude to new heights of national attainment? This uncertainty gave rise to a widespread sense of dissatisfaction with the very real achievements of the Italian kingdom and was largely responsible, as we shall see later on, for the bizarre circumstances surrounding Italy's intervention in the First World War.

With the advent of Mussolini, however, the majority of Italians became convinced that their country had entered on another of its epochs of greatness. And for fifteen years the outside world thought so too. The fact that the Fascist experience ended in disaster—that the dream of a regenerated Italy turned out to be a sham—is the bitterest of the many disillusionments that Italians carry in their memories. In the Second World War Italy sank again into the depths of humiliation—the ally first of one side, then of the other, called traitor by both, respected by neither. Not since the Middle Ages had the Italians seen their beautiful countryside so terribly ravaged. This experience is the freshest of all in Italian memories; it is the psychological wound with which the American must always reckon if he is to try to understand contemporary Italy.

In this alternation of glory and humiliation, as in so much else, the South cannot fully share. With southerners the memories are nearly all of one type: for seven hundred years, in open or in mitigated form, they knew nothing but subjection to alien rulers. A sense of inferior status is deeply rooted in their consciousness. In sheer self-defense they have developed the qualities that make them despised and distrusted—the passive acceptance of oppression, the suspicious reserve, the constant resort to guile, and the pessimism as to any future improvement of their lot: these are the traditional defenses of peasant peoples against those more powerful and better educated than they.

The southerners have much in their history to be proud of. They can recall the splendor of the Greek colonies—Syracuse and Rhegium, Tarentum and Neapolis, centers of commerce to this day. And they can think of the medieval republic of Amalfi and the Kingdom of Sicily, founded by the Normans in the early twelfth century and continued by the Hohenstauffen emperors, which in its day led Europe in the arts and in statecraft. More recently, they can point out that the South has contributed a disproportionate number of Italy's greatest thinkers: Giordano Bruno, Giambattista Vico, Gaetano Mosca, and Benedetto Croce, to mention only the most distinguished.

Yet even these achievements are essentially the achievements of foreigners—or of highly endowed individuals far removed from the life of the southern masses. To the bulk of the people, the decisive experience has been the six centuries of foreign exploitation—an experience begun in 1266 with the conquest of the southern mainland by the French House of Anjou, continued by the House of Aragon, then by the Spanish monarchy itself, then for two decades in the early eighteenth century by the Austrian Hapsburgs, and finally by a younger branch of the House of Bourbon. This succession of ruling houses is actually a continuous history, in which the

Spanish influence predominates. It is a record of nearly uninterrupted decay brought on by neglect, absenteeism, and a profound ineptitude in fiscal policy. In the thirteenth century, the South was not notably inferior to the rest of Italy in culture and living standards. Two centuries later the gap was already great: the South scarcely participated in the creative endeavors of the Renaissance. To this day, the gap has grown ever wider.

Thus when the unification of the country finally came about, most southerners watched the great event as passive spectators. Those who actively participated in the political ferment of the Risorgimento were a narrow segment of the population, drawn from the middle classes and the more progressive aristocrats. The southerners did not rise in defense of their Bourbon king—they had little enough reason to love him. But at the same time they regarded with suspicious detachment the arrival of the unifiers from the North. Only in the more emotional moments of their "liberation" did they show any true enthusiasm—when Garibaldi and his legendary force of a thousand men conquered in ten weeks the island of Sicily or during the popular plebiscite that ratified the annexation of the Kingdom of Naples to the new unitary state. Most of the time, it was all one to the southern peasant: he had simply changed his old foreign master for a new one.

2. THE MANNER OF UNIFICATION

The way the unification was carried out could not fail to intensify this suspicion that the South was again being subjected to foreign rule. As opposed to the formation of the United States—or even of Germany—Italy was not created as a federation of formerly sovereign states which maintained their identities within the new nation. The old Italian states simply disappeared, swallowed up by the state of Savoy-Piedmont (or the Kingdom of Sardinia, as it was rather inappropriately called, from the desolate island the powers had awarded it in 1720). In many ways, Piedmont was an illogical area to become the nucleus of the new Italy. Tucked away in the northwest corner of the country, with a ruling family and aristocracy that generally spoke French rather than Italian, it had only recently come into the front rank of Italian development. Several decades of a progressive economic policy, however, and the strong international position won for it by its prime minister, Count Camillo Benso di Cavour, had enabled Piedmont to become the chosen vessel for the aspirations of Italy. By the sheer force of personality and logical persuasion, Cavour, the greatest statesman of modern Italy, had induced his countrymen to accept the House of Savoy as their rulers. This was not the solution that most Italians had originally preferred. The other two of Italy's trinity of founders, Mazzini and Garibaldi, had dreamed of a democratic republic. Somewhat earlier, a more conservative circle of patriots had talked of an Italian federation under the presidency of the Pope.

What Italy got, in any case, was Cavour's solution. This meant that the Piedmontese constitution, the *Statuto* granted by King Charles Albert in 1848, was simply extended to the whole country. Along with it went the other Piedmontese institutions: administrative structure, laws, taxes—and conscription. These were mostly of foreign inspiration and were a hybrid of British and French models. The Parliament reflected the British example: it consisted of a Chamber of Deputies elected by the more prosperous citizens, and a Senate appointed by the King. The economic policy was likewise English-inspired in its doctrinaire insistence on the principle of free trade. Local administration, on the other hand, was basically French. It was almost an exact replica of the highly centralized system developed by Napoleon. Municipal and provincial councils were elective, but their powers were limited. Ultimate authority rested in the prefect, the governor of the province, who was an appointed official. He owed his appointment to the Minister of the Interior in Rome; he reported and was responsible solely to him, and he could be recalled by him at any time. To many it seemed that the Minister of the Interior and the 90-odd prefects were the real rulers of Italy.

Hence areas that a few months before had been sovereign states now found themselves uniformly managed from the center. To a country as localist in tradition as Italy, this was a tremendous shock —although perhaps an essential one, if the unity of the new country was to be made a reality. Quite naturally, it was most bewildering in the South. Here, since loyal administrative talent of local origin was scarce, the new government tended to appoint trusted northerners as prefects. These officials descended on the South in a manner not unreminiscent of American carpetbaggers and proceeded with more zeal than tact to "piedmontize" the provinces committed to their charge.

The result was a subordination of southern to northern interests. The process was not wholly conscious. The national government and the local officials simply did what their training, administrative and ideological, had taught them was proper. Thus they embarked on the great program of public works and railroad building that alone could give tangible unity to the Italian state. And to balance these enormous expenditures they imposed new taxes and sold royal and Church lands in a hurry for whatever prices they could get. True to their free trade principles, they extended the low tariff policy of Piedmont to the entire peninsula. The combined effect of these measures was a total upset in the traditional economic arrangements of the former Kingdom of Naples. For all their callousness and inefficiency, the Bourbon kings had maintained a fiscal policy which, while it might be retrograde in the eyes of nineteenth-century reformers, at least prevented too heavy a tax burden from falling on the peasants. They kept taxes low on articles of basic consumption and relied on import duties to balance the budget. The new policy was just the reverse. Practically over night the South changed from a country with one of the lowest tax rates in Europe into an area with one of the heaviest, and from high tariff protection to practically none at all. Southern industry—an anemic growth at best— sustained a shock from which it never recovered. Meantime the peasants were seeing their domestic handicrafts undermined by the machine-made products from the North that began to arrive over the new roads and railways. No wonder that so many southerners regarded the foundation of united Italy as a dubious blessing and that the peasants of so many areas gave active support to the anti-Piedmontese "Brigandage" of the early 1860's.

Thus the new Kingdom started on its career with its southern half in a state of smoldering discontent. This would not have been so grave if the unifiers of Italy had not simultaneously alienated the greatest moral force in the peninsula, the Roman pontiff. The Pope had been outraged by the Piedmontese policy of dissolving religious congregations and confiscating Church lands—a policy extended in the 1860's to the rest of the country. In addition, the foundation of the Italian Kingdom in 1861 had deprived him of most of his territorial domains. Nine years later, with the completion of the unification, he lost Rome itself, which thereupon became the national capital. This forcible termination of his temporal sovereignty the Pope refused to accept. He rejected the law passed by the Italian Parliament guaranteeing him the free exercise of his spiritual and diplomatic functions—although he tacitly profited by its provisions. He excommunicated the founders of the new state and cautioned good Catholics not to vote or to accept public office. A prisoner by his own choice, he shut himself up in the Vatican.

Even the death of the old Pope Pius IX in 1878 did not alter the situation. The new pontiff, the great Leo XIII, maintained his predecessor's attitude of intransigence. In practice, however, it proved impossible to erect an impregnable wall between Catholicism and the new Italy. Through a complex network of semiofficial intermediaries, Church and state worked out a *modus vivendi* for arranging, in characteristic Italian fashion, the countless questions of mutual concern in education and appointments to ecclesiastical office. At the same time, good Catholics gradually began to participate in public life. They were tacitly permitted to make a distinction between national politics, which remained a forbidden field, and local affairs, in which they might freely vote and hold office. After the turn of the century, even participation in national elections was not wholly banned. In 1904 and still more explicitly in 1909, Pius X relaxed the *non expedit,* the Papal admonition against voting. By the outbreak of the First World War, practicing Catholics were almost ready for full participation in national life.

By this time, however, the harm had already been done. The intransigent attitude of the Church toward the new nation had prevented a normal development of Italian political activity. By keeping practicing Catholics out of public life, it had sharply reduced the reservoir of support and talent on which the new regime could draw. More particularly many conservatives of the Center and the South, loyal to religion and to their old sovereigns, were led to regard the Italian state with sullen distaste. And the same was true of the mass of the peasants, practically none of whom, in any case, could qualify as voters. Hence the human material both for a truly conservative and for a truly popular party was lacking. Politics became the exclu-

sive domain of the middle classes and the more "enlightened" segment of the aristocracy—in a word, of those who subscribed to the
fashionable doctrines of anticlericalism and *laissez faire*. Within the
governing class, there was near unanimity on basic ideological and
economic questions. Under these circumstances, party distinctions
naturally could mean little, and the terms Right and Left soon
became blurred and confused. From the 1870's to the First World
War, Italian politics had a curious air of unreality.

This development was particularly serious, since it came in a
country with a Latin tradition and a long experience of government
by outsiders. It seemed to confirm the attitude, so widespread in
Latin countries, that the government was something detached from
the life of the individual, and for which he bore no responsibility.
The government might oppress and defraud him—sometimes even
grant him a favor—but it was not *his* government and it was not up
to him to see that it functioned properly and gave impartial treatment to all. Rather it was an alien power to be propitiated and
cajoled on a strictly personal basis. Thus the circumstances of the
unification encouraged the Italian tendency to think of public (and
even religious) affairs in terms of subterfuge and *combinazione*. And
the mechanics of the parliamentary regime lent itself to such practices. Within a decade of the completion of Italian unity, the halls
of Parliament in Rome had become a vast market-place for the trading of political influence.

3. THE PARLIAMENTARY REGIME

In theory, the *Statuto* of 1848 had left to the King more than merely
nominal functions. It had made the Piedmontese monarchy a constitutional regime, but it had not specified that the King would
always permit his ministers to act for him and that these ministers
must necessarily command a majority in the Chamber of Deputies.
This interpretation of the *Statuto* simply developed in practice, as
Victor Emmanuel II chose to behave as a constitutional sovereign. It
received its formal ratification in 1876, with the fall of the old Right.

This event marks the founding of modern Italian politics. The
fifteen previous years had been a transition period in which it was
not yet clear what course the new parliamentary regime would take.

In June 1861, Cavour had died, just three months after the proclamation of the Italian Kingdom, but his political heirs had carried on in the path that he had marked out. This group of political leaders, known as the parliamentary Right, were almost uniformly men of the highest integrity. Wealthy landowners or prosperous professional men by origin, they were able, personally honest, and devoted to the public service. Yet at the same time they tended to be old-fashioned and unaware of the true character of the new state they had brought into being. Like the American Federalists, they had an aristocratic aloofness and rigidity that disqualified them to continue the work they had begun in so lofty a spirit.

Facing them on the benches of the Chamber of Deputies sat the Left, a motley assortment of oppositionists, most of whose leaders came from the South. They were generally of less exalted origin than the men of the Right, their manners and principles were less impeccable, and their loyalty to the Savoy monarchy was doubtful, since many of them had originally been Mazzinian republicans. Yet they represented more adequately than the Right the anticlerical, commercial-minded middle class that was actually the backbone of the new regime. In March 1876 they put the government in the minority. Whereupon the King called one of the leaders of the Left —admittedly among its tamer spokesmen—Agostino Depretis, to the premiership. His act not only fixed the developing precedents of the constitutional regime; it inaugurated the era of *trasformismo*.

The latter term is an Italianism rich in innuendo. It signifies the dissolution of political parties that followed the coming of the Left to power and more particularly the extension of the suffrage six years later. For once in office the leaders of the Left behaved much like the Right. They became loyal monarchists and continued the policies of administrative centralization and economic *laissez faire*. Moreover, it soon developed that their chief interest was to stay in office at all costs. To accomplish this, Depretis worked out a new technique for assuring himself of a safe majority, a technique that his rivals among the leaders of the Left were quick to imitate. Casting aside any unnecessary scruples about political principles, Depretis simply picked up his majority where he could find it. He made bargains with one and all, whether from the Left or from the Right. Any deputy willing to support the government could thereby acquire a claim to a suitable share of official patronage. And many members of the Right, weary of perpetual and hopeless opposition, were quite ready to play Depretis' game. The result was *trasformismo*—the "transformation" of deputies from supposedly reliable members of the opposition to stalwarts of the government majority.

Hence the Italian parliamentary regime developed in conformity with neither of the more usual European models. It did not take form as the alternation in power of two large parties on the English model. Nor did it evolve into a game of constructing coalitions among a number of parties basically ideological in nature, as in France. In the Italy of the 1880's organized political parties virtually ceased to exist. The Italian Parliament degenerated into an amorphous mass of deputies, dependent on the skillful orchestration of an official majority-monger. He alone was able to make the system work. For this reason some historians have called it a regime of parliamentary dictatorship. The term is not entirely apt, since it implies a loss of civil liberties, which in Italy before 1922 was definitely not the case. Yet it is difficult to find a better name for a system in which a talented prime minister regularly managed to dominate the political life of his country for a decade at a stretch. The political history of Italy from 1876 to 1914 is the story of three of these parliamentary dictatorships, broken only by a confused era of social disorder and extraconstitutional rule at the turn of the century. From 1876 to 1887, Depretis was the ringmaster. He was succeeded by Francesco Crispi, who maintained a more intermittent supremacy until 1896, when his efforts to found an Italian colonial empire ended in humiliating defeat by the Ethiopians at Adua. The third was Giovanni Giolitti—master of Italy from 1901 to 1914— the supreme virtuoso of *trasformismo*.

Under Giolitti the art of manufacturing majorities reached a perfection of technique. He combined the usual methods of post-election bargaining with an extremely effective pressure on the elections themselves. In the North, elections were conducted with relative honesty. But in the South a mixture of bribery and intimidation, and even occasional murder, resulted in the return of a bloc of loyal Giolittian deputies distinguished for little more than their voting regularity. The South naturally lent itself to the game of *giolittismo*. In an impoverished area where real political power rested with very narrow cliques, it was relatively easy to "buy" the vote of a whole constituency.

This sort of bargain was the crux of the system. Administrative centralization combined with the supremacy of Parliament to produce a situation in which the business of government rested on a regular traffic between the two poles of authority—the prefects and the deputies. The chief local officials, the prefects, depended on the Minister of the Interior and through him on the government in power. The government, then, expected the prefects to help in preserving its majority in the Chamber of Deputies. Hence a prefect who hoped for promotion was virtually required to make a suitable display of zeal in working for the election of deputies loyal to the government. And similarly, in return for their support, the deputies besieged the government for favors—a new road or other public improvement for their district that would help them to get reelected. As a result, everybody was poking into everyone else's business: the deputies were meddling in administration, and the prefects in politics. Between the two, the concept of the public interest was in danger of becoming lost entirely.

The parliamentary system as developed in the 1880's certainly could not be described as democratic. In 1882, the electorate was enlarged from somewhat more than half a million to about two million. Yet still the mass of peasants and workers remained unenfranchised. It was not until 1912 that Italy acquired something approaching universal manhood suffrage. Basically, the Italian government deserved the epigram that it was a rule over "thirty millions by three thousand for the benefit of three hundred thousand."

Yet one should not exaggerate the faults of the system. Italy had, after all, a free government, based on liberal, constitutional principles. Moreover, by the 1890's Italian politics was beginning to take on a new vitality. In 1892, a regular Socialist party was organized through the union of an earlier labor party with a group of Socialist intellectuals under the leadership of the brilliant, lovable Filippo Turati. Despite a certain verbal immaturity and a tendency to internal factionalism, the Socialists were a real party, grouped around a fairly coherent ideology. They had the bulk of the Italian industrial workers behind them and even a part of the peasantry. Along with the Republicans—the gallant vestigial remnant of the

Mazzinian faith—and the more amorphous Radicals, the Socialists constituted the *Estrema* of the Chamber, the Extreme Left as opposed to the now virtually meaningless Left itself. During six years of social ferment, from 1894 to 1900, the *Estrema* was threatened with dissolution. And indeed the whole concept of constitutional government was in danger as a succession of authoritarian prime ministers resorted to police repression and martial law. But the final result was salutary. Constitutionalism was restored, and the *Estrema* emerged from its trials fortified both in temper and in electoral support.

Similarly the more conservative political leaders found their own principles reinvigorated. These now began to speak of themselves as Liberals. The term Liberal was far from clear. In the South it might mean little more than membership in Giolitti's caucus. But in areas like Piedmont to be a Liberal meant to favor a constitutionalism that was both conservative and open-minded. Like the members of the *Estrema,* a great many northern Liberals actually stood for something. And the same was true of the Catholics, when after the turn of the century they began to participate more regularly in Italian political life. The more democratically minded of the Catholic leaders proposed to act as spokesmen for the peasantry, which had remained leaderless and inarticulate in the new Kingdom. By the outbreak of the First World War, then, Italy was on her way to acquiring a set of regularly functioning political parties.

She was similarly on the way to democracy. In the election of 1913, the mass of the Italian workers and peasants voted for the first time. The new extended suffrage had been Giolitti's gift to the Italian people about whom he frequently seemed so cynical. And this action was more typical of the man than might appear at first sight. For all his shameless manipulation of the electorate, Giolitti had a basic patriotism and sense of what was good for his country. Despising rhetoric and the display of high principles, he seldom revealed the emotional wellsprings of his own conduct. The virtues he exemplified were not exciting—realism, moderation, good sense. But through their systematic application to the problems confronting him, through tact and patience, he had succeeded in accomplishing a great deal. What he had done was to prepare the Italian people for democracy, by extending educational facilities, encouraging trade unions and cooperatives, and making a start on social legislation. It is not going too far to say that he had given modern Italy the happiest and most prosperous decade that she had yet known.

Giolitti's aims may have been modest, but at least he did not promise more than he could accomplish. Eight years after the end of the Giolittian era, Italy acquired a new master. Initially, Mussolini appeared to offer her far more than Giolitti. In the end, he proved to have given her less. And in retrospect the evils of Giolittian corruption seemed as nothing compared to the evils of Fascist tyranny. It was this comparison between Giolitti and what followed him that induced such eminent scholars as Gaetano Mosca and Gaetano Salvemini to revise the harsh judgment they had earlier rendered on his regime. Most students of Italian politics have followed their lead. Today historians readily grant that Giolitti has a permanent claim on the gratitude of his countrymen for the way he enlarged the effective range of Italian public life by bringing vast new strata of the population into active political participation.*

4. PRELUDE TO A NATIONAL REVIVAL

At the time, however, few could take so long a view. All that was young, active, and intelligent in Italian life seemed to be in opposition to Giolitti and Giolittianism. The first decade of the twentieth century saw a notable renaissance in Italian intellectual and literary creativity. Once again Italy was producing intellectual leaders who could command the respect of all Europe. The philosopher Benedetto Croce was subjecting to a searching critique the pedestrian ideology of the Italian ruling classes and developing a new and flexible form of historical idealism that was to serve as the philosophic credo of educated Italians for the next half century. The political theorists Vilfredo Pareto and Gaetano Mosca were mercilessly exposing the shams of parliamentarism and elaborating a doctrine of rule by elites that both reflected the political realities in their own country and foreshadowed a new bluntness in the application of political power. The poet Gabriele d'Annunzio, with torrents of heady lan-

---

* This is substantially the thesis of A. William Salomone's excellent study *Italian Democracy in the Making: The Political Scene in the Giolittian Era 1900–1914* (Philadelphia, 1945).

guage, was seeking to raise his countrymen from dullness and mediocrity to an appreciation of the glories of the sensual world. And a number of lesser writers were offering variations on similar themes.

All of these writers, either directly or by implication, attacked the bourgeois caution and self-satisfaction symbolized in the person of Giolitti. The Socialists might have been expected to respond in loud assent. Actually the master of *trasformismo* had succeeded in domesticating even the Socialists. While they did not sit in his government, they enjoyed his favors and sometimes praised him openly. It was not until the latter part of his long rule that they regained their revolutionary militancy. The chief political expression of the new literary stirrings came rather from a more conservative direction. In December 1910, at a congress in Florence, an Italian Nationalist party was organized. The Nationalists, like their fellows in other countries, were monarchist, anti-parliamentarian, and proponents of an intrinsic national dynamism. More particularly, they were disgusted with the policy of caution in foreign affairs to which the Italian government had adhered—except during Crispi's era of African adventure—ever since the unification of the Kingdom. The Nationalists argued that it was time for Italy to play a more aggressive and glorious role. In short, they wanted warfare and an empire.

And so in 1911 Italy went to war to conquer Tripoli from the Turks. It would be incorrect to say that Nationalist agitation alone pushed Giolitti into a venture that seemed so alien to his nature. Actually the Ministry of Foreign Affairs had been preparing for the occupation of Tripoli for more than two decades by obtaining the assent of the great powers one after another until all had finally agreed. From a narrowly patriotic standpoint, the Tripolitan venture was a success. Although it took years to complete the conquest and pacify the country, Italy had at last obtained something resembling a colonial empire. To the pathetic strips of east African coast that were all that remained of Crispi's brave dreams, Giolitti had now added a real colony, barren and unpromising it is true, but extensive in area and gratifyingly close to the mother country.

Yet the precedent of a war encouraged by Nationalist propaganda was to have a more serious sequel. In 1914, on the outbreak of the First World War, Italy elected to remain neutral. Although technically in alliance with Germany and Austria, Italy had better reason to favor France and Britain, since it was the Austrians who held the Italian-inhabited areas, the South Tyrol and Trieste, coveted by Italian patriots. These—and other, non-Italian areas besides—the Entente powers dangled before the eyes of the government in Rome as the price of the latter's intervention in the war. But Germany and Austria were likewise willing to pay for Italian neutrality. Giolitti believed this to be the better bargain. And not only his followers—a majority of the Chamber of Deputies—but the politicians who spoke for the Italian masses, the Socialists and the Catholics, agreed with him. Giolitti, however, was now out of power. The government that had succeeded him had fallen under the influence of the Nationalists and the King. And these had decided for war.

Italy actually entered the war through a combination of hard bargaining and mob pressure. By the secret Treaty of London, of April 26, 1915, in return for specific promises of territorial gain, she agreed to declare war on the side of France and Britain within one month. But how was this to be accomplished? The mass both of the Italian people and of their elected representatives opposed the step. Time dragged on, and the period specified in the secret treaty was running out. In the end it took a frenzied series of street demonstrations led by the poet D'Annunzio himself to induce the reluctant deputies to vote for war.

It was no wonder, then, that the war was unpopular—that morale was low and desertion a commonplace. Nor did the fighting itself go very well. After two years of inconclusive combat with the Austrians in heartbreaking mountain terrain, Italy sustained one of the worst defeats in her history. On October 24, 1917, the Italians' lines broke at Caporetto and for several days it appeared doubtful whether they could recover at all. Eventually they made a stand on the Piave river, just short of Venice; they regrouped and regained their nerve, and in the end they participated in the general Allied victory. But the total military record was far different from what the patriots and war enthusiasts had originally expected.

The Peace Conference added to their disappointments. Italy received as promised the South Tyrol and Trieste, including the largely Slavic hinterland of that city. But President Wilson drew the line at turning over to Italian rule the overwhelmingly Slavic population of the southern Dalmatian coast, which had also been specified in the Treaty of London, and the city of Fiume, which the Italians had rather unwisely added to their claims. Whereupon Italian patriots raised a great cry of protest, and the Italian premier and foreign minister walked out of the Conference. But their gesture accomplished nothing. Wilson's verdict stood. Italy may have fought on the victorious side, but her patriots remained convinced that they had been cheated of their fair reward. The whole Nationalist wing of public opinion was stirred by a profound discontent.

Their grievances were matched by a still more widespread dissatisfaction among the Italian laboring masses. These had never understood why Italy was in the war at all. In 1915 the Socialist and Catholic leaders had given the watchword of a merely passive opposition to the war effort. The poor people of Italy had continued to work in the factories and on the land or to perform with sorrowful resignation their service in the trenches. They suffered and died and could see no meaning to it. It was only at the very end of the war that they began to discover that some positive gain might come out of the slaughter. A few found this positive message in Wilsonianism —in the doctrine of international understanding among free peoples. Something of the same feeling had already inspired a minority of Italian democrats who had favored a war policy not, as with the Nationalists, for narrowly egoistic reasons, but as an expression of solidarity with the two great European democracies. This sort of appeal, however, was too abstract for the Italian masses. The average worker needed a visible symbol to set his imagination aflame. He found it in the Bolshevik Revolution. For the Italian masses, the Russian uprising of November 1917 was the great revelation of the war years. It was an example that seemed to cry out for imitation. What the Russian workers had accomplished their Italian brothers could do also. The hour of millennial justice long promised by the Socialist leaders appeared at length to have arrived.

Hence in a country shaken by all the usual economic problems of a war's aftermath—shortages, unemployment, inflation—nearly everyone was discontented. Two rival doctrines of political renovation strove to win mastery of the state. Their conflict was to dominate the next three years of Italian history.

5. THE COLLAPSE OF ITALIAN DEMOCRACY

Initially the popular movements led by Socialists and Catholics seemed to have the better of it. For in 1919 Italy had become, in theory at least, a full electoral democracy. In the elections of that year, the first under universal manhood suffrage, the parties that claimed to speak for the Italian workers and peasants won an overwhelming triumph. Out of 500-odd seats in the Chamber of Deputies, the Socialists gained 157, and the Popular party, which had just been organized as the vehicle of political Catholicism, won another 100. Between them it looked as though they were about to establish a true Italian democracy.

The reverse occurred. Three years later Mussolini came to power and proceeded to the systematic destruction of democratic institutions. Within three more years, the leaders of Italian democracy had been reduced to a role of impotent opposition. They had failed catastrophically, and their failure has overshadowed Italian political history to this day.

The Socialists bear the primary responsibility. The Italian Socialist party, like the corresponding parties in other countries, was not nearly so revolutionary as its language implied. Theoretically loyal to the doctrine of Marx, in practice it accommodated itself to the realities of Italian parliamentarism. Under the leadership of intellectuals like Turati, it had developed into a reformist party that was quite willing to let the revolution come by way of the ballot and to strive rather for electoral democracy than for social overturn. True, there had always been a violent and self-consciously revolutionary wing, and this wing had succeeded in dominating the party from 1912 to 1914. But during the war years Turati and his legalist friends had partially re-established their authority. The election of 1919 had made the Socialists the strongest party in the Chamber. Together with the Popular party they could command a majority. It seemed that all they needed to do was to enter into an alliance with the Catholics and proceed to make Italian democracy a reality by embarking on a broad program of social reform.

This might perhaps have been possible had it not been for the example of the Bolshevik Revolution. The Italian workers—who periodically grew restive at the cautious policy of the parliamentary Socialists—now felt that the time for gradual measures was past. With the millennium just around the corner, it would be foolish to let the opportunity for revolution slip by. This apocalyptic enthusiasm had contributed heavily to the Socialist victory at the polls. And the hundred-odd new Socialist deputies whom the election had brought into the Chamber were mostly inexperienced men who mistook words for actions and revolutionary slogans for a social program.

The result was the phenomenon of "Maximalism"—the fatal weakness of Italian Socialism. Maximalism meant adherence to the maximum program of the party—a program of final aims as opposed to the gradualist minimum program that the party leadership had pursued in practice. In the Socialist party of 1919–22, the Maximalists were in a majority. But it was an incoherent majority, without leadership and without a clear idea of how it proposed to achieve its goals. The talent, the leadership of the party, lay to the right or the left of this amorphous Maximalist center. On the one side, Turati and his friends were trying to maintain a shaky pre-eminence and to preach moderation and patience. On the other side, a group of practical revolutionaries were demanding immediate action instead of violent words. These latter— disgusted with the incoherencies of the majority—were to secede from the main body of the Socialists in January 1921 to establish the Italian Communist party.

Meantime the Maximalists floundered in a morass of words, apparently under the illusion that the revolution was so inevitable that one needed to do nothing to bring it on. Mass meetings and popular enthusiasm would suffice. As opposed to the policy of Turati's moderates on the one side and of the Communists on the other—either one of which would have made sense—the Maximalists' activities made no sense at all. They fell neatly between the proverbial stools. In practice they did nothing to bring on the revolution. But at the same time by their verbal violence they alienated and frightened the more conservative elements of the population that might have welcomed, or at least accepted, a parliamentary program of social reform.

This incoherence revealed itself in dramatic form in the movement that was to mark the high point of the working-class agitation of the postwar years. In September 1920, the industrial workers of the north Italian cities—more particularly the metallurgical workers of Milan and Turin—staged the "occupation of the factories." This was what later became known as a sit-down strike. In general it was carried out in a disciplined and non-violent fashion. But it accomplished nothing. The Socialist leaders failed to capitalize on it, and the Prime Minister—once again Giolitti, now aging, but still the master of *combinazione*—persuaded the workers to end the occupation without granting them any immediate and tangible concessions. From this point on, the Italian working-class movement began to decline. Discouragement and defeatism set in as the workers gradually realized that their millennial hopes had come to nothing. After the occupation of the factories, the initiative passed from the Socialists to the forces of reaction. When in a last desperate effort to stop the Fascist advance the working-class leaders called a general strike in midsummer 1922, the outcome was a debacle—the "Caporetto" of Italian Socialism.*

The Catholic responsibility in the failure of Italian democracy has a direct connection with the mistakes of the Socialists. For the *Popolari*—the leaders of the new Popular party—could scarcely be enthusiastic about alliance with people who preached violence and social overturn. They might perhaps have come to an understanding with Turati and his moderates. But even with them, the ideological distrust between anticlerical Socialists and anti-Marxist Catholics set up a nearly impassable barrier. And when it was not Turati but the Maximalists with whom the *Popolari* would have to deal, a real parliamentary alliance became impossible.

On their side, many among the *Popolari* would not have wanted an understanding with the Socialists on any terms. The founder of the People's party—the astute and high-minded Sicilian priest Don Luigi Sturzo—was an advocate of social reform, as were the more aggressive deputies of the new party, among them a wiry

* A. Rossi, *The Rise of Italian Fascism: 1918–1922*, translated by Peter and Dorothy Wait (London, 1938), pp. 231–232.

younger leader from the newly annexed Trentino called Alcide De Gasperi. These people quite properly thought of themselves as Christian Democrats. Their reform program, while milder than that of the Socialists, was by no means timid, particularly on peasant questions; it included a fairly radical proposal for splitting up large landed holdings. But alongside the official leadership, the party included a conservative wing, whose allegiance to the cause of reform was uncertain. Defender of the interests of the Church before those of democracy, they were the heirs of the clericals who had gradually entered local politics in the latter part of the nineteenth century. Quite naturally, they feared and distrusted the Socialists. For them, the idea of a parliamentary alliance with the other great party of the Italian masses was out of the question.

Basically, the *Popolari* fell victim to their own virtues. A parliamentary party before all else, the *Popolari* put their sole reliance on legal methods and parliamentary activity. And they expected their opponents to behave in the same fashion. They did not understand that they were living in a revolutionary period, in which the proponents of direct action had all the advantages. Hence they recoiled from the armed self-defense that could alone have saved them. They refused to fight back and bowed their heads in Christian resignation as the rising torrent of Fascism engulfed them. To the last they remained true to their doctrines of peaceful negotiation and sweet reason.

The final responsibilty for the collapse of democracy in the years 1919–22 rests with the government itself. The four ministries that followed each other in these years were far different from the long-lived, solid governments over which Giolitti had presided in the years before the war. The postwar ministries were makeshift affairs living from day to day as best they might. No longer could they rely on a majority of loyal deputies who owed their election to the local prefects. The new system of proportional representation that had been inaugurated in 1919 ruined the traditional electoral contrivances. It not only resulted in the return of masses of Socialists and *Popolari;* it reduced the Liberals and Giolittians to a pallid reflection of their former power. Under these circumstances, the government was at the mercy of the two large popular parties. And the Socialists and *Popolari,* while they criticized freely the conduct of the government, were not ready to take over the responsibility themselves. Hence nobody really governed: the nation drifted, while the countryside sank into endemic civil war.

As the Socialists revealed their ineptitude, and the *Popolari* their resignation, the propertied element in the country began to gather courage. In 1919 and 1920, social revolution had seemed virtually inevitable. By 1921, the initiative had passed to the counterrevolutionaries. Mussolini's Fascists, who had stolen the Nationalists' fire, had become bolder and stronger. And the men of property, seeing that the Fascists were prepared to take on the Socialists and *Popolari* in open combat, began to give them avowed or covert support. At the end of the year 1920, the Fascists launched a regular campaign of rural terror. In town after town, they sacked or burned the local Socialist, *Popolare,* or trade-union headquarters, meeting only mild or insignificant resistance. Those who tried to oppose them suffered merciless beatings or administrations of castor oil. By the autumn of 1922, the peasants and workers, at least in the North, had been terrified into submission.

Meantime the police did almost nothing to protect them. In the spring of 1921, the government had begun a policy of winking at or even openly encouraging the Fascists' depredations. Francesco Saverio Nitti, the first postwar prime minister, had been a sincere democrat, but vacillating and ineffective. His successor, the old Giolitti—returned as though from the grave to save his distracted country—had thought that he could use the Fascists, as he had used so many and such various political forces in earlier years, to buttress his regime. In the second postwar election campaign, held in April and May 1921, he gave them their head to threaten and beat and burn. But times had changed. The pre-election terror failed of its effect. The Socialists returned to the Chamber of Deputies only slightly reduced in strength, and the *Popolari* even more numerous than before. Giolitti had simply unleashed on the country a force that he could no longer control.

Hence when the old master of *trasformismo* resigned for the last time and was succeeded by another well-meaning democrat, Ivanoe Bonomi, it was too late. The Fascists were now the masters of the streets and the countryside. Bonomi could not stop them. And his successor, Luigi Facta, scarcely tried. He resumed Giolitti's policy of official connivance. It was only at the end, in late October 1922, when the Fascists were preparing to march on Rome, that Facta seriously proposed resistance. On October 28 he went to the King with a proclamation of martial law ready for signature. But the King refused to sign, and the following day called on Mussolini to form a ministry. Two days later the Fascist blackshirts, weary and rain-drenched, began slogging through the streets of Rome. Mussolini himself had arrived more comfortably in a sleeping car from Milan.

4

The Legacy of Fascism:
The Corporate State

THE FAILURE of the attempt to establish an Italian democracy in the three years following the First World War has about it an air of historical tragedy. Much in it was accidental, and still more was due to the inexperience and overconfidence of the leaders of the new mass parties. Yet any such view of the democratic collapse is too simple and attributes too much importance to the failings of individuals or political machinery. It begs the question whether Italy possessed the social foundation on which a viable democracy could be based—and we have seen already that this was more than doubtful. If the Italian society of the early twentieth century was really two societies—existing together in time and space yet worlds apart in their mental attitude—then this very cleavage offered an initial reason to question democracy's chances for survival. But the cleavage meant more than social incoherence. Actually neither of the two societies provided a suitable base for democratic construction. Such was obviously true of the old hierarchical society. But it was also true of the new industrial one. This second society was in its way too attuned to its own time to adapt its economic conflicts to the institutions of liberal democracy. In the eighteenth and nineteenth centuries, Italy had been unready to found a middle-class democracy on the French model. By the twentieth century it was possibly too late. In 1920 neither of the contending classes in Italian industrial society honestly subscribed to the give-and-take principles of liberal democracy. The workers were aspiring toward a class dictatorship—milder than the Soviet, but still intolerant of its class adversaries. The employers were passing from a state of near-panic to a new-found resolve to maintain their rights of ownership at all costs; if it came to a final choice, the greater part of them were prepared to jettison the historic principles for which their grandfathers had fought on the barricades. This new realism on the part of the propertied classes is at the very center of the Fascist phenomenon.

It is no accident, then, that Italy should have produced the first Fascist party and the first Fascist state—the party and state that gave their name to the general movement which was to bulk so large during the next two decades of European history. As fascism spread to other countries, it soon became apparent that the same kind of social conditions that had favored its development in Italy produced similar political effects elsewhere. The coexistence of a patriarchal rural society with a modern industrial one—and a corresponding weakness of old-fashioned middle-class values—everywhere offered the conditions propitious to its rise. In addition, the circumstances of the postwar era created a favorable psychlogical atmosphere. Unemployment, especially among war veterans, class conflict, and inflation produced a sense of general insecurity that could easily lead to the acceptance of authoritarian solutions. Among members of the salaried middle class in particular, the great fear was of losing status, of sinking to the level of the industrial proletariat in living standards and social prestige. And this fear operated as a powerful argument in favor of a movement pledged to maintain the values of social and political hierarchy. In countries that had either lost the war, or, as in Italy, where patriots felt that the war had in effect been lost, all these conditions applied with redoubled force. For to a middle-class citizen threatened with *déclassement,* his own plight and that of his country merged into an undifferentiated sense of injury and humiliation. Against such slights and dangers, firm leadership, both in repressing subversion at home and in defending the national interests abroad, seemed to offer the only dependable recourse.

In Italy, finally, the feeling of injured national pride was by no means a new sensation. In one form or another, it had figured in the Italian consciousness for a half century—ever since the completion of national unification had brought to an end the era of the

Risorgimento. Since that September day of 1870 when Rome had at last been conquered from the Pope, Italian patriots had felt oppressed by disappointment. The dream had been realized, but it had turned out quite differently from the original expectations. United Italy had proved to be neither a fraternity of free men nor a sober, high-minded constitutional monarchy. It had simply become a quite ordinary and unexciting—and periodically corrupt— parliamentary state. Decade by decade, this sensation of frustrated hope had gained in intensity. In the first part of the new century it had exploded in the wholesale attacks on Giolittianism and the pro-war agitation of the years 1911 and 1914-15. Then had come the Italian intervention in the First World War and the disillusionment that followed it. By the early 1920's, the postwar disappointments had added their venom to the old familiar bitterness. Italians sick to suffocation of the parliamentary game were looking for something new, something young and virile, to sweep away the musty trappings of the constitutional state. Fascism would do it. Fascism would chase away or discipline to their duty the quarreling deputies in what Mussolini was to call the "gray and squalid" halls of Parliament. A party of youth, as its anthem proclaimed, Fascism would rejuvenate Italy. It would revive the tradition of the Risorgimento—dormant for fifty years but ready to be reawakened by a fighting chieftain who could be relied on to give a clear lead for the future.

In 1922, then, as Mussolini assumed power, Italy came once more to the attention of the world at large. For the next twenty years, the Duce was to make news, if nothing else. The Fascist experience seemed to be pulling Italy out of its rut of mediocrity and gave Italians the feeling that they were again playing a leading role in history. This is one reason for considering it in some detail. A second, however, and more important reason is that Italy proved to be not only the first Fascist state but also the one most representative of the rest. Germany under Hitler went faster and farther, but found fewer imitators. The milder Italian form of Fascism proved more appealing. Thus a study of the Mussolinian example illuminates not only the problems of contemporary Italy but also the broader nature of social forces and political action in the second quarter of the twentieth century.

1. THE THEORY AND THE PRACTICE

In October 1922 Italy offered Europe the first example of the twentieth-century counterrevolution, a phenomenon that subsequently became depressingly familiar. Since the thing itself was new, it was no wonder that Italians were at a loss to determine the exact meaning of the March on Rome and to guess Mussolini's intentions for the future. Few realized that he was out to establish a dictatorship that would bring to an end the constitutional, parliamentary regime. Hence many of them made compromises with the new government, and even praised it, in actions or words they were later to regret. We, however, who have the advantage of hindsight, may do well to exercise charity in judging them. All that many conservative Italians knew was that a party pledged to preserve property and order had come to power, and this they could only applaud.

Actually, Mussolini proceeded rather slowly to the consolidation of his authority. He took four years to accomplish what Hitler was later to do in six month. Initially he left the parliamentary system as it was, and members of other parties beside the Fascist, including representatives of the *Popolari,* distrustful but willing to give the new regime a try, sat in his first government. It was not until the year following the March on Rome, with the merger of the Fascist and Nationalist parties and the dismissal of the *Popolari* ministers, that Mussolini's government became a single-party affair. It was only in 1924, by a combination of pre-electoral violence and a tricky new electoral law contrived to favor the strongest party, that Fascism obtained a reliable majority in the Chamber of Deputies. And it was to be two more years before the opposition parties found themselves expelled from the Chamber and officially banned. The real consolidation of the dictatorship, then—in the imposition of press controls, the Fascist organization of the professional classes, and the rounding up of political adversaries—dates from the years 1924 to 1927. Through all these changes, the old *Statuto,* in theory at least, remained intact; up to 1930 the only significant institutional innovation was the establishment of the Grand Council of Fascism, an advisory body of about twenty-five members, as a supreme coordinator between the two poles of public authority, the government and the party.

When these events were new and Fascist tyranny had not yet become as familiar as it is today, students of Mussolini's Italy took pains to analyze at some length the institutions and practices of the single-party state. It is in no sense a disparagement of their efforts if we conclude that today we may be much more brief. All this is old stuff to us—again we have the advantage of hindsight. Suffice it to recall that Fascist Italy in time acquired the full paraphernalia of modern dictatorship: the unquestioned "leader" (*Duce*)— doubling as party chief and prime minister—a title Mussolini was the first to bear, either in the Fascist or in the Communist world; party chieftains, devoted or time-serving depending on their natures, but all alike at the mercy of the Duce, who believed in keeping them on their toes by frequent "changes of the guard"; a party militia, wearing a colored shirt, in this case black, and fatigued or exalted, as the case might be, with frequent public exercises; youth organizations, regimenting the extracurricular activities of the young Italian, boy or girl, from the age of six to twenty-one, when, if he was a boy, he was eligible to join the party itself; above all, the contrast between the party members, pledged to apply the spirit of Fascism in all their public and private concerns, and the mass of the population, who were expected to follow, with as much enthusiasm as they could muster, the lead given by the favored minority.

Such, in theory, were the institutions of Fascism. In practice, things worked out rather differently. Although Mussolini apparently coined the word "totalitarian" to describe his regime, the Duce's Italy, as compared with the subsequent development of the Nazi and Soviet states, scarcely deserved that title. The Fascist control over public life, or even over party members, was something less than complete. Laxity began at the top and extended right down to the base of the Fascist hierarchy. As the regime consolidated itself and Italians realized it was likely to last, the party became flooded with new adherents, who had joined simply from self-interest. And Mussolini actually encouraged the process, by obliging civil servants, school teachers, and similar people to become party members. Meantime, even the stalwarts of Fascism's heroic days grew soft and corrupt. They relaxed among their wealth and privileges; they engaged in favor-mongering on the side; they spouted the conventional party phrases with more volubility than conviction. Moreover, two decades of power bred a second generation of party leaders who were obvious mediocrities and sycophants. These people fooled nobody: by the mid-1930's the regime was visibly beginning to rot at the top. A creeping apathy engulfed the country. As late as 1933, only about half the youth of Italy was enrolled in the various Fascist formations; the upper and middle classes sent them the overwhelming majority of their children, but the working class and peasantry were frankly uninterested.

Why was this the case? Why was Mussolini unable to do what Hitler and Stalin were to accomplish with comparative ease? Initially, of course, the Duce had more difficult human material to work with. Both the Fascists and the general public had grown up in an atmosphere of skepticism and slovenliness, of individualism and indiscipline, that quickly transformed the rhetoric of political enthusiasts into bitter mockery or a good-humored shrug of the shoulders. It took no very profound observation to arrive at the conclusion that Fascism was alien to the Italian popular tradition. Mussolini himself, in his more objective moments, apparently realized this perfectly well. In his fashion, he tempered his heroic doctrines to the realities of Italian life. Thus his secret police never operated with such ferocity as in the Nazi or the Stalinist state, and a merely conventional phrase or even silence was usually considered an adequate expression of respect for the ideology of the regime.

This ideology itself, however, created a further difficulty. Italians might well be puzzled as to just what Fascism meant, despite the constant barrage of definition to which they were subjected. If the Latin tradition of Italy was mostly a matter of sentiment, it at least gave Italians the idea that words were supposed to signify something clear and tangible. Under such critical scrutiny, the doctrines of Fascism crumpled up. When closely examined—and particularly when compared with the actual history of the party—they revealed themselves as a jumble of platitude, inconsistency, and untruth, in brief, an enormous deception.

Perhaps most damningly they carried the mark of political and class betrayal. Benito Mussolini had originally been a Socialist, like his father before him, an honest, large-hearted blacksmith from the stormy Romagna. After a wandering youth of odd jobs and political agitation, Benito had risen early in life to a position of influence in the Italian Socialist party. His unusual gifts as a journalist and orator, his personal magnetism and wide if rather unsystematic reading, had everywhere created the quite understandable impression that here was a superior man. He early identified himself with the revolutionary wing of the party; in his emphasis on force and rough solutions, in his impatience with parliamentary methods, he was to remain consistent throughout his career. In 1912, when he was just turning twenty-nine, he took the lead in swinging over the party congress at Reggio Emilia to vote the expulsion of the reformist leaders Bissolati and Bonomi. For the next two years, as editor of the party journal *Avanti,* Mussolini was the most influential figure in Italian Socialism. Then suddenly the outbreak of war changed everything. After a few months of hesitation, the future Duce, who had been one of the most violent opponents of the Tripolitan campaign, declared for Italian intervention on the side of the Entente powers. It was an act of political suicide. Mussolini was deprived of his editorship and shortly afterwards expelled from the Socialist party; very few followed him into the wilderness.

For the next five years Mussolini wandered in a political limbo. He who had once been proud to be a draft-evader now answered the call of his country and served at the front. Seriously wounded and mustered out of the army, he resumed the task of trying to gather around himself a new political movement. At first he could enroll only bits and pieces—a few ex-Socialists like himself and a handful of revolutionary syndicalists left over from an even earlier Socialist purge. By the end of the war, he was ready to attempt something more systematic. In March 1919, he organized his first action groups, the *Fasci di Combattimento,* which were to give the movement its name. But even these, although they had an appeal for the demobilized army officer and the young student who had just missed the adventure of war service, languished without notable success for another year. During this same year, the poet D'Annunzio led a fantastic filibustering expedition to the disputed port of Fiume and proceeded to occupy it and even rule it in his own eccentric fashion until Giolitti finally expelled him. D'Annunzio's heroics came to nothing. But from them Mussolini profited vastly: he not only recruited for his *fasci* the veterans of the Fiume fiasco who were drifting back to Italy; he also learned from D'Annunzio the stage tricks that were later to make him famous—the Roman salute, the rhetorical questions to the crowd, the disciplined, almost bestial responses of the *Arditi*—and even the windy pseudo-economics of the "corporative state."

From this point on, Fascism became somthing to be taken seriously. It also began to assume the character of eclectic conservatism that was to distinguish it later on. Originally it had been an undefined movement of protest, combining nationalist appeals and semi-socialist promises in illogical juxtaposition. Now it began to turn conservative, as propertied people realized its advantages as a weapon of counterattack against the Socialists and the more radical wing of the *Popolari*. Tough young leaders such as Balbo, Grandi, and Farinacci, who posed as the defenders of rural property, directed the movement toward the class warfare that inflamed the northern countryside. Then Giolitti inaugurated the policy of official connivance. By May 1921, when they succeeded in electing thirty-five deputies, the Fascists had nearly completed their metamorphosis into defenders of property and the established order. The last step was a pledge of loyalty to the monarchy: an astute reassurance to the conservative classes given by Mussolini just before the March on Rome.

Nor did Mussolini's evolution stop with his attainment of power. We shall see later that it was only after the March on Rome that the understanding between Fascism and the major Italian industrialists could be elaborated. Similarly, it was not until he reached power that Mussolini showed a proper appreciation for the Nationalists, whose slogans and following he had gradually stolen. As participants in his government and later as assimilated Fascist leaders, the chief Nationalists—men like Corradini, Federzoni, and Rocco—brought to the movement a much-needed increment of intellectual distinction. In addition, they confirmed its new monarchism and they gave it a heightened respect for rank and hierarchy—and even, eventually, for the Church.

By 1925, when Mussolini's evolution had been virtually completed, he had come a long way from Socialism. He had become the idol of the propertied classes—the defender of the state, the army, the monarchy. Mussolini was not one to worry about inconsistencies. He shrugged them off as inseparable from the dynamism of genius, and most of the time refrained even from trying to explain them. A consummate actor and speaker, the Duce, unlike Hitler, was never carried away by his own oratory. At the very height of his rhetorical passion, he remained cold inside, secretly despising the rabble that applauded him. But his earlier Socialist utterances were too much even for this sort of cynicism to brush aside. In his later years, he went to some pains to cover up his past and tried to suppress what he had said and written before the war. And at the same time he attempted to give his movement an ideological paternity.

The job fell to Giovanni Gentile—a reputable idealist philosopher, who had parted company with Croce shortly before the First World War and had eventually found his way into Fascism. For the better part of a decade, Gentile served as the official philosopher of the movement. He actually wrote the article on Fascism for the *Enciclopedia Italiana,* which, under Mussolini's signature, finally defined the Fascist revolution ten years after the event. The article added little to what observers might already have deduced from the actions of the regime: it attacked the "sentimental" illusions of liberalism, democracy, and socialism; it established the state as an "ethical" entity, "an embodied will to power and government"; and it called for "faith," "heroism," and "education to combat."* Moreover, by the time it was written Gentile had fallen from influence; even the official philosophy had become obsolete.

Mussolini himself—who prided himself on his culture—took delight in discoursing to foreign visitors about his ideological forebears. He would speak of Nietzsche and Pareto and Sorel— and even Willian James. All of these, he felt, were realists, men disgusted with the hypocrisies of nineteenth-century thought who appreciated the fact of power and its application through systematic violence. They were all, he reasoned, pragmatists rather than ideologues. And to this extent he had chosen his masters wisely. It has never been proved that any of them—with the possible exception of Sorel—exerted any direct influence on his career. Mussolini let himself be guided by circumstances, and usually with uncanny accuracy: even his apparently suicidal change of front in 1914 in the end proved well-advised; he seems to have sensed that Italian Social-

---

* The authorized English translation, under the title "The Political and Social Doctrine of Fascism," was published in *International Conciliation,* No. 306 (January 1935), pp. 5–17.

ism was bound on a course that would lead only to ruin and that the way to power lay elsewhere. Power and domination were what he pursued with single-minded resolution, to be put off by no feeble charge of inconsistency. In this sense, he was the supreme pragmatist.

For those who had suffered from his shifts and betrayals, however, it was no comfort to realize that they were witnessing the evolution of a master political tactician, and that Mussolini in power was proving himself an energetic, efficient, and hardworking administrator of the state. To them—and to a large part of the Italian people—all that seemed important was that a former revolutionary had carried out a successful conterrevolution. The erstwhile champion of the workers was now running a government that functioned unashamedly in the interest of the propertied classes. This was the deepest reason for the disillusionment and apathy that in the end reduced the work of Fascism to a hollow sham.

2. THE INSTITUTIONS OF THE CORPORATE STATE

Nowhere did the contrast between the theory and the practice of Fascism appear more starkly than in the institutions of the so-called corporate state. In this field, as with the concept of totalitarianism, Mussolini was the innovator who set the example for subsequent dictatorial regimes. Before the advent of Italian Fascism, corporatism had existed as a theory, as a vision of a harmonious economic order that would transcend the century-old conflict between capital and labor. But it had not yet been put into practice. Mussolini was the first European ruler to embody corporatism in the official ideology of his regime. Indeed, he placed it in the very center of that ideology. Next to the energetics of national dynamism, the new corporative institutions of the Italian state became the most advertised feature of Mussolini's Fascism. This it was that particularly impressed foreign visitors, who on their return home spread word of the novel institutional devices that were on the way to solving the universal problem of class conflict. Such visitors, overwhelmed with a surfeit of official phraseology and statistics, usually swallowed what was fed them with the docility of wishful conviction. They wanted to believe—and hence few found time and energy for the painful labor of comparison and criticism that would reveal the disparities between official doctrine and economic reality.

To the minority of scholars who bucked the pro-Fascist current and searched for the truth concealed beneath the official torrent of words, all students of contemporary Italy owe a massive debt. By the mid-1930's a number of critics of diverse nationality—such men as Herman Finer, Louis Rosenstock-Franck, Gaetano Salvemini, and Carl T. Schmidt—had been able to piece together the main outlines of what had actually occurred. The present discussion of Fascist corporatism rests almost entirely on their work.* Briefly, what they argued was, first, that Italian corporative doctrine represented an amalgam of contradictory traditions; second, that the corporative institutions themselves had come into being late in time and for the most part as rationalizations of accomplished facts; third, that these institutions had few powers or functions and served chiefly as an impressive façade to mask the harsher features of class rule.

For the theory of corporatism, Mussolini had two traditions on which to draw. The first, the Catholic doctrine of class collaboration, which had received papal endorsement in Leo XIII's encyclical *Rerum Novarum* of 1891, was by far the more moderate. As elaborated in the late nineteenth and early twentieth centuries, Catholic corporative theory was an attempt to answer Marxism. It was an effort to supersede the class warfare preached by the Marxists, through the creation of new institutional devices that would call forth a spirit of class reconciliation. Among the devices suggested, two in particular commended themselves to the more radically minded among Catholic political leaders. As a substitute for the nationalization or socialization of basic industry, the corporatists suggested a system of associating the workers in the actual operation of the factories, through part ownership, profit sharing, and participation in the councils of management. Similarly, to replace the usual method of parliamentary representation by territorial constituencies—which the corporatists considered both artificial and easily subject to manipulation by political parties—these innovators proposed a system of representation by class or economic function; a new sense of actuality, they believed, would enter political life if deputies should sit in legislative bodies not as the representatives of a largely mythical universal electorate but as the spokesmen of

* For complete titles, see Appendix II. Suggested Reading.

clearly defined economic groups whose needs they understood and could express with conviction. For it was the corporatists' contention that the way to overcome class conflict was not to pretend that it did not exist, as so many conservative European statesmen were trying to do, but to recognize it frankly, and by incorporating the pressures of the various economic interests into the very structure of government, to provide a forum in which these conflicts could be honestly discussed and reconciled. In this way, they hoped, the European working classes could eventually be lured away from their allegiance to the subversive doctrine of Karl Marx.

Owing to its moderation and religious pedigree, this sort of corporative doctrine enjoyed a widespread prestige, and among the most various political groupings, in the years immediately following the First World War. It was again Mussolini's sure sense for the politically expedient that caused him to apply to his regime the adjective "corporate" or "corporative" long before any such institutions existed in fact. The word dazzled and misled the run of foreigners. Actually, Italian Fascism borrowed little from the Catholic corporative tradition. And what it did take it had learned in perverted form from the resounding verbiage of D'Annunzio's constitution for his ephemeral "regency' in Fiume. Moreover, before many years of Fascist rule had passed, Mussolini had reduced to silence all but the most conservative wing of Catholic political leadership. In the historical development of Italian Fascism, it was a second type of corporative tradition—the tradition of syndicalism— that was alone to play a significant role. And even here, once Mussolini's power had been consolidated, the syndicalist doctrine gradually fell into disuse—or was reduced to the same sort of verbal jugglery that gave the word "corporative" its continuing appeal.

Initially, there had been nothing corporative about the syndicalist tradition. A derivative of the French or Italian word for trade union (*syndicat, sindicato*), syndicalism before the First World War had stood for a militant doctrine of working-class revolution. It distinguished itself from the more usual forms of Marxism by its insistence that the workers should do the job themselves, through the medium of the general strike, rather than by trusting to the leadership of a political party, which might be Socialist in theory, but in practice had succumbed to the middle-class ideology of legal methods and parliamentary activity. For this heresy, the Italian Socialist party had expelled its syndicalist wing as early as 1908. Subsequently, the expellees had gone in various directions, while syndicalism as a whole lost strength nearly everywhere. One group of them—in total contradiction to their earlier professions—had become enthusiastically nationalistic. These people, whose erratic course had anticipated Mussolini's own, allied themselves with the future Duce during the war years. As in the case of Mussolini, their conversion to nationalism entailed a revision of their previous emphasis on class struggle. In place of unions consisting exclusively of working-class members, they began to advocate "mixed syndicates" of workers and employers. Thus they eventually came to propose a doctrine of class collaboration and of political representation by economic function which, despite its widely contrasting origins, bore a superficial resemblance to the theories of the Catholic corporatists.

At the time of the March on Rome, then, the economic and social doctrines of Fascism rested on a syndicalism that had diametrically shifted its ideological axis and a corporatism in which the gentle preachings of Catholic theorists had been diverted by D'Annunzio to nationalist ends. This theoretical ambiguity is the initial aspect of Fascist corporatism on which its critics have laid stress. The second is the fashion in which the corporative institutions themselves came to be established. In its historical sequence—and divorced from the subsequent rationalizations that surrounded it—the organization of Fascist institutions appears as a pragmatic process of adaptation to the pressures of class interests indispensable to the consolidation of Mussolini's authority. Fundamentally, it was a process of conciliating the class of industrial employers.

We have seen that this group had, as a whole, been slower about going over to Fascism than either agricultural proprietors or members of the urban salaried classes. At the time Mussolini came to power, only a minority of them actively supported the Fascist cause. The majority had adopted an attitude of alert—and receptive—waiting. Before committing themselves, they wanted to see how the Fascist regime would develop, and in particular how the new Fascist "syndicates" would behave toward the representatives of organized capital.

These syndicates were in theory mixed organizations of workers and employers. In practice they contained few employers and their working-class adherents were of a rather curious sort. Some were unemployed or otherwise disillusioned war veterans who had reached Fascism through personal conviction. But the majority were simply the debris of earlier unions, Socialist-oriented or Catholic, who, through terror, apathy, or calculation, had let themselves be swept up by the Fascists in the wake of the latters' campaign of systematic union-smashing. The Fascist leaders were under few illusions as to the political solidity of these new recruits: among themselves, they jocularly referred to them as "prisoners of war."

Such were the cadres around which, in January 1922, nine months before the March on Rome, the Fascists organized a National Confederation of five "syndical corporations." (Herewith begins the confusion and overlapping of syndicalist and corporative terminology that befogs the history of Fascist economic organization.) There was to be one for industry, one for agriculture, one for commerce, one for the merchant marine, and one for intellectuals. Naturally the first of these was the most important and was to figure most prominently in the tortuous game of alternating threats and negotiation with the industrial employers that went on for the next four years.

Surprising as it may seem, it took Mussolini nearly that long to reach a *modus vivendi* with the chief Italian industrialists. Although the Duce was a firm bargainer and in 1925 even encouraged a metal-workers' strike to put further pressure on the recalcitrant employers, in the end the latter gained most of what they wanted. By the Palazzo Chigi agreement of December 1923 and the Palazzo Vidoni pact that followed twenty-two months later, the industrialists established for themselves a position of substantial autonomy within the Fascist state. In return for recognizing the Fascist syndicates as the sole agents for the Italian working classes—and thereby ridding themselves of the Socialist and Catholic unions that they had never liked in any case—the industrialists obtained from Mussolini the most extraordinary concessions. The Fascist syndicates were no longer to be "mixed"; they would represent the workers alone. For their part, the industrial employers would retain their own organization, the Confederation of Industrialists—a kind of national chamber of commerce—which would receive official recognition as the bargaining agent for Italian industry. In addition, the employers obtained the suppression of the chief weapons available to the workers in wage negotiations—the election of factory committees and the right to strike. From this point on industrial strife in Italy practically ceased; the number of strikes dwindled to the vanishing point. Here again foreign visitors were impressed by the ease with which Mussolini had "solved" the strike problem. They failed to see that the solution—far from being a reconciliation of conflicting interests— was a thoroughly one-sided affair.

The quiet and (at the time) scarcely noticed Palazzo Vidoni agreement of October 1925 is the key to the subsequent organization of the corporate state. As an unofficial charter of independence for the Italian industrialists, it was far more substantial than the official and highly advertised Charter of Labor proclaimed with such ceremony a year and a half later. In essence the difference in the Fascist treatment of capital and labor was as follows: while the former was permitted to manage its own affairs, subject only to a few very general official directives, the latter was grouped into Fascist-organized bodies, which were trade unions only in name, since they possessed none of the usual instrumentalities for collective bargaining. This blunt fact was to become increasingly apparent as the Palazzo Vidoni agreement began to be given official application.

By the law of April 3, 1926, there came into being the "syndical state" (not yet "corporative"; the first word still had favorable connotations in the eyes of Italian workers). This law transformed the five former "syndical corporations" into confederations for employees alone. Or at least it so transformed four of them, leaving as "mixed" by its very nature the organization of the intellectual classes. To these four it added two further confederations for banking and internal transport. Corresponding organizations in the same six fields were designated for the different categories of employers. These latter, in most cases, were simply reincarnations of previously existing bodies —the Confederation of Industrialists and similar organizations in the other areas of economic activity.

During the next four years, Mussolini and his colleagues tinkered considerably with this "syndical" machinery. But no amount of grouping and regrouping, or of official declarations on Fascist economic theory, could conceal the fact that the structure was incomplete. The Fascist state might be corporative in doctrine, but in fact no corporative institutions existed. The "confederations" organized under the law of April 3, 1926, could properly be called officially recognized pressure groups; the workers' organizations were in fact dependencies of the Fascist party. But they had not yet been incorporated into the structure of government.

A first step in this direction came in 1930 with the establishment of the National Council of Corporations. A large and unwieldy body, including representatives of both employers and employees in all the different syndical categories, it was intended to serve as an advisory council on economic affairs. Four years later the corporations themselves finally came into existence. These were not unlike the earlier syndical "confederations" of employers and workers in that they were conceived as self-governing bodies for the different fields of economic activity. But in the case of the new corporations the economic pie was sliced rather more finely: there were to be twenty-two of them, including separate organizations for the specialized branches of agriculture and industry. Moreover, a third functional element had now appeared on the scene; in each corporation, alongside the representatives of employers and employees, were to sit spokesmen for the public—and who else did these turn out to be than Fascist bureaucrats from the Ministry of Corporations? Finally, in 1938, the corporative structure was completed and definitively merged with the government itself. In that year, Mussolini decided to do away with the old Chamber of Deputies—which under the dictatorial regime had lost all semblance of legislative power and in 1929 had become simply a gathering of deputies nominated by the Fascist party. In its place he substituted a Chamber of Fasces and Corporations. This new body appeared to be a direct outgrowth of corporative theory, since it was based on the principle of representation by function rather than by territorial constituencies. Actually it was a hybrid. It was formed by merging two previously existing bodies—one of which was in fact corporative but the other strictly political: the advisory National Council of Corporations and the National Council of the Fascist party. Alongside the representatives of self-organized capital and state-organized labor, there were to sit the local hierarchs of the Fascist party—as though to symbolize the fact that at the apex of the corporative pyramid final control was reserved to the political authorities and, ultimately, to Mussolini himself.

Such, indeed, is the final verdict on all the elaborate syndical and corporative institutions established under the Fascist regime. When we come to the third and last aspect of the critique of these institutions—the analysis of their powers and functions—we find that they did comparatively little. Essentially the corporative machinery existed to rationalize decisions that had already been taken on the political level. Or, to put it more precisely, the corporative bodies could perform three functions that were extremely useful to the Fascist regime. They could explore the economic ground by engaging in academic discussions of problems that might assume importance in the future. They could clarify for the political authorities the play of interests, the real pressures of organized economic groups, that would further or jeopardize the success of some contemplated policy. Finally, and perhaps most important, they could serve as organs of self-regulation: for purposes of statistics-gathering and production control they could take over much of the work that would otherwise have entailed the organization of an expensive and unwieldy bureaucracy—much as in the NRA period of the New Deal American business undertook to regulate its own doings. In Italy, this function of self-regulation assumed particular importance after the spring of 1936, when Mussolini, threatened with economic sanctions by the League of Nations, launched the slogan of national "autarchy."

Yet even these modest functions could not be performed by the corporative bodies in an even-handed spirit of class reconciliation. For most of the time it was only the employers who could make their voices heard there. Theoretically, in the corporative organizations, workers enjoyed equal representation with employers. But those who sat for the employee groups were not representatives in any proper sense. The real spokesmen of the Italian working classes —the leaders of formerly independent trade unions, Socialist or Catholic as the case might be—had been silenced: they were dead or in prison, in exile or in hiding. In their place, the officials of the Fascist workers' "syndicates" occupied the seats reserved for labor in the corporative bodies. Some of them were simply party careerists. Others were sincerely anxious to advance the interests of the Italian working classes: former syndicalists with a revolutionary past, they were distressed and bewildered as they saw the Fascist regime steadily moving in a pro-employer direction. As the years went by, however, more and more of the syndical officials became mere bureaucrats with no real link to the workers themselves. Only on the lower levels were they elected, even in theory. They might conscientiously try to do their best in disputes over wage rates and working conditions, but the leverage they could exert was extremely limited. Caught between the precise orders of the Fascist party and the sardonic distrust of their presumed constituents, these syndical officials lived in a constant state of frustration in which they were almost fully occupied in maintaining their own personal prestige.

The employers, on the other hand, were present in visible corporeal form. Or at least, the larger employers, who dominated the organizations of industrial and agricultural proprietors, had no trouble in making their desires known. This is not to say—as some critics of Italian Fascism have implied—that the regime simply acted as a police agent for organized Italian capital. Ultimately, authority rested with Mussolini and the party, not with the Italian industrialists. But subject to the final orders of the dictatorship, the Italian employing classes—and the industrial employers in particular— were granted a wide sphere of independence. Provided they followed the general economic line laid down by the regime, they were safe from the threat of nationalization and could manage their businesses as they pleased. Nor was this line too difficult to follow, since the employers themselves, through the corporative bodies, and perhaps still more through direct personal intervention, had had a share in drawing it up. In most cases, the interests of the regime and the interests of large capital ran parallel. Both were anxious to see labor curbed, industry and agriculture protected by tariff barriers, and war production expanded. Moreover, the authoritarian philosophy of the regime led it to favor large over small enterprise as more efficient and easier to deal with. Two decades of Fascist rule mightily encouraged the tendencies already existing in Italy toward concentration of capital and semimonopolistic agreements on prices and production quotas. Some of the officially recognized employers organizations behaved, in fact, more or less as legalized cartels. This monopolistic understanding between government and the larger economic interests was to prove the most pervasive and lasting feature of Italian corporatism. It is today what most people, both inside and outside Italy, have in mind when they speak of the "corporate state."

From the overblown verbiage of corporatism, then, only two realities emerge: the political dictatorship and the strong position of the employers. The rest was wind. The elaborate corporative machinery served largely as a façade to lead the outside world—and even, perhaps, some people in Italy—to believe that Mussolini had eliminated class antagonism in his new state. In actuality, below the surface of apparent harmony, the conflict of class interests raged as bitterly as before.

3. THE GOVERNMENT AND THE CLASSES

In analyzing the position of the different social classes under Fascism, we are handicapped by the fact that in the twenty-one years of Mussolini's rule, there is no period we can call "normal"— no base line for purposes of comparison. Each succeeding epoch of the Fascist era was an epoch of crisis. The Italian people lived through the two decades of the Fascist experience in a perpetual state of tension and excitement, of straining toward some distant economic goal. (Actually, of course, this applied only to the politically active sector of the population; the mass of the Italian people lived as always, in an attitude of weary resignation.) Such an atmosphere of tension appears inseparable from totalitarian or attempted totalitarian rule: we have seen the same forces operating in more rigorous form in Stalinist Russia and in Nazi Germany. In Italy, however, this crisis attitude had a peculiarly forced and synthetic quality. Behind the brave phrases, the exhortations to renewed exertion, we occasionally catch glimpses of the reality—a patient, long-suffering people pitted against a heartbreaking complex of nearly insoluble problems. For twenty years, Mussolini struggled in vain to arouse the Italians to a sense of heroic endeavor; he urged them to "live dangerously" and phrased his economic policies in terms of successive "battles." In the end, the blunt facts of Italian economic geography took their revenge on him.

The first four years of Mussolini's rule represent the culmination of a protracted period of postwar inflation. There follows nearly a decade of deflationary policy, launched in the summer of 1926 as the "battle of the lira." In 1935 a third phase begins, a phase of partial war economy and attempted "autarchy" that was to last right through to the fall of the regime eight years later. For from 1935 on, Italy was practically always at war. On the Ethiopian War there followed the Spanish Civil War, and after that conflict, with only a year of respite, came Italy's intervention in the Second World War. In brief, the decade of deflationary policy marks the central and the sole comparatively "normal" period of Fascist rule; the succeeding era of war economy in retrospect appears as simply a long preparation for a virtually inevitable collapse.

It is only giving Mussolini his due to say that his deflationary policy stabilized a potentially dangerous situation. And it was of course beyond his control that Italy in the early thirties should have been drawn into the world-wide economic depression. In terms of the Italian people, however—in terms of wage rates and living standards—the depression began in Italy three to five years earlier than in the rest of Europe. In this sense, the whole period from 1927 on ranks as one long depression. The beginning of the policy of war preparation alleviated the situation somewhat: in the second half of the 1930's wages and living standards improved. But in Italy, as in Germany, the improvement was largely fictitious. The real economic difficulties were masked by a state of partial mobilization, economic and military, based on the presumption of a victorious war.

The same verdict applies to Mussolini's whole social and economic policy. It was a policy of short-run solutions, of showy triumphs over limited areas calculated for their propaganda effects. Actually nothing was permanently "solved." Italy's long-term problems were simply concealed from general view. With the loss of the war and Mussolini's overthrow, the same problems were to re-emerge, basically unchanged, and rendered even more acute by two decades of failure to face up to economic reality.

Moreover, what gains Mussolini had been able to register were at the expense of the Italian laboring classes. This statement we may document by examining the impact of the Fascist economic policies on the various social strata of the Italian population.

In the field of agriculture Mussolini professed to believe that a strong, laborious peasantry was the backbone of the Italian state. He liked to display himself to his people as a son of the soil—toiling like a peasant in the fields, his muscular torso bared to the burning heavens—and he made much of his aim to "ruralize" Italy. Some of his most strenuous exertions he poured into the "battle of wheat" and an extensive program of land reclamation. The first of these, launched in the year 1925, was a kind of dress rehearsal for the later autarchy policy. It aimed to make Italy as nearly self-sufficient as possible in the production of basic foodstuffs. Technically it could be called a success. By a variety of devices, chief among them the imposition of a heavy tariff, wheat imports were virtually wiped out, and the area sown to wheat was increased by about 13 per cent. But this increase occurred almost wholly in the South and the islands. And the fact that the change occurred there symbolized what was wrong with the entire program.

In 1925, Italy had 35 per cent of its sown area under wheat—the highest percentage in Europe. Italian wheat cultivation, particularly in the South, was already overdeveloped at the expense of other crops; a great deal of the land devoted to wheat was unsuited to its production. The "battle of wheat" only intensified this imbalance. The raising of such products as livestock and fruit—for the latter of which southern Italy was particularly well suited—suffered through the concentration on wheat cultivation and through the retaliation by foreign countries that the high tariff policy brought on. Moreover, the social effects were equally questionable. During the first decade of the new policy, the consumption of wheat in Italy, as opposed to its production, actually declined. Mussolini's "battle" had succeeded in raising the Italian price to double the world price, and thus the poorest groups in the population were obliged to reduce the quantity of wheat products they ate. Ironically enough, those who felt the pinch included an important part of that very peasantry who were supposed to be aided by the wheat policy—agricultural laborers and others who were primarily consumers rather than independent producers of foodstuffs. Only the larger cultivators had benefited.

The second of Mussolini's major efforts had similar, if less drastic, effects. Land reclamation was a highly laudable aim in itself. To drain the swamps and bring into production the barren areas that disgraced the otherwise intensively cultivated Italian landscape had been the ambition of generations of Italian reformers. And the government of united Italy, from 1860 to 1922, had made real progress in this direction, notably in the lower Po area. Mussolini, besides taking credit for work that had been practically completed before his accession to power, threw himself with enthusiasm into a number of new projects. The chief of these was the reclamation of the Pontine marshes. Here, in an area close enough to the capital to impress the foreign visitor, Fascism could score one of its most notable successes. In fact, Mussolini concentrated effort and expenditure on the Pontine reclamation scheme to the neglect of less showy areas: in the five years 1932–37, nearly one-third of the national budget for land improvement went to this area alone. In the end, the achievement was scarcely commensurate with the expense: only about 19,000 people were settled on the newly reclaimed land—a drop in the bucket in comparison with Italy's total population problem.

Here at least the veterans' organization that managed the resettlement did it on a non-profit and equitable basis. Elsewhere, land reclamation projects were frankly profitable, and sometimes speculative. In the government-assisted consortia that undertook such projects the large proprietors dominated—since a majority of the total land, rather than of the total number of owners, was deemed sufficient to bind the rest. Nor did the government, which frequently supplied the bulk of the funds, exercise any control over how the proprietors administered their land, once the improvement project had been completed; it did not inquire into the speculative profits that certain prominent Fascists had been able to harvest by getting in on one of the consortia. In short, Mussolini's government did not in any systematic way use land improvement as a device for combatting the problem of Italy's landless peasantry.

The net result of twenty years of Fascist rule was in fact the contrary. Within three months of the March on Rome, Mussolini had either repealed or withdrawn the major measures, enacted or pending, that had been devised during the period of postwar democracy to favor the Italian peasants—measures for limiting rent raises and the eviction of tenants, for ceding land to cooperatives, and for making a start toward dividing up the great estates. And by the end of a decade and a half of Fascist rule the number of peasants who owned their own land had actually decreased. At the same time, and rather puzzlingly, the total number of landless agricultural workers showed an even greater decline. Part of this change can be ascribed to a rise in tenancy and a slow population shift from the country to the city. During the Fascist era perhaps a million former farm laborers became urban workers, as the Italian population for the first time ceased to be predominantly rural. Another million, however, failed to turn up in new occupational categories: in all probability, the greater part of these people went into the ranks of the unemployed, who in rural areas were most inadequately registered or cared for. In general, the government left them to their own devices, subject to the provision that they might be sent back to their native villages if they failed to find work elsewhere.

In this regulation—which sought to limit the influx into the large cities of unemployed farm hands looking for work—some critics of the Fascist regime have discerned a species of neofeudalism. And they have applied a similar epithet to Mussolini's efforts to encourage the spread of *mezzadria,* or share tenancy. This system of tenure is extremely equivocal: we shall see later how it has changed from a source of rural stability and contentment into an inefficient and reactionary device that lends itself to political extremism.* Certainly in encouraging the *mezzadria* relationship Mussolini was seeking something more than a stalwart peasantry rooted in the soil; he was also aiming to group the poorer peasants in his Fascist cadres. It is significant that in the Fascist syndical organizations, share tenants fell into the same category as workers, while cash tenants were grouped with the employers. A peasant holding his land under *mezzadria* contract could not enroll himself in the semiautonomous organization of agricultural proprietors. He was placed firmly under the control of Fascist officials in one of the party-organized workers' syndicates.

In a sense, however, *mezzadria* prospered under Mussolini's rule. The number of share tenants, indeed of tenants of all sorts, increased markedly. To give these tenants a sense of added status, Mussolini promulgated a Charter of Mezzadria. Ostensibly a device for protecting the peasantry by codifying the standard provisions of tenancy contracts, the charter actually registered the extent to which the customary norms of share tenancy had turned against the peasants during the first decade of Fascist rule. By a gradual process of attri-

* See Chapter 8.

tion, the agricultural proprietors had strengthened their position relative to that of their tenants. And similarly in their relations with agrarian labor. During the Fascist period, the Italian agricultural workers forfeited most of the gains they had made in the years of postwar struggle: the eight-hour day, the right to unemployment insurance fell into disregard. Real wages decreased as the system of payments in kind—another reactionary device—became increasingly the rule.

When we turn to the industrial classes, we find a similar worsening of the workingman's legal status. This is exactly the contrary of what Mussolini claimed, and what most foreign observers imagined. They saw that Fascist Italy was in many respects a welfare state, and was farther advanced in terms of social legislation than, for example, either France or the United States. This situation the half-informed foreigner, taking the regime at its word, ascribed to Mussolini's personal initiative. In fact, the government-supported insurance systems against unemployment, old age, accident, and invalidity were for the most part legacies from the era of the much-maligned Giolitti or from the semirevolutionary year 1919. What Mussolini did was to rationalize them and extend their range while simultaneously whittling down other workers' rights that were already in existence. Even the celebrated Charter of Labor, like the Charter of Mezzadria, did little more than codify the extent to which the workers had already lost ground. It omitted all mention of the eight-hour day, and although it set certain specifications for labor contracts, it often seemed to Italian workers that this elaborate machinery existed merely to cushion the shock of the constant wage reductions that marked the period of deflation. Moreover, the government frequently winked at the widespread violations by the employers of the norms specified in the Charter, and in its own sphere, was either unwilling or unable to live up to the promises contained in earlier legislation. It sometimes diverted to other purposes the reserve funds of the various public insurance systems, and it totally failed to cope with the mass unemployment of the early 1930's. Economists have estimated that by 1932 about half Italy's industrial labor force was totally or partially unemployed, and that fewer than half of these were being cared for by the government.

There was very little, then, of "socialism" in Mussolini's treatment of Italian labor. Nor can this word with any more justice be applied to the Fascist attitude toward organized capital during the depression of the thirties. We have seen that Mussolini's regime had come to rely heavily on a tacit understanding between business leaders and the government. In the thirties, however, this official attitude appeared to be changing. The depression and the drive for war preparation together seemed to be leading the regime toward sterner courses. Here again, foreign visitors usually misjudged what was happening. Impressed by the new economic control devices instituted from 1931 on, they concluded that Italy was turning toward socialism. And some members of the vestigial Fascist "Left" at the same time began to pluck up hope. Actually the new machinery of controls changed little in the structure of the Italian economy. Like the corresponding measures adopted in the same era by Britain and the United States, they were technical devices for dealing with temporary problems, not steppingstones toward socialism. The most prominent of these measures, the IRI* program of government acquisition of industrial holdings, instituted in 1933, was not an effort to nationalize basic industry. Like its American counterpart, the RFC—which, we may remember, dates from the Hoover administration—IRI was a stopgap expedient for rescuing concerns that had fallen into financial difficulties. Although this government-financed corporation eventually acquired control of a massive percentage of Italian industry, it behaved for the most part as a trustee for private capital. It did little beyond buying up the depreciated securities of concerns threatened by bankruptcy and regrouping those concerns on a more rational basis, while leaving management as it was before.

The only large organized sector of Italian capital to suffer seriously from official regulation was banking. In 1934 and 1936, two sweeping decrees reduced the major Italian banks to a position of nearly complete subordination to government orders. This, however, was an exception to general practice and reflected the hostility so often discernible in fascist movements to banking as opposed to industrial capital. We may make another exception for retail com-

* *Istituto per la ricostruzione industriale.*

merce and small industry, which, like banking, suffered severely from the imposition of economic controls in the period after 1934. Smaller concerns could not adjust to the new regulations as well as large ones, and a good many of them were eventually forced to go out of business; between 1934 and 1937 the total number of industrial establishments in Italy declined by about five thousand. On balance, we may conclude that the policy of economic controls and autarchy in the 1930's strengthened the already existing tendencies toward industrial concentration and monopoly.

The plight of small business in the second decade of Mussolini's rule leads us to the problems of a final social category, the urban middle class. The term middle class is, of course, extremely imprecise, and it is almost impossible to make generalizations about so heterogeneous a group. Moreover, we lack the sort of statistical material on wages and working hours that illuminates the situation of industrial or agrarian labor. This much, however is clear. The urban white-collar groups that had originally given Mussolini the bulk of his adherents fared less well under his rule than they had been led to expect.

This relative disfavor was not immediately apparent. The deflationary policy of the late twenties worked, if anything, to the advantage of most of the urban middle class—particularly those on fixed incomes. But the economic controls imposed in the succeeding decade had the opposite effect. Holders of government securities suffered a reduction of income through a series of conversions that lowered the interest rates on successive bond issues. Moreover, like small tradesmen, members of the free professions found their business slowing up and their income declining in the period of war economy. The position of the professional and intellectual classes in the later years of Fascism is, in fact, one of the clearest indications of what was happening to the regime.

Originally, when Mussolini was just establishing his rule, Italians with a university degree—provided they were willing to make an adequate profession of enthusiasm for Fascist ideals—found the doors of advancement wide open to them. Intellectual talent was in demand, and jobs were plentiful. Not only were there the vacancies left by non-Fascists retired or purged from the civil service and the teaching profession. There were also a whole range of new positions in the rapidly expanding bureaucracy of the Fascist party and its dependent organizations. But this happy period lasted only a few years. By 1927, the intellectual job market was drying up. The positions had all been filled—and by younger men who could not be expected to die or retire for years to come. Hence from this point on Italian intellectuals and professional men lived in a state of increasing insecurity. The familiar European phenomenon of an intellectual proletariat again made its appearance. Thousands of university-trained Italians were out of work, and only a handful of positions were falling vacant annually either in the civil service or in the professions—where, in true corporative fashion, the self-governing bodies of lawyers, doctors, or journalists drastically limited the number of new men certified to practice. In the early 1930's, for example, only one out of every two hundred graduates of the various law faculties was admitted to the bar.

Long before the fall of Fascism, then, the younger Italian intellectuals were beginning to grow skeptical about the regime. And many of them, driven to desperation by a situation in which every outlet to their talents seemed blocked, transferred their allegiance to a doctrine of radical social overturn. In the intellectual unemployment of the later Fascist period, we can find one explanation for the tenacious hold of Communism on the generation of Italians graduated from the universities in the thirties and early forties.

For those who actually had jobs, however, the situation was totally different. The period of the thirties was to see an increasing cleavage in attitude between the bureaucracy—at least those in its higher ranks—and the mass of Italians with university training. For the bureaucrats enjoyed precisely the security that the others lacked. Their incomes remained steady, and their prestige increased as the institution of economic controls brought new power into their hands. By the mid-thirties it was becoming apparent that Fascist Italy was acquiring a fairly homogeneous ruling class. In the institutions of the corporate state, the two chief supports of the regime, the industrialists and the higher bureaucracy, were beginning to merge in attitude and even in function: as the officers of corporative bodies, the industrialists were turning into bureaucrats, while the higher civil servants, through jurisdictional overlapping, social contact, or marriage, were being brought into increasingly close relations with private enterprise. Hence the Italian man in the street was not far wrong when he confused the two in his mind. His image of the typical Fascist was of a prosperous middle-aged man, corpulent and balding, somewhat lazy and self-indulgent after the fatigues and enthusiasms of his youth, ready to relax now with his fine automobile, his villa, and his title of *commendatore*. This was not the sort of leadership calculated to inspire devotion among the populace. Nor was it a very sure support for a Mussolini who was himself ill and aging as the crisis of the regime drew closer.

5

The Legacy of Fascism:
The Church and the Opposition

1. THE RECONCILIATION WITH THE CHURCH

THE HISTORY of the social policies of the Fascist state has taken us far beyond the mid-point of Mussolini's rule and into the era of his declining fortunes. It has perhaps given the impression of a more widespread dissatisfaction with the regime than was actually the case. Through most of the Fascist period—and particularly during the central years 1926 to 1936—the mass of the Italian people accepted the new dispensation, even when they suffered under it. The decade from the mid-twenties to the mid-thirties may have been one of deflation and depression—but at the time it appeared to be an era of substantial achievement. By 1936 Mussolini had disciplined the country to an unquestioned "Roman" order; he had ended social strife; he was draining the swamps; he had conquered an empire. Above all, he had done what no previous regime had been able to accomplish: he had brought about a reconciliation between the Papacy and the Italian state. This achievement had more to do with winning over non-Fascists to support his government than any other of Mussolini's acts, and 1929, the year of the great reconciliation, marked the high point of his prestige and popularity.

We must add that the Duce had only to give a final impetus to a development that had been long in progress. For nearly half a century, as we have seen, the official irreconcilability on which both Church and state insisted had reduced itself in practice to a workable, if rather complex, system of mutual forbearance, in which the remaining elements of misunderstanding acted as irritants rather than serious hazards. Particularly after the war ended, with practicing Catholics fully and influentially engaged in national politics, it had become generally apparent that a regularization of the *de facto* situation was overdue. At the Peace Conference of 1919, an unofficial spokesman for the Vatican had taken soundings with Prime Minister Orlando. But the brief life of the postwar ministries had precluded any serious negotiations.

By 1925, with Mussolini firmly installed, the question could be taken up again with some hope of continuity in negotiation. Moreover, the Duce was fortunate in the antagonist with whom he would be dealing. In February 1922, only eight months before Mussolini himself came to power, the College of Cardinals elected a new Pope who by background and temperament was well equipped to carry out the work of reconciliation. Pius XI was a practical man, with the traditional tenacity and hard-headedness of the Lombard bourgeoisie from which he sprang; scholarly, conservative, and somewhat authoritarian by nature, he was deeply impressed by the peril of Communism, which he had experienced at first hand as nuncio to Poland from 1919 to 1921. Fascism the new Pope saw as a bulwark against atheistic Bolshevism. While not precisely pro-Fascist, as some of his detractors have asserted, he was sufficiently convinced of the merits of the new movement to adopt toward it an attitude of sympathetic understanding. And this even at the expense of jettisoning the new Catholic party, the *Popolari,* whose foundation and growth his predecessor had tacitly fostered. Pius XI was distrustful of political Catholicism; he preferred to see the faithful grouped into nonpartisan laymen's organizations under the guidance of their bishops. Hence by a series of small but significant slights and warnings he disavowed the Popular party, which thereby found itself grievously handicapped in its struggle for survival against Fascist terrorization.

Mussolini, for his part, was aiming at the total destruction of the *Popolari.* This was one of his main reasons for desiring a reconciliation with the Church. For once the Fascists could pose as the defenders of religion, the Popular party would find the ground cut out from under it. And Mussolini's regime would be immensely strengthened: the idea of national unity, of profound popular sentiment incarnate in Italian Catholicism would reinforce the Fascist state and give it enhanced prestige in the eyes both of Italians and of the outside world. Mussolini, then, sought a settlement for essentially practical reasons. He himself was far from being a religious

man. In his youth, he had been distinguished even among the anti-
clerical Socialists for the violence of his sacrilegious utterance; among
other things, he had written a lurid novel entitled *The Cardinal's
Mistress*. And this strong dislike for the Church he had taken over
with him into Fascism; most of the early Fascists were anticlericals
—one of the rare exceptions being Mussolini's younger brother
Arnaldo, the only real friend, by his own admission, that the Duce
ever had, and an ardent promoter of the reconciliation. The former
Nationalists were pushing in the same direction. And so Mussolini,
who prided himself on his pragmatism, did not find it too difficult
to make one more ideological flip-flop. In his heart, he probably never
changed. He simply kept his own counsel to the end.

Yet the settlement, when it came, offended the more extreme and
doctrinaire wing of the Fascist party. This was one reason why the
negotiations took so long and why Mussolini felt that public opinion
needed to be carefully prepared for the change. He began with a
series of significant gestures: the restoration of crucifixes to public
buildings; the appointment of former clericals as local officials; above
all, the reintroduction of religious teaching in the curriculum of the
state schools and the concession of a vastly more favorable competitive position to educational institutions run by the Church. With
these tokens of his good intentions in hand, Mussolini was ready to
enter into full-scale negotiations for a settlement. The Pope was also
prepared to talk. The negotiations began in 1926, to be continued
for nearly three years, in close secrecy and at first only through semiofficial intermediaries. At the very end, the Duce himself took over
the task and drove it through to a successful conclusion. In February
1929 an astonished world learned of the signature of two accords
ending a controversy that had endured nearly sixty years—the
Lateran Treaty and the Concordat.

The division of the settlement into two separate documents symbolized the fact that the "Roman Question" had actually been twofold—both political and religious. The former, covered by the
Lateran Treaty, was by far the easier of solution. By the creation
of the tiny state of Vatican City the Pope was restored to a position
of territorial sovereignty; while he renounced all but a few acres
of the extensive domain that had formerly been his, he gained the
essence of what he had always sought—a position of juridical inde-

pendence from control by any temporal authority. The second question, whose solution was embodied in the Concordat, was more difficult by its very nature. It included the whole complex of quasi-religious problems—the ramifying questions of ecclesiastical appointments, Church property, marriage law, and education that had been at issue ever since the Piedmontese monarchy in the 1850's had embarked on a policy of separating Church from state, dissolving monastic bodies, and severely limiting the activities of the remaining religious associations.

The Concordat reversed the whole tradition of Church-state separation. It restored the Catholic Church to the position it had always occupied by the letter of the Italian constitution as the "sole religion of the state." In the future, religious bodies would suffer no limitations in their right to teach and to hold property, and Church marriages would be legally binding in the eyes of the civil authorities. It was on the question of marriage that the Pope gained his greatest victory. Previously in Italy, as in France, a civil marriage ceremony had been obligatory; a Church wedding from the legal standpoint ranked as no more than an optional supplement. By the terms of the new Concordat, Italians, like Americans, might choose whether they wished to be married by a civil ceremony or in Church; and in practice, since 1929, most of them have chosen the latter. Beyond that, however—and here the Concordat diverged from the American example—Mussolini undertook to bring the marriage law of the Italian state into conformity with canon law. Similarly, Church courts were to have sole jurisdiction in questions involving the dissolution of the marriage tie.

Although these provisions on marriage law made no very great difference in practice—we have already noted the hostility of most Italians to the idea of divorce—they raised a grave question in the minds of both non-Catholics and Catholics of liberal views: what was a Protestant or Jew to do if he wished to have his marriage dissolved? He had no other recourse than to bring his case to the ecclesiastical courts of a Church that was not his own. The question of marriage law focused attention on the inferior legal status the Concordat assigned to the non-Catholic minority faiths. As opposed to the official "religion of the state," they were to be simply "admitted cults." Unlike Catholics, Protestants and Jews were required to comply with a marriage procedure that was. essentially civil rather than religious. And they were obliged to ask official permission if they wished to open a new church or temple. These limitations might be minor and the members of the admitted cults might be few in number, but the subordinate position assigned to them under the Concordat revealed to that minority of foreigners who took care to scrutinize its provisions in detail, what was illiberal and anachronistic about the whole document

The few doubting voices that dared make themselves heard, either in Italy or abroad, were drowned in a chorus of general jubilation. It was too much to expect that the mass of Italians, who had suffered for more than half a century from a painful division of their national and religious loyalties, should now question a settlement that laid their scruples to rest. Only in the Senate did any coherent opposition manifest itself; and even there no more than five elderly Liberals joined the revered philosopher Benedetto Croce in voting against the ratification of the accords. In general, anti-Fascists saw the reconciliation with the Church as a severe blow to their hopes for a change of regime. They lost heart as they heard Catholics all over the world hail Mussolini as a great statesman and benefactor of his people.

The wave of pro-Fascist sentiment produced among Catholics both inside and outside Italy by the settlement of 1929 might well have raised doubts in the Pope's mind as to the wisdom of what he had just done. For one of his main purposes in entering into the negotiations had been to prevent Mussolini from smothering the Church with kindness; by regularizing the relations between Catholicism and the Fascist state he had hoped to disentangle the Church from too close an association with Mussolini's regime. The actual effect was nearly the reverse. Whatever doubts about Fascism the Pope himself might entertain were not shared by most of the Italian clergy. These interpreted the accords of 1929 as a blessing bestowed on all the Duce's works—as was to be apparent six years later when a number of the highest-ranking Italian ecclesiastics actively endorsed Mussolini's war of conquest in Ethiopia.

Long before that time the false harmony of the year of reconciliation had disappeared. Indeed the accords had scarcely been signed when the first misunderstandings over their interpretation arose. The crucial issue concerned education and the control of youth organizations—an issue on which either Fascism or Catholicism could give ground only at the risk of losing its hold on the rising generation. Two years of spirited polemics culminated in a struggle between Church and state bitterer than any similar controversy Italy had experienced since the turn of the century: the fight over Catholic Action of the year 1931.

Catholic Action, the nationwide laymen's organization in favor of which Pius XI had sacrificed the Popular party, represented a potential threat to Mussolini's totalitarian pretensions. As the only important organization in Italy that had not been brought under Fascist control, it was growing steadily in size and popularity. Its youth groups in particular looked like a dangerous exception to the Fascist monopoly of Italian thought and action. In May 1931, after a preliminary warm-up of press attacks and physical violence, Mussolini dissolved the Catholic youth and university associations. The justification he gave was that Catholic Action was mixing in politics and was under the influence of former Popular party leaders—a specious pretext, although there was naturally considerable overlapping in membership between the two organizations, and they had tended to become confused in the public mind. The Pope, stung to anger by the threat to the association he had so sedulously fostered, took up the challenge with vigor; in the encyclical *Non abbiamo bisogno* he unmasked the "pagan" intentions of the Fascist state. All summer long the controversy raged. Then suddenly in September the Fascist attacks ceased. Mussolini, evidently impressed by the near unanimity with which the foreign press had supported the Pope's stand, had decided to compromise the issue. Catholic Action was saved: it was permitted to resume its youth activities, but only subject to drastic limitations calculated to reduce their competitive appeal. Yet the organization continued to prosper. And, ironically, it in the end became in fact what Mussolini had accused it of being: a focus of political opposition in which the Popular party was gradually able to reconstitute its shattered cadres.

Once more a compromise had been patched up. But this time the fragility of the settlement was apparent to all. Pius XI had lost whatever illusions he may have originally harbored about the Christian intentions of the ruler of the Italian state. In his last years, the "old lion," as the people began to call him, was seldom silent: with fiery indignation and mordant wit, he kept up a running skirmish with Fascist publicists who could not match him in polemical agility. Where fascism appeared to stand for the preservation of religion and the established order, as during the Spanish Civil War, the Pope continued to support it. But where, as in Germany, it was coupled with the doctrine of racism, he condemned its un-Christian cruelty. And so, in 1938, when Hitler induced Mussolini to copy his anti-Semitic legislation—to limit the right of Jews to marry, to engage in professions, or to educate their children as they chose—the Pope once again raised his voice in protest.

This was Pius XI's last battle. He died in February 1939, on the eve of a great address that was to mark the tenth anniversary of the Concordat with the Italian state. The College of Cardinals, in a gesture widely interpreted as a rebuke to the two fascist dictators, chose as his successor Eugenio Pacelli—Pope Pius XII—who as Papal Secretary of State had been closely associated with the policy of the deceased pontiff. As the Second World War approached, the Italian state and the Catholic Church confronted each other in an attitude of uneasy truce.

2. THE OPPOSITION

The history of the organized opposition to Mussolini begins with the "Aventine" secession. In June 1924 the moderate Socialist deputy Giacomo Matteotti—who had courageously denounced the terrorism by which the Fascists had just gained their first electoral victory—disappeared and was later found to have been murdered. It was universally suspected, and subsequently proved, that his assassins were acting on official orders. The event shook the whole country: such happenings were not yet as familiar as they became during the next two decades. Mussolini was visibly worried, and it appeared doubtful whether his regime could last.

In protest some hundred and fifty deputies walked out of the Chamber—the Socialists, the Republicans, some Liberals, and most of the *Popolari*. They called themselves the Aventine, taking their name from the hill to which the Roman plebs had retired under the leadership of Caius Gracchus. In the Aventine was nearly all that was most distinguished in Italian political life. Yet it failed totally.

It consumed its time in sterile debate and took no action. As the months passed and the threat to his authority failed to materialize, Mussolini regained his confidence. Striking out in a bold counter-attack, he accepted general responsibility for all that had happened. In the autumn of 1926, the rump Chamber of Deputies voted to deprive the members of the Aventine of their seats in Parliament, and all political parties other than the Fascist were dissolved. The first experiment in united opposition was over.

Historians have freely condemned the Aventine for irresolution and ineptness. It is true that they relied exclusively on legal methods and the pressure of public opinion. Yet it is difficult to see what else they could have done. They could scarcely have raised the standard of armed revolt: the military forces and police were thoroughly under Mussolini's control, and even if they had not been, the country would have recoiled from a revival of the civil strife that had plagued the years 1920-22. In sum, the members of the Aventine were right in thinking that their only chance lay in an appeal to the King: he had appointed Mussolini; he could now dismiss him. Victor Emmanuel III, however, rebuffed the tentative advances of the secessionists. Despite all the evidence that his prime minister was implicated in political assassination, the King remained loyal to him. This is the second major reason—the first being his refusal to proclaim martial law in October 1922—why anti-Fascists demanded that Victor Emmanuel follow Mussolini into retirement after the collapse of 1943.

With the failure of the Aventine, the opposition fell to pieces. In this welter of conflicting attitudes three major currents are discernible. The first was a tolerated opposition whose locale was the Senate. The Italian upper house, we may recall, was an appointive body, consisting largely of older men, a number of whom had been chosen for their distinction in the field of letters rather than of politics. Since senators were appointed for life, the anti-Fascists among them continued to hold their seats even after the dissolution of the opposition parties. For a few years after 1925, the Senate provided the only free forum in Italy: world-famous scholars like Benedetto Croce and Gaetano Mosca assailed the regime in measured but unmistakable language. Yet this sort of opposition declined steadily: its members died off or succumbed to discouragement. After 1929, even Croce ceased attending Senate sessions.

Croce, however, continued his opposition in another form. In the columns of *La Critica,* which he edited throughout the Fascist period, the great philosopher maintained the tradition of liberal thought in Italy. As the one dissenting voice still permitted to speak out, Croce became the symbol of a lofty and dignified refusal to compromise with Fascism. The more scholarly and conservative among the opponents of Mussolini looked to the Neapolitan philosopher as a guiding light and a rallying-point for the future.

Why did the Duce permit Croce to continue to publish his dissenting opinions? Why did he not shut down *La Critica* as he had suppressed every other opposition journal? The question puzzled both Italians and foreigners at the time, and even today has not been entirely cleared up. It is probable that Mussolini, with his pretensions to culture, cherished a grudging admiration for the philosopher who refused to be overawed by him. Moreover, he saw that Croce's continued independence had propaganda value for the regime: like the presence of one Negro in an American professional association, it served as an argument that no real discrimination or denial of freedom existed. Conversely, the suppression of *La Critica* would have created an extremely unfavorable impression in foreign intellectual circles. Finally, and most calculatingly, Mussolini doubtless realized that Croce's type of opposition carried no real threat to the regime. As a conservative and a man of thought, Croce abhorred the idea of revolution and would never knowingly have incited anyone to it. In a sense, then, he served as an intellectual lightning rod by deflecting to the field of abstract speculation the more inquiring among the youth of Italy who might otherwise have espoused revolutionary doctrines.

The men in the universities and in other intellectual pursuits who admired Croce and followed his lead, although they did not dare to voice their opinions openly, fell into a second category of opposition —a quiet opposition. These people enjoyed no official tolerance like Croce. Outwardly they were obliged to conform to the dictates of Fascism. In 1931, the government forced all university professors to take an oath of loyalty to the regime. Only eleven refused. But dozens of others, unwilling to see their families destitute, or, in the case of the Catholics, having received ecclesiastical permission to take the oath with reservations, complied with it simply as an irksome formality. In their hearts they dissented: they lived a life of what anti-Nazi Germans later called "inner emigration." Through them, despite all Mussolini's efforts to indoctrinate the youth of Italy, the universities increasingly harbored small but influential circles of independent thought.

Even more characteristic of the quiet opposition was the attitude of millions of devout Catholics. While a large minority of Catholics applauded Mussolini as the friend of the Church, a majority, particularly after the Catholic Action controversy of 1931, shared the Pope's suspicions about the regime and sought to shield their children from Fascist influence. Among them were the former leaders of the *Popolari*. The Popular party had paid heavily for its mistake in joining Mussolini's first government: it had seen its more conservative wing won over to Fascism and its beloved leader, Don Luigi Sturzo, hounded into exile. But few of Sturzo's followers had taken the same road. In a spirit of Christian humility, the *Popolari* had submitted to the dissolution of their party after the failure of the Aventine and had tried to return to their normal lives. In general they refrained from active opposition and lived quietly and obscurely. Denied passports and advancement in their professions, they suffered from economic hardship and moral isolation. Yet few were seriously molested by the Fascists. An exception was the last party secretary, Alcide De Gasperi, who was arrested in 1927 while trying to escape abroad. But even he, after his release sixteen months later, abandoned political activity; as a minor functionary in the Vatican Library, he received sanctuary in the Pope's new state. When the fall of Fascism finally came, De Gasperi and the other Popular party leaders enjoyed the enormous advantage of having remained in their own country and never having lost touch with the Italian people.

The leaders of the other Aventine parties had had the opposite experience. Most of them had found that they either were too devoted to principle or had already exposed themselves too thoroughly, to take the course of passive protest. They form the third and most significant segment of the opposition—the militant opponents of the whole Fascist dispensation.

For them there were only two choices: clandestine activity inside Italy or exile. The former was of course extremely dangerous. Sooner or later most active anti-Fascists inside Italy landed in the hands of the police. Once captured, however, they experienced relatively merciful treatment—at least in comparison with the practice of Nazi Germany or Stalinist Russia. Mussolini operated no true concentration camps. In their place, he sent his opponents to *confino,* a kind of internal exile. The milder form of *confino* was banishment under police surveillance to some desolate southern town, as in the case of the writer Carlo Levi. More drastically interpreted, *confino* meant detainment on a barren, wind-swept island in the Tyrrhenian Sea: here the elite of anti-Fascism spent years of discomfort and frustration, reading, plotting escape, or endlessly chewing their ideological cud. Oppositionists considered by the regime to be particularly dangerous went to prison, and a few were sentenced to death. Others died from their sufferings while in prison or *confino* —like the remarkable thinker Antonio Gramsci, the patron saint of the Italian Communist party.

In general, it was the younger men who elected to remain inside Italy. The older and more prominent leaders, wisely and with the full approval of their followers, went into exile. These émigrés included several of the leading figures of Italian politics: besides Don Luigi Sturzo, there were Francesco Saverio Nitti, the first postwar prime minister, and Count Carlo Sforza, foreign minister in Giolitti's last government and a vigorous opponent of Italian hyper-nationalism. Most of the earlier exiles left their country legally, by train and equipped with passports. But those who fled later, after the regime had begun to clamp down on the opposition, were obliged to make their escape in more dangerous and unconventional fashion: Pietro Nenni and Giuseppe Saragat, the future chiefs of Italian Socialism's rival factions, walked over the Alps, while Filippo Turati, the patriarch of the Socialist movement, who was too old for mountaineering, was smuggled out from the Italian Riviera to Corsica in a motor boat.

Among those who managed Turati's escape were two of the most promising of the younger generation of anti-Fascists: Carlo Rosselli and Ferruccio Parri. On their return to Italy they were captured by the police and sent to *confino* on the island of Lipari. Here their courses diverged. Parri elected to serve out his sentence. On his release, he went to Milan, where he worked quietly for the Edison Electric Company. As an active organizer of the clandestine opposi-

tion inside Italy, he became universally respected for his disinter-
estedness and bravery—qualities that were later to win him leadership in the wartime resistance and, eventually, the premiership of
Italy. Rosselli, on the other hand, felt that he could accomplish more
in exile. After an escape even more daring than Turati's, he arrived
in Paris in the summer of 1929.

Rosselli's arrival galvanized the emigration into new life. Paris
had naturally become its center—since the French Republic had a
long tradition of hospitality to political dissenters, and the Italian
exiles, nearly all of whom spoke French, could quickly make themselves at home there. In 1927, they had united to form an Anti-
Fascist Concentration. But this union was too loose and conventional
to be really effective. As simply a revival of the old Aventine parties,
it could offer no new political message to the Italian people. This
was what Rosselli sought to provide. Shortly after his arrival in
Paris, he gathered together a number of like-minded friends to form
a new movement, *Giustizia e Libertà* (Justice and Liberty), that
aimed to transcend and supplant the older parties.

During his confinement on Lipari, Rosselli had had more than
enough time to think through the problem of why Italian democracy
had failed. He concluded that one of the basic reasons had been the
split between the liberal and the socialist traditions. What Italy
needed, he believed, was a new political creed that would merge
the liberal emphasis on individual freedom with the socialist striving
for economic welfare. Hence he arrived at a doctrine of "liberal
socialism." This new socialism would no longer rest on the flinty
foundation of Marxist economics; it would be a vaguer and more
tolerant creed of universal humanitarianism.

Rosselli was no very coherent political theorist, and in his "liberal
socialism" there lurked a number of theoretical ambiguities. But as
the instigator of a political movement, he offered a remarkable
combination of qualities. The descendant of a distinguished Jewish
family that had played a prominent role in the Risorgimento,
Rosselli possessed a thorough humanistic education, considerable
literary talent, overflowing energy and optimism, and, not least,
a fairly large personal fortune. Hence he not only had the requisite
qualities of intellect and character to found a new movement; he
also had the means to insure its continued existence.

During the first few years after its foundation, *Giustizia e Libertà* was the most active among the anti-Fascist groups in exile. Intellectuals in particular enthusiastically endorsed its program. In the establishment of clandestine cells inside Italy, it was rivaled only by the Communists, who eventually had a particularly large number of their leaders in *confino*. At first, *Giustizia e Libertà* tried to emphasize its claim to be more than a mere political party by remaining outside the Anti-Fascist Concentration. In 1931, however, it joined up with the others—just in time to participate in the crisis and dissolution of the Concentration itself.

The early thirties were a period of transition and upheaval in Italian anti-Fascism. After 1931, the police began to gain the upper hand in identifying and rounding up the oppositionists inside the country; they smashed cell after cell until by 1936 organized anti-Fascism inside Italy was nearly extinct. The national unity inspired by the Ethiopian War—the first of Mussolini's major foreign adventures and the only one that was genuinely popular—had finished it off. Meantime in Paris the exiles began to succumb to discouragement. In May 1934 the Anti-Fascist Concentration broke up.

The date 1934 is significant. It gives a clue to a second reason besides discouragement why the Concentration was dissolved. In that year, the French Communist party launched the policy of the Popular Front. To Italian Communists in exile, this development meant a radical change of tactics. Previously they had worked in isolation, suspicious of and suspected by the parties in the Anti-Fascist Concentration. Now they moved toward alignment with the Italian Socialists. And the Socialists were ready to meet them. In 1930, the two wings of the Socialist party, the Maximalist and the moderate or "Unitary," had patched up their differences and reunited. Subsequently, with the death of the older Socialist leaders like Turati, the headship of the party had fallen to Pietro Nenni, a strong advocate of working-class unity. Three months after the dissolution of the Concentration, in August 1934, Nenni signed his first "unity of action" agreement with the Communists.

The year 1934, then, marked the end of the Aventine idea—the concept of a loose union of already existing political parties—as the focus of Italian anti-Fascism. Now there were again two rivals for the allegiance of the emigration and the clandestine opposition inside Italy. But this time Rosselli's *Giustizia e Libertà* was faced by a far stronger competitor in the new coalition of the Communist and Socialist parties. The Spanish Civil War, from 1936 to 1939, was to provide the stage for their rivalry—and for the eventual triumph of the Marxist bloc.

In Spain, the Italian anti-Fascist exiles at last found their chance. Here, with Mussolini actively intervening to support Franco's cause, the Italian enemies of Fascism could meet their foe on a foreign battleground. Some five thousand Italian émigrés enrolled in the Loyalist ranks. These amateurs soon became seasoned soldiers: at the battle of Guadalajara they helped defeat the professional forces that Mussolini had sent to Spain under the guise of volunteers. Eventually, of course, they lost—as the Spanish Republic went down, overwhelmed by foreign arms. But almost as serious as the lost war was what the Spanish experience had done to the anti-Fascist cause. It had given the Communists a new position of near supremacy. By the ruthless use of the superior organization and material means at their disposal, the Communists had squeezed out or suppressed their rivals. It was they who organized and dominated the International Brigades, in which the Italians were a leading element. Not all the International Brigade commanders were Communists: the Republican Randolfo Pacciardi, for example, led the chief Italian unit, the celebrated Garibaldi Brigade. But the Communists held the key positions of influence: such men as Luigi Longo and Giuseppe Di Vittorio gained in Spain the experience that was later to prove invaluable in organizing the Partisan movement in northern Italy.

The Communists had similarly hampered the efforts of *Giustizia e Libertà* to aid the Spanish Republicans. Within a few weeks after the outbreak of the Civil War, Rosselli had organized a small volunteer "column" to fight on the Catalonian front. Rosselli's column had gone into action nearly three months earlier than the Communist-organized Brigades. But when these latter did get into the fighting, their greater strength and prestige had proved too much for the smaller unit, whose effectives began to melt away. In June 1937 Rosselli, worn out and seriously ill, withdrew to France to recover his health. On a lonely Normandy road, in the company of his brother Nello, he met his death at the hands of French

Cagoulards—local fascists serving as the paid agents of the Italian government.*

The murder of Carlo Rosselli—which closed the phase of opposition activity that the assassination of Matteotti had inaugurated—dealt a grievous blow to the whole non-Communist sector of Italian anti-Fascism. *Giustizia e Libertà* never recovered from it and, in an organizational sense, nearly ceased to exist. Mussolini had chosen his target well. During the next two years, the Communist-Socialist bloc dominated the anti-Fascist emigration. And—unlike such alliances elsewhere—it was only temporarily shaken by the Nazi-Soviet pact.

The approach of the Second World War gave hope to the whole emigration that the end of Mussolini's tyranny might now be near. But at the outbreak of the war itself, the anti-Fascist opposition was as far as ever from the attainment of its goal. For all its heroism and sacrifice, neither the emigration nor the clandestine opposition inside Italy had been able to encompass Mussolini's fall. Their best efforts had shattered against the technical defenses of the modern police state, which, in Italy as elsewhere, proved impervious to the sort of old-fashioned ideological attack that was all the opposition could bring to bear. In the end, the Fascist regime simply succumbed to the accumulated mistakes of a disastrous foreign policy.

3. THE RECKONING

Had Mussolini refrained from throwing in his lot with Hitler, he might have ridden through the Second World War without mishap, and, like Franco, in due course have become the ally of the United States against the Communist menace. The speculation is rich in historical irony; one might even find retrospective justification for Mussolini in the resemblances between his 1933 proposal for a Four-Power Pact directed against the Soviet Union, and the postwar alliance of Britain, France, Germany, and Italy for anti-Communist defense.

This proposal came at a time when the Duce still enjoyed a good reputation as a constructive statesman and, basically, a defender of the peace. Two years later, he shocked the Western democracies

* Aldo Garosci, *La vita di Carlo Rosselli* (Florence, 1945), II, 277–284.

by the sudden assumption of a warrior role. Mussolini's war of conquest in Ethiopia lost him his reputation for moderation and brought down upon him concrete retaliation in the form of economic sanctions voted by the League of Nations. The imposition of sanctions infuriated Mussolini and left him with the permanent conviction that the British and French were his enemies. This, plus his involvement in the Spanish Civil War, which broke out only ten weeks after the end of the Ethiopian conflict, persuaded him that he needed a reliable ally. The result was the establishment of the Rome-Berlin Axis in October 1936.

From that date on, Mussolini was caught in a trap from which he seemed unable to escape. As an old-fashioned tyrant, with vestiges of personal honor and humanitarian scruples, the Duce was no match for his German partner. Almost from the start, the Axis became an unequal union. The annexation of Austria in the spring of 1938 set the pattern for what was to follow: with cavalier unconcern, Hitler withheld from his ally any accurate knowledge of his plan to absorb the small state whose independence Italy had protected for more than a decade; only after the deed had been done, did he assure Mussolini that he would "never forget" the splendid way in which the Duce had swallowed his humiliation. The same thing occurred at the time of the final annexation of the Czech lands, in March 1939, and again with the signature of the Nazi-Soviet pact and the attack on Poland that launched the Second World War. Mussolini was left to pick up what scraps of information he could —and to receive the Führer's thanks when there was no longer anything he could do about it. Desperate for some kind of compensation, he could think of nothing better to do than to annex the kingdom of Albania, which was already virtually an Italian protectorate.

For one brief moment Mussolini enjoyed the role of mediator and maintainer of the peace. As the architect of the Munich meeting of September 29, 1938, that postponed the general war for another year, Mussolini seemed to have become the arbiter of Europe. In Italy, he began to regain his popularity, which had been slipping ever since the intervention in Spain and the proclamation of the Axis. Yet he failed in his efforts to repeat the act a year later. Hitler was determined that this time his Italian ally would not defraud him of his war. And so in early September 1939, Mussolini could see no other course than "nonbelligerence"—an attitude of benevolent neutrality toward the Nazi war of conquest.

Once again, as in 1914, Italy had failed to declare war on the side of her German ally. And once again the British and French hoped that the Italians might at least remain neutral, since this time they could scarcely be expected to change camps. All through the winter of the "phony war," Mussolini hesitated. Prematurely aging, and tortured by doubts and a duodenal ulcer, he balanced between his frustration at seeing his ally win the military victories for which he longed, and the sober advice of his diplomatic and military chiefs that Italy was totally unprepared for war. Hitler's invasion of the West decided him. Dazzled by the rapidity of the German victory over France, and convinced that the defeat of England was now only a matter of time, Mussolini determined to take the plunge: Italy, he reasoned, could not afford to be absent from the kill. Never did a calculated decision prove more calamitously wrong.

The Duce's foreign policy had failed. Italy had won an empire in Ethiopia and an ideological ally in Spain, but she was now about to lose both of these—and everything else besides. Mussolini had maneuvered himself into a position from which he must either triumph or see his whole achievement collapse into dust. The test of war revealed the shakiness of the regime the Duce had established. Originally it had rested on something that might be called "idealism." But by the late thirties it had come to be based on little more than the self-interest of those whom it had elevated and enriched or whose class position it had protected.

Mussolini, as we have seen, had not fundamentally altered the structure of Italian society. He had simply shored up the propertied classes that had been so scared and shaken by the revolutionary ferment of 1919 to 1921, and had temporarily stimulated them with a shot of Fascist dynamism. This had not been his original intention: he had hoped to replace a worn-out old elite with a new and sturdier elite of Fascist youth. But the forces of inertia had proved too strong for him. His followers had grown elderly and fat and had been absorbed by interest and attitude into the already existing propertied classes.

To these people—Fascist and non-Fascist alike—Mussolini's regime was good only so long as it brought results. They would support it only if it continued to keep the poor in check, guarantee profits, and win easy diplomatic victories. If the opposite happened, they would jettison it and try some other *combinazione*. This character of temporary expediency was of the essence of Italian Fascism: it marked its difference both from Nazism and from Soviet Communism. In the Soviet Union no independent grouping, no corporate body, no autonomous focus of allegiance existed outside the party-state. In Nazi Germany, such bodies continued to maintain themselves—we may think of the army, certain branches of the civil service, the larger industrial combinations, and, above all, the Churches—but they led a precarious existence, essentially on sufferance of the regime. In Italy the situation was reversed. The independent bodies appeared to be much the same as in Germany. Actually they were far stronger: in Italy it was the regime, rather than they, that lived on sufferance. Of course these constituted powers would not have dared to overthrow Mussolini if all had been going well: he was too popular for that, and his control of the police and Fascist Militia was too solid. But when things began to go badly, they found their chance. Mussolini himself was not totally deceived. Despite the fawning and flattery that prosperous citizens lavished on him, he never lost his scorn and distrust for the Italian bourgeoisie.

Yet this was not all. In Nazi Germany or in Soviet Russia, Hitler or Stalin stood alone: he had no rival for the allegiance of his people. In Italy, there was still the King. In this, as in so many other respects, the Fascist revolution had been incomplete. By leaving intact the institution of the monarchy, Mussolini, as he later bitterly lamented, had sanctioned a situation of "dual command" or "dyarchy."* Victor Emmanuel III had proved himself weak-willed and lacking in principle. He had irrevocably compromised himself with the excesses of Fascism. But he was still there—a cipher, perhaps, but an alternative symbol of loyalty. To traditionalists—to the aristocracy, the officers of the army and navy, the diplomatic corps, and the older senators—the King rather than the Duce was the chief.

In Italy, these older ruling classes still wielded great influence. Particularly in areas where the values of the hierarchical society persisted they retained their traditional prestige, and, through their

---

* Benito Mussolini, *Memoirs: 1942–1943*, translated by Frances Lobb and edited by Raymond Klibansky (London, 1949), pp. 154–157.

extensive landholdings, a secure economic base. During most of the Fascist period, they had gone along with the regime, but they had been less deeply involved with it than the newer ruling class of industrial capital. Many members of the older aristocracy had remained skeptical of Fascism; a few, indeed, had been strongly hostile to it. And now, with defeat piling on defeat, they were nearly unanimous in their conviction that Mussolini must go. More timidly a large number of industrial capitalists agreed with them. So did a growing band of dissidents among the Fascist party leaders themselves. All these diverse malcontents were united in looking to the King. And, by the spring of 1943, they had the overwhelming mass of the Italian nation with them. For twenty years, Victor Emmanuel had connived in the deception of his people. But now this people, nearly to a man, looked to him for deliverance. What the devotion and talent of the anti-Fascist opposition had been unable to bring about, the old King, for all his moral feebleness, was alone in a position to accomplish.

6

The Second World War

MUSSOLINI'S decision to enter the war at Hitler's side was based on the idea that the period of Italy's active participation would be very brief. Indeed, he had feared that if he did not intervene in June 1940 he might never get a chance to fight at all. A short war was the only type of war that made any sense from the Italian standpoint. The Italian military commanders had laid their plans on that basis, as anyone with even a superficial understanding of the country's geographical and economic limitations might readily have guessed. Moreover, they had told the Duce that they would not be prepared to fight until 1942 at the earliest. Hitler had refused to wait that long: by precipitating the war in the late summer of 1939 he had given his Italian ally a plausible excuse for remaining nonbelligerent. But then the sudden collapse of France had forced Mussolini's hand. In the summer of 1940 the Duce found himself at war under circumstances that were far from his choosing and that gradually revealed themselves as unfavorable in the extreme.

Italy's unpreparedness was not merely a matter of military equipment—although that was bad enough. Under the best of circumstances it would have been difficult for Italian industry to equip a modern army. But with Fascist officials and their industrialist friends making an easy profit out of shoddy supplies or supplies that did not exist, the results were lamentable. The Italian armed forces went into battle ill equipped and inadequately supported from their home base. It is no wonder that the average Italian fighting man soon lost confidence in his country's war leadership.

In addition to this physical unpreparedness, the Italian people were psychologically unready for the rigors of a long conflict. Again, as in 1915, Italy had intervened in a struggle that had no meaning for the mass of its people. But this second time public morale was still lower than in the earlier conflict: the years of foreign adventure from 1935 to 1939 had created an atmosphere of war weariness even before there was much to be weary of, and had deepened the general conviction that Fascism and war were synonymous. From 1940 to 1943, the Italians fought with less than half their hearts. Certain picked professional units, particularly in the navy and air force, displayed a dash and bravery that won the admiration of their enemies. But among the bulk of the Italian armed forces, caution, apathy, and defeatism reigned nearly unchecked. British and American war writers have freely mocked the Italians for their undistinguished military record. It is easy to hurl the charge of cowardice —but it is also a cheap and superficial way of dealing with the question. It is more revealing to ask, as so many Italians did at the time, what was the point of showing bravery in a futile war for a bad cause. Rather than taking a high moral line with the Italians, we, the victors, might have done better to have recognized the extent to which their attitude of weary realism had facilitated our own victory. In his sober and unheroic fashion, the Italian soldier who fought listlessly, who deserted, or who surrendered to the enemy had made the only contribution he could to the triumph of the Allied cause, and with it, the liberation of his country from Fascist tyranny.

The average Italian had expected little from the war, but what actually happened surpassed his most gloomy anticipations. More than three years of combat on the Axis side—years of constant defeat and humiliation—were to be followed by nearly two additional years of a "liberation" that proved even more ruinous than the lost war itself. This war could have been of advantage to Italy only if, as Mussolini had hoped, it had brought quick and easy gains from the collapse of the French and British positions in the Mediterranean. But right from the start such easy conquests proved illusory. In the two weeks' war against France the Italian performance was so mediocre that Hitler decided his laggard allies had not deserved the rewards they had intended to carve out of French territory; moreover he wanted to win over the Vichy government as a still newer and potentially more valuable ally. Defrauded of his plunder in the western Mediterranean, Mussolini turned toward the east.

But here he came up against the power of Britain and Britain's allies. After the defeat of France, the British had failed to collapse according to schedule. Driven off the Continent and confined to their own island, they proved not only that they could defend themselves from German air attacks at home, but in the Mediterranean and Africa they were still strong enough to meet and defeat the main power of Italian arms.

This for Italians was the first great humiliation of the war—to be beaten by mere detachments of the British army, navy, and air force in the sea that Mussolini had so proudly told them was their own. During the first year and a half of fighting, the Italian army was twice pushed back from the Egyptian frontier deep into Libya, and the whole of Italian East Africa, including the newly conquered Empire of Ethiopia, fell to a small British expeditionary force. On the sea and in the air, the Italian record was equally disastrous: at Taranto and Cape Matapan the British crippled the Italian fleet for a negligible loss of their own aircraft. And when, in the autumn of 1940, Mussolini decided to take on a weaker adversary, the results were no better. The Italian invasion of Greece met a stern resistance that drove it back into the Albanian mountains. Here—as in North Africa—the Italians could resume the offensive only after the Germans had come to their aid. And when Greece was finally overwhelmed, the Italians were made to realize that the victory had not been theirs: German rather than Italian influence was to predominate in the Balkans—an area that Mussolini had long ago staked out as a preserve for future Italian expansion.

By mid-1941, then, it was clear that the Italians had nothing to hope from the war. Victory would simply confirm their subordination to the Germans—and what this meant in human terms was apparent from the sufferings of the expeditionary force that Mussolini had contributed to the invasion of Russia. Moreover, the events of late 1941 made an Axis victory appear increasingly unlikely. The German halt before Moscow was impressive enough. But it was the American intervention that convinced most Italians that the war neither could be won nor deserved to be won. It was the cruelest blow of all—the last and worst of a series of crushing disappointments—to have as an enemy the nation where millions of their countrymen had found new homes and for which they had always cherished a particular admiration.

The year 1942 brought the last Axis victories. But these were German victories, not Italian, even in the Mediterranean, where Rommel's advance into Egypt owed little to Italian initative. And when the Axis retreat in the desert began, the German commander showed what he thought of his Italian troops by leaving them to fend for themselves without water or transport. From this point on, the Italian military experience was one long martyrdom. The Anglo-American landing in Morocco and Algeria, the closing of the Allied pincers on Tunisia, the bombing attacks on Italian cities, and the invasion of Sicily—these were the steps in a protracted road of suffering that led closer and closer to catastrophe. By the spring of 1943, the war for Italians had reduced itself to one desperate question: how could they detach themselves from their dreaded ally and save their country from further destruction?

1. THE FALL OF MUSSOLINI

Beginning in March 1943 the opposition to Fascism inside Italy dared come into the open. On March 5 the workers of the FIAT plant in Turin—the traditional center of revolutionary consciousness in the skilled mechanical trades—launched a strike that was clearly political in inspiration. The previous months had seen a number of smaller strikes: already the workers were showing that they no longer feared the Fascist regulations against industrial agitation. But the strike at the FIAT plant was the first conscious and overt move against Mussolini—indeed, the first such demonstration that Italy had experienced for nearly twenty years. During the next few days the strike spread to other factories in Turin and eventually to the whole of northern Italy. Everywhere, under the guise of economic demands, the underlying purpose was the same: to force Mussolini to make peace. It was easy for left-wing agitators to fan antiwar sentiment among urban workers who were the chief sufferers from food shortages and Allied bombings.

At the same time the opposition political leaders—both those who had lived quietly through the Fascist period and those who had engaged in clandestine activity—began to reconstitute their parties and to seek out one another for consultation. Besides the Socialist and Communist parties, which had never lost their organizational identities, two further important political groupings secretly established themselves in the spring of 1943. The remnants of *Giustizia e Libertà* united with a newer movement of "liberal-socialist" intellectuals to found the Action Party (*Partito d'Azione*). Similarly, the former leaders of the Catholic *Popolari* revived their party under the new name of Christian Democracy. A number of the more conservative political figures left over from the parliamentary era were also carrying on individual negotiations. Of these the most active was Ivanoe Bonomi, a former Socialist turned conservative and the next to the last pre-Fascist premier of Italy. Bonomi had been Mussolini's enemy for more than thirty years—ever since the latter had had him expelled from the Socialist party in 1912. While he had not actively opposed the Fascist government since the election of 1924, he had never compromised with it. Now as a respected elder statesman, with acquaintances in all camps and a gift for negotiation and compromise, Bonomi was the ideal man to serve as the connecting link among all the disparate elements in the anti-Fascist opposition.

Through Bonomi, the political opposition was in contact with the first of two groups that were actually in a position to encompass Mussolini's fall—the King's entourage and the dissidents in the Fascist party. Both of these groups had long hesitated over what to do about the Duce: they quite naturally feared that to jettison Mussolini completely would be to unleash a revolutionary tempest that might sweep away their own positions along with him. But by July 1943 they could no longer afford to hesitate. With the Allies overrunning Sicily, an invasion of the Italian mainland threatening, and the Germans unwilling either to reinforce the peninsula adequately or to let Mussolini make a separate peace, there was no recourse left but to get rid of the Duce. Each of the two dissident groups within the ruling classes of Italy arrived at its decision separately. That is why the circumstances of Mussolini's fall have appeared so puzzling: it came about through the convergence of two distinct but overlapping conspiracies.

In the first of the palace plots were the King, the Minister of the Royal Household Duke Acquarone, the old former prime minister Vittorio Emanuele Orlando, and Marshal Pietro Badoglio. The last of these, the conqueror of Ethiopia and the recipient of countless Fascist honors, was, to say the least, a very recent convert to anti-

Fascism. But he could easily sympathize with the highly conservative aims of the royal plot—the replacement of Mussolini's government by an aristocratic regime basing itself on a strict interpretation of Italy's monarchical constitution.

The second group was not yet certain of its course when the news that the King was about to act forced its hand. The Fascist conspiracy, which was less integrated than the royal one, was the work of the so-called moderates in the party—particularly the two former foreign ministers, Count Dino Grandi and Count Galeazzo Ciano, the latter of whom was Mussolini's own son-in-law. Their aim was to replace the Duce's government with a more "respectable" type of Fascism that could arrive at an understanding with the Allies. They did not plan to eliminate Mussolini entirely; they would simply take his power from him. And by calling on the King to resume his constitutional position as supreme military chief, they hoped to share with him the responsibility for the disastrous war that the Fascist party had up to now been shouldering alone.

In an atmosphere heavy with anger and suspicion the Grand Council of Fascism convened on the evening of July 24. After a tense and confused debate, the motion offered by Grandi was carried by an overwhelming majority. The surviving founder of the Nationalist party, the two remaining "Quadrumvirs" of the March on Rome—nearly everyone except a handful of Fascist extremists voted for it. Yet few of those in the majority realized what they were doing. The motion seemed innocuous enough: it merely called on the King to take over "effective command" and the "supreme initiative of decision" in the conduct of the war. Mussolini knew better what it meant. As he adjourned the ten-hour meeting, he told his faithless followers: "You have provoked the crisis of the Regime."

Even the Duce, however, did not know the whole truth. He, like his enemies in the Grand Council, assumed that Fascism in some form or other would continue to guide the destinies of Italy. The whole truth came out only the following afternoon when Mussolini went to report to the King what had happened. For at this point the other plot—the King's own plot—took over. Victor Emmanuel received the Duce with an unexpected air of resolution. For Mussolini's own good and the good of the country, he told him, he was divesting him of his functions: Marshal Badoglio would be the new prime minister. Mussolini was stunned. As he walked from the royal presence, a *carabiniere* captain approached him and told him that he was under orders to protect the fallen Duce's personal safety. Mussolini was the King's prisoner: the twenty-year adventure of Fascism had just come to an end.

So ended modern Italy's great day of dupes. It was not yet clear who had had the last laugh. Both Mussolini and the Fascist opposition had been tricked by the wily King. But had Victor Emmanuel himself really won the game? Had the effort of the old conservative classes to save themselves by an artful *combinazione* actually succeeded? At the time—and for the next two years—the idea seemed preposterous: everywhere the prestige of the intellectual anti-Fascists and of the Italian working classes was in the ascendant. But after a few more months had passed—by the end of 1945—the victory of the anti-Fascists was no longer so apparent; the old ruling classes were returning in full force.

In itself, the success of the two converging palace plots had not constituted a true revolution. That was to be the major problem of the next two years, linked and sometimes in conflict with the other great issue of how Italy could best contribute to the victory of the Allies—would the fall of Fascism develop into that profound social and political revolution for which the militant opposition had so long been working?

2. *THE FORTY-FIVE DAYS AND THE ARMISTICE*

In the streets of Rome the news of Mussolini's fall set off an unprecedented explosion of popular joy. Long before the new Badoglio government had taken any official action, the Fascist regime simply disappeared under the pressure of a public revulsion that was nearly universal. In fact, the Italians were neither politically free nor out of the war; but they felt themselves to be so.

This was the central paradox of the "Forty-Five Days" from July 25 to September 8, 1943—one of the strangest epochs in contemporary history. For a month and a half Italy lived suspended between two worlds, its people torn between anxiety and a feckless confidence that their troubles were over. The country was unsure and hopeful at the same time, with the remnants of Fascism and the practices of a new and intoxicating freedom shifting in uneasy balance as the dominant element in its public life.

The Badoglio government reflected the popular uncertainties. On the one hand, it dissolved the Fascist party and its subsidiary organizations; it began to set up the machinery for a purge of Fascist hierarchs and profiteers; it liberated all political prisoners; and it restored a limited freedom of organization to Italian labor. At the same time, the bureaucracy, convinced that the new government would not last, sabotaged its liberalizing measures. And the government itself perpetuated many of the practices of the fallen regime. It severely censored the articles of the pre-Fascist newspaper editors who had everywhere replaced Mussolini's spokesmen, and it refused to give legal status to the anti-Fascist political parties.

During the Forty-Five Days, organized anti-Fascism found itself in a most curious situation. The opposition political leaders were the heroes of the hour: their years of exile, prison, or uncompromising withdrawal from public life had given them an unquestioned prestige. Immediately after the fall of Mussolini, they had formalized their previous personal understandings into a loose alliance of six political parties. Besides the Socialists and Communists, Christian Democracy and the Action Party, the six parties now included the Liberals and the Democracy of Labor. The former were the heirs of the major tradition of Italian parliamentary politics: basing itself on the personal distinction of five or six elderly leaders of conservative views and lofty principles, the revived Liberal party looked to Benedetto Croce for intellectual guidance. The Democracy of Labor was a more nebulous affair, which had little to support it but the prestige of Ivanoe Bonomi, its ideological mentor. Standing outside the alliance of the six parties were the traditional Republicans, who, though anti-Fascist to the core, refused to recognize even by implication the continued existence of the Italian monarchy.

It was Bonomi, as might have been expected, who presided over the meetings of the six-party leadership. These leaders operated as a kind of shadow government. Yet the parties they represented enjoyed no legal recognition. Moreover, the King had refused to permit Badoglio to take even the more conservative political leaders into his ministry; terrified of the spread of Communism, he had insisted that the government be restricted to nonpartisan "technicians." Hence the party leaders were reduced to a role of prodding and exhorting Badoglio to more energetic action. In particular, they reproached him for hesitation and delay in arriving at an armistice with the Allies.

In his first proclamation to the Italian people, Badoglio had declared: "The war goes on." But no one had believed him—neither the Italians, nor the Germans, nor the Allies. And in fact as early as July 29 or 30, he had begun his efforts to establish contact with the British and Americans. For Badoglio and the King—indeed, for the whole Italian nation—the overriding question was how to change sides in the war without provoking a German occupation of the peninsula. Under the most favorable circumstances, this problem would have been nearly insoluble. With Badoglio and the King in charge, the assignment was hopelessly bungled.

The story of the Armistice is a tragicomedy of illusions, blunders, and misunderstandings. On the Italian side, Badoglio must be charged with procrastination and overcaution, to say the very least. He took his time about sending an emissary to treat with the Allies; and then he confused the issue by dispatching three separate missions. Moreover, the chief negotiator, General Giuseppe Castellano, was instructed to remain in Lisbon after his assignment was accomplished, thereby wasting several precious days. It was not until September 3—five weeks after Badoglio had begun to send out peace feelers—that General Castellano, on his third visit to the Allies, was at length empowered to sign the Armistice.

The long delay had been partly the result of difficulties in communication; but it was chiefly due to the illusions that Badoglio entertained as to Italy's bargaining power. The Italian Prime Minister—and with him, most of the Italian people—thought that his country could discuss terms with the British and Americans on a basis of near-equality. In restrospect, this claim does not seem so exaggerated as it did at the time: had the British and Americans behaved more generously toward the Italians, they might have eased their own burden by obtaining more enthusiastic cooperation from their late enemies. But to expect this sort of trust and understanding in the late summer of 1943 was totally unrealistic. The Allies—and particularly the British—could not forget so soon that the Italians had been partners to their planned destruction. And so President

Roosevelt and Prime Minister Churchill had empowered General Eisenhower to discuss nothing except unconditional surrender. The Italians must either take it or leave it.

Yet Badoglio's emissaries continued to ask the impossible: they wanted to know the date of the major Allied landing on the Italian peninsula and they insisted that this landing should be in sufficient strength (fifteen divisions, they said) and near enough to Rome to protect the capital and the government from German retaliation. Eisenhower's deputies could agree to none of this. The landing had already been set for a place far to the south of Rome, it could not possibly be in the strength demanded, and the Allies certainly did not trust the Italians sufficiently to tell them when it would occur. The farthest they would go was to offer an air-borne landing to aid in the defense of the capital and to drop a few hints as to the general period during which the main landing might be expected.

These modest concessions probably did as much harm as good. They gave the Italians the illusion that they had gained more than they actually had and that they could afford to leave to the Allies the primary responsibility for the defense of Rome. Vacillating between confidence and discouragement, Badoglio let the six days between the signing of the Armistice and the Salerno landing slip by without arriving at a coherent plan. Then in the early morning of September 8 his illusions vanished. To his dismay he learned that the landing would take place the next day. Vainly he pleaded for a postponement of the Armistice announcement, which had been scheduled to come a few hours before the main landing. Again the Allies were adamant: their only answer was to cancel the air-borne operation near Rome and to go on with the Armistice announcement as planned. All that Badoglio could do was lamely to follow suit; in confused and uninspiring language, he told the Italian armed forces to "repel attacks from whatever quarter." Italians might find this hard to comprehend: the Germans understood immediately. Within a few hours after Badoglio had announced the Armistice, the latter began to occupy the capital city. Resistance appeared hopeless. In the early morning of September 9, at the very time that the Americans were going ashore at Salerno, a motor convoy with dimmed lights left Rome by one of the eastern gates; it was bearing to safety the Prime Minister and the royal family. The capital had been abandoned to its fate.

If we may reproach the British and Americans with excessive rigidity and lack of comprehension in conducting the Armistice negotiations, we may charge Badoglio with far worse. He himself sought to excuse his delays and hesitations by pleading the necessity of deceiving the Germans as to his real intentions.* But this argument lacks substance. We now know that the Germans were not deceived for a moment. As soon as they heard of Mussolini's fall, they began to send additional troops to the peninsula. The only question in their minds was whether they would have sufficient time to consolidate their position in Italy before Badoglio changed sides. In late July they were prepared to abandon Rome and to attempt to hold only the area north of a line between Pisa and Rimini—a line, incidentally, which it was to take the Allies a full year to reach. Six weeks later, when the Armistice was actually announced, the Germans had poured so many troops over the Brenner that they were in a position not only to capture Rome but even to imperil the whole Allied landing south of Naples.

Badoglio, then, accomplished nothing by delay. He could hardly have done worse, and he might have gained a great deal, if he had thrown caution away and boldly announced—even before any armistice negotiations had started—that Italy was changing over to the side of the Western democracies. Besides whatever military advantages such an announcement might have brought, the moral effect would have been enormous. It would have given the Italian people a clear lead: it would have told them that the aberrations of Fascism were over and that Italy had embarked on a new course. As it was, the way the Armistice came about had nearly the opposite effect: it left the Italian people confused, discouraged, and deeply resentful.

That is not to say, as some critics have asserted, that the Allies should never have made an armistice with Badoglio at all. The main concern was to get Italy out of the war; the instrument of the change did not matter. As they had already done in French North Africa, and as they were later to do in Japan, the British and Americans simply accepted the surrender of whoever was in a position to sign

---

* Pietro Badoglio, *Italy in the Second World War: Memories and Documents,* translated by Muriel Currey (Oxford, 1948), pp. 48–51.

the capitulation. Such an acceptance need have implied no endorsement of the signer. When he had done his work of surrender, he could have been dismissed, and the frankly anti-Fascist political leaders could then have taken over. This was the logic of the Italian situation after September 9, 1943; but the Allies—and more particularly the British—took nine months to realize it.

3. THE GOVERNMENTS OF THE SOUTH

At the Quebec conference of August 1943, President Roosevelt and Prime Minister Churchill had agreed that the Italians, once they had surrendered unconditionally, would be given a chance to "work their passage home" by contributing military assistance to the Allied cause. The prospect mitigated the bitterness of the harsh Armistice. In effect, the surrender was to be unconditional only in name; in a very short time Italy was to progress from the status of a defeated enemy into a twilight zone of "co-belligerency" that implied an increasing role of military cooperation. But the process was never fast enough or complete enough to satisfy the Italians. Most of them were no doubt apathetic toward the Allied war effort, as they had been indifferent to the campaigns waged by Mussolini. But there was a large minority, both among civilians and in the armed forces, who earnestly desired to fight. The Americans and British never adequately mobilized this reserve of military strength. The former lacked the imagination to visualize the possibilities of Italian aid; the latter were reluctant to put so much confidence in their recent enemies and made no secret of their intention to keep them in a state of inferiority and dependence.

The Italian navy and air force were able to make a contribution from the start. Owing to their mobility and the decisive action of their commanders, the major units of the fleet and air force reached Allied-held territory shortly after the Armistice was announced. Throughout the rest of the war, they rendered valuable if inconspicuous service, particularly in convoy and reconnaissance. For the Italian army, the problem was much graver. Bogged down without transport or fuel, demoralized and uncertain what to do, most of the army units in the Balkans and in northern and central Italy simply allowed themselves to be overpowered and disarmed by the Germans. The situation of those units that found themselves in Allied-held territory was not much better. They too lacked adequate equipment and vigorous leadership. The greater part of them proved to be fitted only for guard and supply duty in the rear of the Allied fighting forces.

Eventually, an Italian Corps of Liberation was organized and sent into battle. But the Allies limited it to 14,000 front-line soldiers and dissolved it in the middle of 1944 after the fall of Rome. During the following autumn, they set up a more extensive Italian force consisting of six small-sized divisions, or combat groups, of 9000 men each. These new units, which had been trained by the British and had received up-to-date Allied equipment, made a valuable contribution to the final victorious advance into northern Italy. In the end the Italians succeeded in establishing a respectable military record. But their full potential was never utilized.

Proceeding on the assumption that the officers of the regular Italian armed services were loyal to the King rather than to some more nebulous idea of anti-Fascism, the British and Americans hesitated to upset the regime that had emerged from the *coup d'état* of July 25. In themselves the leaders of this regime were not particularly prepossessing. After their flight by car across the peninsula and by corvette down the Adriatic coast, the King and Badoglio had arrived pathetic and destitute at the southern seaport of Brindisi. Here they awaited the arrival of General Montgomery's Eighth Army, which had landed on the toe of the Italian peninsula six days before the main landing at Salerno and had subsequently swung over to the east. On September 11 the British troops made contact with the King. This was the beginning of the royal government of southern Italy—first established at Brindisi, later shifted to Salerno, and finally, after the liberation of Rome in June 1944, transferred back to the national capital itself.

The Allies reserved to their own Control Commission and Military Government a veto power over all the decisions of the King's ministers. The provinces nearest to the fighting lines they governed themselves, and only gradually returned the rear area provinces to Italian administration. Meantime, Badoglio carried on as prime minister; as during the Forty-Five Days, his government consisted only of "technicians." This the Allies found to be an entirely satisfactory arrangement. They had come rather to like Badoglio and, despite his dubious past, to trust him. They believed that he alone could guarantee the loyalty of the Italian armed forces and faithfully carry out the Armistice terms, which at the time seemed to be the overriding considerations.

But this was to take a short-run view of the matter. If the Allies simply wanted a minimum contribution by regular Italian armed units, the King and Badoglio might do. But if they wanted to mobilize the mass of the Italian people for a vigorous effort to win the war, then something more inspiring and less intimately associated with Fascism was required. The anti-Fascist party leaders in southern Italy were acutely aware of this need. And during the autumn and winter of 1943-44 they kept up a steady propaganda in favor of a change.

It is true that southern Italy was the least favorable area of the country in which to launch the perilous experiment of a revived democracy. And it is also true that the South lacked party leaders of acknowledged stature; most of these were either in Rome or in the North. But there were enough of them around Naples to serve as the nucleus of a government: among others there were the revered Croce and Count Carlo Sforza, since Rosselli's death the leading figure in the emigration, who had returned to his native country shortly after the Armistice.

Croce and Sforza were the chief speakers when the six anti-Fascist parties met in January 1944 at Bari for the first free political convention that Italy had seen for nearly two decades. The Bari congress demanded a party government and the abdication of the King. But neither Victor Emmanuel nor the Allies were in any hurry to comply. During the whole winter and early spring of 1944—a period of discouragement when the British and American armies were stalled south of Rome at Anzio and Cassino—the political deadlock continued. Whatever the King and the Allies might say, Badoglio knew that he needed the party leaders to strengthen his government. Yet these leaders refused to serve as the ministers of Victor Emmanuel III, and Badoglio was too timid a man and too good a monarchist to force his sovereign to abdicate.

Two parallel developments resolved the impasse. In late February a distinguished Neapolitan jurist and political leader, Enrico De

Nicola, had persuaded the King to accept a formula by which, without formally abdicating, he would turn over his powers to his son Umberto as soon as Rome was liberated. This arrangement was still technically a secret when a sudden upset in the whole political situation necessitated that it be divulged immediately. On April 1, with their customary unpredictability, the Communists changed their line. Palmiro Togliatti, the unquestioned head of the party, who had been a guest of the Russians since the mid-twenties, had just arrived in Italy with a new directive from Moscow: in the interests of unity in the war effort, the Communists would accept office under any terms. Togliatti's announcement threw panic into the leadership of the other parties. They realized that the Communists' change of tactics had undercut their whole position and that they must reach a settlement as soon as possible. Within a few days after Togliatti's arrival the leaders of the six parties accepted De Nicola's formula for dealing with the King, and on April 21 Badoglio announced the formation of a predominantly political ministry.

This first party government had little time in which to function. Six weeks after its formation, the Allied armies marched into Rome. The liberation of the capital necessitated a further government reshuffle, since it made available a reservoir of experienced party leaders. After the German seizure of Rome, the representatives of the original six-party alliance had gone into hiding. Under Bonomi's presidency they had constituted themselves a Committee of Liberation to coordinate the underground resistance to the Germans. They had met in convents and other places presumed to be secure, but at the same time they had run great risks and had maintained their role of popular representatives under trying circumstances. Hence it was obvious to nearly everyone—except to Badoglio and the Allies—that Bonomi was the man to head the new government. After an initial Allied resistance, Bonomi received the mandate from Prince Umberto; besides the members of the Rome Committee of Liberation, he included in his ministry Count Sforza and a number of the more prominent leaders who had been in the South.

The formation of the Bonomi government greatly clarified the situation. With the King and Badoglio gone, the rulers of southern Italy were now definitely anti-Fascists, although they could not yet lay claim to democratic election. Yet the troubles of the Italian government were far from over. The Allies—and more particularly the British, who usually overshadowed their less experienced American colleagues—still hampered the government at every turn and showed a profound lack of understanding for the aspirations of the anti-Fascist leaders. Under Churchill's inspiration, the British not only hindered these leaders' efforts to make the fall of Fascism a reality by projecting reforms and eliminating Fascist officials from the administration; they even tried to undo what had already been accomplished. In November 1944, the British encouraged the Liberals and the other conservative political elements inside and outside the government to press for a reorganization of the ministry. A government crisis followed. In the course of it, the British Embassy in Rome let it be understood that Count Sforza, who by his prestige and previous experience was the obvious candidate for foreign minister, would not be acceptable to them. The American Secretary of State retorted that the question was "purely an Italian affair." But the veto on Sforza stuck. The two parties of the moderate Left, the Socialists and the Action Party, which had aligned themselves with Sforza, refused to serve in the new government. Hence Bonomi formed his second ministry through the illogical juxtaposition of the Communists and the more conservative parties. The absence of the Socialists and the Action Party was an ominous foretaste of what was to happen to the democratic Left in the period after 1945.

Denied real power and frustrated in their efforts to reform the state, the leaders of the anti-Fascist parties turned to pure politics. They argued endlessly, they spun ideological webs, they jockeyed for position, as Rome began to exude the close, heavy atmosphere of old-fashioned parliamentarism. The Bonomi government was going stale; it was whirling in a void where its words and actions mattered very little. Reality lay elsewhere. As the spring of 1945 approached, all eyes turned toward the North.

4. THE PARTISANS IN THE NORTH

During the twenty months when Italy was cut in two, the populations of the two halves of the peninsula went through very different experiences. In the South the Italians were the wards of the Allies—scorned, misunderstood, suffering from every kind of shortage and privation, yet for the most part free from danger and permitted to live their own lives. For them, the war had really ended with the arrival of the Allies; what followed was a painful and mostly incomprehensible epilogue in which they felt they had no part. North of the fighting lines, the situation was radically different. Here the war was by no means over; its cruelest period had just begun. And it was now not merely a foreign war: it was a civil war in which the forces of revived Fascism and the forces of liberation were joined in a combat that knew no mercy.

On the one side, there was Mussolini's neo-Fascist Republic. Four days after the announcement of the Armistice, a daring German glider raid had liberated the former Duce from the Apennine ski resort where the Badoglio government was holding him captive. Suitably cajoled by the German Führer, a weary Mussolini had allowed himself to be persuaded to re-establish his authority. And so on September 15, 1943, he announced the formation of his new government. The neo-Fascist Republic of the North never became a functioning reality. It was derisively known as the Republic of Salò, from the small town on Lake Garda where it had its head-quarters—Rome being considered too exposed to Allied attack. And the support on which it rested was perilously meager. The only thing truly popular about it was the word Republic in its title: this offered a welcome contrast to the worn-out institution of the monarchy that encumbered the government of the South. But Mussolini's efforts to win support for his new regime by advertising an extensive "socialization" program evoked no similar response. The workers of the North soon saw through the Duce's promises. They saw the neo-Fascist Republic for what it was—a puppet regime at the service of the Germans.

Within a very short time, then, the average citizen of northern Italy came to hate the Neo-Fascists even more than the Nazis. For the only function that Mussolini's followers appeared to be perform-ing was to terrorize and murder their fellow-Italians. After a decep-tively tolerant beginning, the new regime inaugurated its campaign of terror in January 1944 with the trial and execution of nearly all the members of the Grand Council of Fascism who had voted against Mussolini that he could lay his hands on; they included the Duce's son-in-law, Count Ciano. From this time on, the Neo-Fascists relied on bloodshed rather than persuasion. In their military and police formations, besides sullen and unwilling conscripts, they were able to enroll little more than the dregs of society. Some of these served in the fighting lines alongside the Germans. Most of them, however, were occupied in holding in check the resistance formations that were harassing with impartial fury the German invaders and their neo-Fascist deputies.

Far more than Mussolini's Republican government, the anti-Fascist resistance expressed the real sentiments of the north Italian population.* Here, as in the South, the majority of the people were no doubt passive and apathetic. But from Rome north a far larger number actively associated themselves in the work of liberation. The chief organs of this resistance were the armed Partisan bands and the Committees of Liberation, which on the model of the Rome committee everywhere established themselves as centers of communication, supply, and political propaganda. It has been estimated that as many as 200,000 people were enrolled at one time or other in the armed resistance of the North. A far larger number gave some sort of aid. The fact that so extensive a resistance movement could be organized in the teeth of German and neo-Fascist repression was a striking proof that the twenty-year efforts of the anti-Fascist opposition had not been wasted. Despite the discouragements it had suffered, it had succeeded in laying the groundwork for a broad popular movement. From exile, from *confino,* from their lives of clandestine opposition, the leaders of Italian anti-Fascism had emerged into the open during the Forty-Five Days. The Armistice and the German occupation had driven them underground again. But during the six weeks of comparative freedom they had been able to get acquainted with each other and to enlist a substantial number of followers. In organizational terms, this gain more than compensated for the extra perils they suffered from the fact of having made themselves known during the brief period of apparent liberation.

In the areas of central Italy freed during the great Allied push from May to October 1944, resistance activity was relatively light. In Rome the number of clandestine fighters was large—perhaps as many as 8000—but their efforts were poorly coordinated. It was only

* For details on the resistance, I am particularly indebted to Charles F. Delzell, *Mussolini's Enemies: The Italian Anti-Fascist Resistance* (Princeton, 1961).

when in early August the Allies reached Florence that they saw what a really active resistance movement could do. There the Partisans liberated the whole Oltrearno quarter before the Americans and British arrived, and subsequently gave major support in the capture of the northern part of the city.

North of Florence the resistance reached its full development. Partisan bands were everywhere—overt formations in the Alpine valleys and clandestine patriot groups in the major cities. These bands were of two types. There were the nonpolitical "autonomous" units —frequently the outgrowth of regular army formations that had taken to the hills to resist disarmament by the Germans—which were generally conservative in orientation. Then there were the political units managed by the anti-Fascist parties, which were usually more leftist. In this latter field, the Action Party and the Communists were the most successful organizers. The "Garibaldi" bands directed by the Communists constituted the largest single element in the resistance: perhaps two-fifths of all the overt Partisans were enrolled in these formations. By no means all the Garibaldi fighters, however, were Communists themselves. People joined one type of unit rather than another for many reasons besides political conviction: mere propinquity or the prestige of some local leader was usually sufficient. Yet once inside a Garibaldi band, the non-Communist recruit was subjected to vigorous indoctrination by a political commissar. Both in organization and in proselyting tactics, the Communists in northern Italy profited greatly from the lessons they had learned in Spain.

These different types of units got along together only passably. Although united in the cause of liberating the country, the resistance leaders well knew that they were also preparing for a postwar struggle for power—a struggle that would decide the political and social character of the new Italy. The armed bands that were now fighting the Germans and Neo-Fascists might later prove to be the decisive force in promoting or hindering a revolution. Hence the different types of Partisan formations regarded each other with a suspicion tinged with hostility. They were jealous of each other's successes and tried to keep other bands out of the territory they regarded as their own.

The local Committees of Liberation did their best to coordinate these disparate resistance operations—although they themselves were torn by the same sort of hostilities and suspicions. Fortunately in the area north of Rome there were only five parties to worry about; here the Democracy of Labor did not exist. Moreover, the Milan Committee had early established itself as a supervisory authority for the whole northern part of the country. Under the name of Committee of National Liberation for Northern Italy (CLNAI), the party leadership in Milan operated as a clandestine government whose orders were more widely obeyed than those of Mussolini's Republic. In December 1944, the Bonomi government in Rome recognized this *de facto* situation by designating the northern committee as its delegate for the still unliberated areas of the country. Two weeks earlier the Allies had granted a corresponding recognition. Along with it, the British and Americans had promised a substantial increase in the shipments of arms, money, and medical supplies that they had been parachuting to the resistance formations.

This aid was essential to maintain the morale of the Partisans during their final and most difficult winter. In the previous summer, when it had seemed as though the Allies were about to break through into northern Italy and that the war would end in a few weeks, the resistance movement had reached its maximum extent. In the mountain valleys of Piedmont and Lombardy, the Partisans had brought wide stretches of territory under their control; in a few places they had even established tiny "republics." But then the Germans had retaliated with savage fury, and the Allied advance had come to a halt just short of Bologna. With another winter of stalemate in the offing, the Allied commander, General Sir Harold Alexander, had made a proclamation to the Partisans urging them to go home and await the spring offensive. Alexander's advice enraged the resistance fighters. For how could they go home—when all that awaited them was torture and death? The hard core of the Partisans chose to wait it out in the hills.

Early the following April the Allied offensive began to roll. Within ten days, it had cracked the German mountain defenses and was about to fan out into the Po valley. Northern Italy rose to meet the liberators. The Partisan bands came down from the hills to join the clandestine fighters of the cities. Together they challenged the Germans to evacuate or to fight it out in the streets. Between April 19 and 28, Bologna, Venice, Genoa, Turin, and Milan virtually accomplished their own liberation.

Mussolini realized that the end had come. In the palace of the Cardinal Archbishop of Milan he met the delegates of the northern Committee of Liberation to discuss terms of surrender. (He did not yet know that the Germans behind his back were simultaneously offering to surrender to the Allies.) But Mussolini never completed the negotiations. Apparently overcome by panic, he fled from Milan with a small group of his closest followers. Near the village of Dongo close to the Swiss frontier, the former Duce was recognized by a local Partisan detachment. His execution followed: the trial had consisted solely of a reading of the sentence of death already rendered by the northern Committee of Liberation. Next morning —the morning of April 29, 1945—Mussolini's body was hanging head down in a Milan square, mutilated nearly beyond recognition by the fury of the populace.

7

De Gasperi and the Triumph
of Christian Democracy

IN 1945, as in 1919, Italy appeared on the verge of a political and
social revolution. Again, as in the period following the First World
War, the laboring classes had been aroused by the war experience
and the example of revolution in other countries to a new consciousness of their power and a lively impatience with their lot. Once again,
the propertied element was frightened and unsure of itself. Most of
the more prosperous Italians had compromised themselves in some
fashion with the Fascist regime. As the war ended, and the reckoning seemed at hand, the wealthy, the conservative, and the well-born
lay low, hoping without much conviction that the revolutionary
storm would pass them by. To save what they could from the wreckage, they were prepared to make the most sweeping concessions to
the unfamiliar principles of democracy and socialism.

Yet once again the revolution failed to occur. Three years after the
revolutionary high tide of May and June 1945, the forces of conservatism won an overwhelming electoral victory. In exactly the
same length of time as it had taken the earlier wave of protest to
spend itself, the second flood of Italian revolutionary consciousness
had ended in frustration and disillusionment.

The parallel was not complete, however. The forces that triumphed
in the election of 1948 were not the same as those that had ridden
to power in 1922. Their leadership—anti-Fascist by conviction and
long experience—kept Italy firmly in the course of constitutional
government and electoral democracy. Thus Americans had good
cause to congratulate themselves on the results of the election of

1948. They were right in believing that the Christian Democratic government whose rule that election had confirmed had profound affinities with American political procedures and ideals. Yet most Americans were in no position to evaluate the election results in their full complexity. They saw that Western democracy had triumphed. What they did not see was that by the same process the social groups which had supported the Fascist regime had managed to climb back into their former positions of influence. Americans could see the upper part of the Christian Democratic iceberg—the part that stood for personal liberty and the Western democratic tradition. They could not see the lower part—larger and more ramifying, where actions and entrenched practices belied the lofty aims of the official leadership.

The present chapter, then, has two purposes. It is intended to demonstrate, first, why the revolutionary hopes of the anti-Fascist resistance failed to materialize—or, to put it more precisely, why the quiet opposition to Fascism triumphed over the militant. Second, it is an attempt to analyze the character and policy of the victors, to define that ambiguous and usually misunderstood political phenomenon which calls itself Christian Democracy.

1. THE "WIND OF THE NORTH"

At the end of April 1945, the anti-Fascist forces of the Italian North rejoiced in the exhilaration of a painfully won victory. For a few weeks of glorious spring weather, the members of the Partisan bands and the local Committees of Liberation enjoyed the unfamiliar sensation of being the masters of the country. Few Italians at the time were bold enough to question their authority. By their staunchness in suffering and their courage in battle, the northern anti-Fascists had won the right to lead their countrymen in fashioning a new Italy. For it was primarily through their efforts that Italy had regained a certain standing among the nations: the achievements of the northern resistance had gradually won the grudging respect of the Allies and given the rest of the Italian people something at last of which they could be proud. In their more optimistic moments, the militant anti-Fascists cherished the illusion that their endeavors had wiped out the record of twenty years of tyranny and the shame

of the lost war, and that the victory of the resistance had automatically installed Italy in the community of advanced democracies.
They forgot that this victory had been the work of a minority—the
work of a large minority, it is true, but still in no sense the achievement of the whole Italian people.

In the anti-Fascist resistance all social classes had played a part.
It was the industrial workers, however, who had contributed most
heavily. Similarly, it was the parties of the Left—the Communists,
the Socialists, and the Action Party—that had taken the lead in the
clandestine struggle. All of these parties in one form or other
espoused socialist doctrines. Hence it was not surprising that the
temporary government of the northern Committees of Liberation
should have had a distinctly socialist tinge. In the factories, the
workers were encouraged to organize plant councils (*consigli di
gestione*) to share in the work of management. And on the national
scene, the Milan Committee, the CLNAI, expressed its frank exas-
peration with the timid and "reactionary" government in Rome: the
day of the antiquated politicians and parliamentarians, it maintained,
was now over; the purifying "wind of the North" would sweep
away Bonomi and his fellows. On this question, the Milan Committee was adamant. After six weeks of tortuous negotiation, the
northern leaders succeeded in imposing one of their own men on
the reluctant politicians in Rome. The new prime minister was to be
Ferruccio Parri, who seventeen years earlier had been Carlo Rosselli's
companion on the island of Lipari, and who had emerged from his
life of clandestine opposition in Milan to assume—along with the
Communist Luigi Longo—the leading position in the northern
resistance.

Parri was affiliated with the Action Party, the heir of Rosselli's
Giustizia e Libertà and the smallest and most moderate of the three
Left parties. Despite this moderation, his government represented
tendencies that were far more revolutionary than those of its predecessor. From Bonomi's second ministry, we may recall, the Socialists
and the Action Party had been absent. With Parri, these two parties
returned to power, while the Democracy of Labor—Bonomi's personal dependency—in fact disappeared into oblivion although it continued to exist in theory. Again there was a government of all the
anti-Fascist parties. But this new government was rather different

from the original six-party front. With the roster of effective parties reduced to five, the Left now held a majority of three to two. Moreover, the coalition rested on a new theory of public authority. The six parties of 1943 and 1944, as the age of their leaders suggested, were the lineal descendants of the Aventine bloc that had originally resisted Mussolini's totalitarian pretensions. Their aim—or at least the aim of the more conservative parties that dominated the coalition —was the restoration of the parliamentary regime as it had existed before 1922. For the five parties in the Parri government, the left-wing leadership envisaged a more ambitious task. Through the CLNAI and the local Committees of Liberation, these parties had already been exercising authority in the North without the benefit of royal appointment or the temperate counsel of the Allies. Deriving their authority from the presumed will of the Italian people, they had been functioning on revolutionary principles as local "committees of public safety." Thus the Parri government was the outgrowth not of the legalist and cautious Aventine but of the extralegal and militant Committees of Liberation. It saw itself as the initiator of a total reorganization of the Italian state and Italian society—of that great revolution, political and moral, which had been hanging fire for a quarter century.

In this task, the Parri government failed. And its failure cast a shadow over the whole subsequent development of Italian politics— bringing with it an atmosphere of weariness and skepticism, and the withdrawal or exclusion of the bulk of the militant anti-Fascists from effective participation in public life. This failure came about partly through the very nature of the situation the Parri government faced, partly through its own mistakes, and partly through the unexpected tenacity of the forces opposing it.

On the surface, the Italian situation in the spring and early summer of 1945 appeared thoroughly revolutionary. Not only were the dominant political parties talking in terms of basic social change; the workers of the North, as veterans of the Partisan formations, had arms in their hands and seemed prepared to use them. But this was an illusion. In reality, the northern resistance held a position of only temporary mastery. The real masters of Italy—now as before—were the British and Americans. Faced with the rapid collapse of the German army and the self-liberation of much of the North, Allied military government had been unable to assume immediate control in northern Italy. As previously agreed, it had left the task of maintaining order to the CLNAI and the local Committees of Liberation —a task, incidentally, which the latter carried out with a moderation marred only by sporadic acts of vengeance against real or suspected Neo-Fascists.

Then, after a month of this sort of self-government, the Allies took over on the first of June. Already the atmosphere was beginning to change. The Partisans, summoned to surrender their arms, had complied with docility. (That is, all of them except certain Communist formations that hid their weapons away against future eventualities.) From special demobilization camps run by the Allies, the resistance fighters returned to their civilian lives—many of them embittered and disillusioned, feeling that their sacrifices had gone unrewarded. It was becoming evident, then, that the armed Partisans would not play their expected role as the people's militia of the Italian revolution. In the same fashion, the other revolutionary institutions that had come into existence in the North soon lost any real function. The workers' *consigli di gestione* were gradually deprived of their powers and dissolved, as the employers, encouraged by the Allies, began to reassert their customary prerogatives. And the Committees of Liberation experienced a similar fate. The main Committee, the CLNAI, had passed into the national government; this latter had its own problems, which we shall come to in a moment. The local Committees simply withered and died: military government had taken over nearly all their functions, and they were reduced to a role of querulous criticism and an increasingly vexatious interference in the lives of ordinary citizens.

By the end of June, whatever slim chances for an Italian revolution had once existed had definitely disappeared. The rank-and-file of the resistance and many of the leaders were surprised and disappointed by what had happened. Not so the chief Communists. Under the guidance of the astute Togliatti, the Communists—who were troubled by no split in ideas between the leadership in Rome and that in the North—early arrived at a correct assessment of the situation. In mid-1945, the Soviet Union was still playing the game of Allied co-operation and spheres of influence. Italy it was leaving strictly to the British and Americans. Hence it would support no revolutionary adventures on the part of the Italian Communists. The Communist party in Italy must do the best it could with its own resources.

With these considerations in mind, Togliatti spoke the language of moderation and sought to quiet the fears of his conservative colleagues in the government. He concentrated on what was practically attainable in an Italy that was moving toward social stabilization. He worked steadily for Communist predominance in the trade unions, he emphasized the need for his party to remain in the government at all costs, and he tried to make a double alliance which would secure the Communist political position for the future. On the one hand, he stressed "unity of action" with the Socialists—a formula that had been renewed and strengthened at regular intervals ever since 1934. On the other hand, he called for an understanding among the three "mass" parties—the Communists, the Socialists, and the Christian Democrats—the last of which Togliatti very early discerned as the Communists' chief rival for the allegiance of the Italian masses.

In neither of these alignments did he find a place for the Action Party. This was intentional. The Action Party Togliatti scorned as a gathering of ineffective intellectuals. And such in fact was what it was rapidly becoming. Despite its great role in the resistance, the Action Party soon proved itself to be an extremely talented elite without any large popular support. In the person of Prime Minister Parri, the Action Party epitomized the vague and widespread longing for an Italy that would be "purer' than the Italy of tradition. But it was unclear what sort of revolution the party was actually aiming at. Would it be a legal revolution, a slow process of socialization with a scrupulous maintenance of personal liberties? Or would it be a more sudden and brutal change, with dictatorial power in the hands of the people's representatives? And how could either of these programs be squared with the position of the Communist party, the strongest single element in Italian anti-Fascism and the known enemy of free institutions and of loyal co-operation among political parties? On these questions the Action Party never gave a clear answer: different leaders proposed different solutions, and the argument gradually spent itself in a flood of words.

If they had allied themselves with the Socialists—as had seemed likely in the previous winter—they might have arrived at a clear-cut and practicable revolutionary program. But this could not be, since the Socialists were committed elsewhere. Under the leadership of Pietro Nenni—a gifted tribune of the people but no match for the wily Togliatti—the Socialists moved ever closer to the Communists. Unaware of the cautious and cynical strategy that Togliatti was following, Nenni let himself be led along blindly. And so by the summer of 1945 the anti-Fascist resistance was succumbing to the dangers that had already been discernible in the late 1930's: Parri and the Action Party were experiencing the fatal consequences of Rosselli's failure in his effort to group all Italians of good will in a broad new movement of liberal socialism, and the Communists were profiting by the position of dominance they had won during the Spanish Civil War.

The Action Party—and the Parri government with it—was doomed by its own mistakes and the superior tactics of the Communists. In the history of postwar Italy, Prime Minister Parri emerges as an appealing and tragic figure. A man of unquestioned integrity, of lofty aspirations and a conscience tempered through long suffering, he has a Lincolnian grandeur. But the very lack of political and administrative experience that made him so attractive as the symbol of a new and better Italy was also his ruin. Scrupulous to a fault, he seemed incapable of rapid decision. And this in a situation where the most desperate problems on all sides cried out for decisive action—separatist agitation in Sicily, Communist violence in the countryside, above all, a totally uncontrolled black market that had reduced the mass of the population to a life of insecurity and privation.

By autumn, then, the conservative forces, encouraged by the Allies and by the ebbing of revolutionary enthusiasm, were ready for another onslaught against the government. Among the people —and particularly in the South—the reaction from the government of the resistance expressed itself in a new and equivocal political movement, the *Uomo qualunque* or Common Man Front. Led by a former playwright and notoriously hazy in its political program, the *Uomo qualunque* was only potentially neo-Fascist. The real reason for its appeal and rapid growth was that it championed all the miscellaneous grievances that ordinary Italians blamed on the Parri ministry: the economic misery, the exactions of the Allies, the petty domineering of the local Committees of Liberation, and the mistakes and excesses committed by the government in its purge of Fascist officials.

Inside the government, the two conservative parties—the Christian Democrats and the Liberals—which had only half-heartedly gone along with the political program of the CLNAI, were intriguing both with the Allies and with certain conservative elder statesmen like Vittorio Emanuele Orlando who were hoping to return to power. In November, this combination of political forces brought the government down. The atmosphere of the moment has been admirably recaptured by Carlo Levi in his series of sketches entitled *The Watch*. And he has dramatically described the culminating scene—an unprecedented gathering of politicians and journalists before which the retiring Prime Minister explained the reasons for his resignation. With sober detail and in a gentle, monotonous voice, he told them how the Fifth Column within the government, after systematically undermining its position, was now going to restore to power the social groups that had formed the basis of the Fascist regime. In a moment Alcide De Gasperi was on his feet. As the leader of the Christian Democrats and Parri's logical successor, he hotly denied the assertions of the outgoing Prime Minister and pleaded with the foreign journalists present not to report what they had heard. But the journalists refused to be convinced; they knew—and most Italians knew with them—that the militant opposition to Fascism had passed into history.

2. THE COMING OF DE GASPERI

In December 1945, with the formation of the first De Gasperi government, the Christian Democrats had gotten their foot in the door. From that time on nothing was to dislodge them, and the next two and a half years were to see them gradually consolidating their position and reducing the power of their rivals until the election of April 1948 carried them to total victory. In this march to power they enjoyed many advantages, some of which we have already noted—the fact that their leaders, with rare exceptions, had remained in Italy during the period of Mussolini's rule and hence could gauge with accuracy the temper of the average Italian, anti-Fascist through experience and necessity, but distrustful of political militancy; the support of the Church and more particularly of the network of local branches put at their disposal by Catholic Action, the sole independent organization that had continued to exist throughout the Fascist dictatorship; finally, the political talent, amounting nearly to genius, of their party leader, Alcide De Gasperi.

At first sight, De Gasperi did not look like a great political leader. He was unimpressive personally and no more than a fair speaker. His assets appeared only gradually—just as it was only gradually that he established his ascendancy over Italian public life. Combining personal integrity and an austere private life with an astuteness and finesse in maneuver that recalled the classic models of the Italian parliamentary tradition, he concealed his unbending purpose under a gentle and conciliatory manner. Such a combination of qualities—nearly unknown in American politics—had gone into the making of the great Italian popes and churchmen. And there was something sacerdotal about De Gasperi: in that sense he appeared a fitting leader for a Catholic party. Looking far younger than his years—when he first came to power he was sixty-four— with a mountaineer's lean and wiry physique, he was able to surmount repeated bouts of illness and political crises until he had either driven his rivals from the field or brought them into service as allies. Chief among his rivals and enemies was the Communist Togliatti. In De Gasperi, Togliatti at last met his match. Similar in mental agility and even in physical appearance, the leaders of the two great parties faced each other—like two Jesuits, as one of their colleagues put it—with quiet deadliness across the ministerial council table. In 1945, the odds were on Togliatti; but it was to be De Gasperi who would eventually outwit his Communist opponent.

In the spring of 1943, De Gasperi had emerged from his Vatican retreat to reconstitute the Popular party under the new name of Christian Democracy. During the next two and a half years he had taken a prominent part in the successive councils that had linked together the anti-Fascist alliance: he had served as the Christian Democratic representative on the clandestine Committee of Liberation in occupied Rome and as a member of the Bonomi and Parri governments; since December 1944, after the British veto on Sforza, he had been Italian foreign minister. In all these posts, without pushing himself too much into the foreground, he had worked quietly and effectively to advance the interests of his party. By the end of 1945, he was ready for a more prominent role. The premiership came to him at exactly the right moment: the militant resistance had failed; the country was ready to let the quiet opposition to Fascism take over.

As prime minister, De Gasperi brought something new to post-Fascist Italian politics—a "sense of the state." A heritage in part from his Austrian upbringing, this concern for the prestige and power of the public authorities was the last thing that most anti-Fascist politicians were worrying about in 1945: the very concept smacked of the Fascist insistence on state power. The difference between De Gasperi and the rest of the political leaders had been apparent as early as the ministerial negotiations of May and June. At that time, the Christian Democratic leader had urged so strongly the need to re-establish respect for the law that even his political adversaries had gone away impressed; one Action Party representative had commented, "This man will govern us for five years."* In actual fact, De Gasperi's rule lasted more than seven.

In the situation of near chaos prevailing at the beginning of 1946, a sense of the state was precisely what was required. At the end of the previous year, Allied military government—having done its work of consolidating the forces of conservatism—had withdrawn its authority from all the Italian provinces except those along the Yugoslav border. The Italian government was now on its own. It was up to De Gasperi to bring order to the Italian countryside and to stabilize as best he could the torrential economic inflation.

In theory the first De Gasperi government was still a government of all the parties. The three parties of the Left continued to sit in a ministry that transparently represented the liquidation of the militant resistance to Fascism for which they had stood. Before this paradox, the Action Party simply collapsed: in early 1946 it split into two independent parts, both equally impotent. The Liberal

* Leo Valiani, *L'avvento di De Gasperi: Tre anni di politica italiana* (Turin, 1949), pp. 23–24.

party—Christian Democracy's ally in the conservative wing of the government—similarly lost all real importance. Its intellectual mentor, Benedetto Croce, had become too old for active politics. With Croce's withdrawal from effective leadership in party affairs, the frankly reactionary segment of the Liberals led the party into an ill-advised and disastrous alliance with the Italian monarchists—a group that had never formed part of the anti-Fascist coalition. Thus by the spring of 1946 the only political forces which really counted were the three "mass" parties—these and the equivocal *Uomo qualunque*. This was to be made apparent in the first nationwide test of Italian political sentiment, the elections of June 2, 1946.

With the first national postwar elections, the situation of political unreality in which De Gasperi had been governing during his first half year of power was suddenly clarified. The elections ended the two great anomalies of the postwar scene—the theoretical parity among anti-Fascist parties that obviously differed tremendously in the popular support they commanded, and the continued existence of a monarchy that since Victor Emmanuel's withdrawal in the spring of 1944 had been little more than a shadow.

Thus the elections of 1946 had a twofold character. On the one hand, they were a plebiscite on the "institutional question"—the question of monarchy versus republic. Originally it had appeared as though the advocates of a republic would win overwhelmingly: all the anti-Fascist parties except the Liberals had declared for the change. But then, less than a month before the voting, the old King had at last taken the step that earlier might have saved the monarchy: he had abdicated in favor of his son Umberto. The new "King of the May", as he was called from his one month's reign, enjoyed a certain popularity. His accession, coupled with the general revival of conservative sentiment, swung a number of votes over to the monarchy. By the final count, the country proved to be 46 per cent monarchical and 54 per cent for the republic. Moreover—and this was the more troubling significance of the plebiscite—the South had voted for the King. The southerners, traditionally retrograde and with their feeling of separation from the national life intensified by their lack of participation in the resistance experience, chose this anachronistic method of protesting against the ideals of the North. But they accepted the results of the plebiscite with their customary resignation. Aside from a minor riot in Naples, the institutional change passed off quietly. And the newly elected deputies wisely decided to conciliate the southerners by choosing as Provisional President of the Republic a Neapolitan—the jurist Enrico De Nicola, who had devised the original institutional compromise of 1944.

In the second aspect of the elections—the selection of deputies to a Constituent Assembly that would draw up a new constitution for the country—the three mass parties won their expected victory. Prime Minister De Gasperi's Christian Democrats came out first with 207 deputies, the Socialists second with 115, and the Communists third with 104. Far behind them, the *Uomo qualunque* gained 30-odd seats. The other main parties got about 20 apiece—among them, the doctrinaire and honorable Republicans, who now that their century-old goal had been attained, felt free to participate in the business of government without risk of monarchical taint. This party was soon to be revitalized by the addition to its ranks of the right wing of the shattered Action Party, which included former Prime Minister Parri and most of the talent of that ill-fated venture in high-minded politics.

His own party strengthened by its electoral victory, De Gasperi reorganized his government on a more realistic basis. He made it a "tripartite" ministry of the three mass parties, to which he added a few Republicans. Yet while the new government accurately reflected the verdict of the electorate, it was no more homogeneous than its predecessor. It was an artificial plastering together of two disparate masses of roughly equal strength—the Christian Democrats, loyal to the Church and public order, and the Socialist-Communist bloc, Marxian revolutionists in theory if not in current tactics. Between these two groups there could be no real understanding or cooperation. Their joint participation in the government was no more than a temporary expedient, a truce in a war of extermination. Eventually one or the other would have to give way. And meantime, outside the circle of recognized anti-Fascist politics, there was the *Uomo qualunque,* steadily gaining strength and turning more and more toward neo-Fascist agitation. This was to be the problem of the next twenty-two months: would De Gasperi be able to survive the onslaughts of Communism from the one side and Neo-Fascism

from the other? By the end of that time he had defeated them both
—and more overwhelmingly than even his most enthusiastic supporters had thought possible.

Besides his own political astuteness, De Gasperi was saved by a
number of external circumstances—Socialist mistakes, Communist
illusions, and support from the United States. Under Nenni's
leadership the Socialists totally failed to exploit their electoral
position as the second strongest party in the country. Like their
Maximalist forebears of a quarter century earlier, they wasted their
time in demagogic oratory and left the tactical initiative to the
Communists, numerically the weaker partner in the Marxist bloc.
In the autumn Nenni strengthened still further his alignment with
the Communists. This proved too much for the right wing of the
Socialist party—the democratically minded minority that followed
the lead of Giuseppe Saragat. In January 1947 Saragat walked out
of the party congress, taking with him nearly half the Socialist
deputies but comparatively little of the rank and file. The secessionists established a new party, which after a complex series of
further secessions and reorganizations, came to be known as the
Social Democrats.

Saragat's defection gave De Gasperi his chance. Nineteen forty-
seven in Italy, as throughout Western Europe, was to be the decisive year of political showdown and victory for the anti-Communist forces associated with the United States. First, De Gasperi
reorganized his government once again. In the ministerial reshuffle
necessitated by the Socialist split, the Prime Minister took care to
strengthen his own party: he installed in the key Ministry of the
Interior, which controlled the whole local administration of the
country, his own man, Mario Scelba, who proceeded with relentless
determination to the task of restoring order and reducing the
power of the Communists in isolated rural areas. Next De Gasperi
approached the more delicate problem of expelling the Communists
and left-wing Socialists from his government. This task demanded
courage and finesse, both of which De Gasperi had in large supply.
Moreover, earlier in the year, on a visit to the United States, he
had received assurances of American economic aid, coupled with
the intimation that his government would enjoy still greater favor
in Washington if the Communists were no longer in it.

Apparently unaware of what was being planned, Togliatti continued to stress the importance of maintaining the governing coalition of the three mass parties. He even went so far as to attempt to gain Christian Democratic favor by directing his party to vote for the retention of Mussolini's Concordat with the Vatican in the new constitution that was being slowly elaborated by the Assembly. This vote—which deeply shocked the deputies of anticlerical convictions, including Togliatti's own Socialist allies—saved the Concordat for posterity. But it could not save Togliatti himself. De Gasperi simply accepted the Communists' pro-Catholic vote in the cynical spirit in which it had been offered and proceeded to carry out his plans of destruction. In May he announced the necessity of enlarging his government both to the Right and to the Left. There followed his own resignation—a feint to put his adversaries off the track—and an interlude in which Francesco Saverio Nitti, another octogenarian from the pre-Fascist era, tried in vain to collect a ministry. Eventually, with all alternative possibilities exhausted, De Gasperi accepted President De Nicola's invitation to form his fourth government. This time it was to be a frankly conservative ministry, including besides the Christian Democrats only the Liberals and a few eminent personalities like Count Sforza. The Communists and left-wing Socialists had been left outside. Togliatti had lost the game.

In their irritation at being outwitted, the Communists threatened that it would prove impossible to govern against them—against the parties that the elections had shown to represent a third of the Italian nation. And many non-Communists agreed in this estimate of the situation. But the summer and autumn of 1947 proved that De Gasperi's courageous gamble had succeeded. First, the economic situation began to stabilize itself. Between August and November, the deflationary program inaugurated by the new Minister of the Budget, Luigi Einaudi, brought decisive results.* Somewhat later the aid from the United States promised under the Marshall Plan began to arrive in encouraging quantities. In the autumn the Communist-led strikes against the European Recovery Program collapsed before the blunt police action directed by Minister of the Interior Scelba. Everywhere the state was vigorously reasserting its authority. Faced with this evidence of De Gasperi's power to govern, the

* See Chapter 8.

propertied classes began to rally to Christian Democracy. They deserted the Christian Democrats' chief rival for the conservative vote, the *Uomo qualunque,* which succumbed to its own internal inconsistencies. In the Rome municipal election at the end of the year, De Gasperi's party simply swallowed up the following of this first postwar venture in neo-Fascist demagogy.

The stage was now prepared for the general election of April 18, 1948—the election that would choose the first Senate and Chamber of Deputies under the new republican constitution completed four months earlier. Prior to going before the electorate De Gasperi decided to broaden the base of his government by taking in the Republicans and Saragat's Social Democrats. With all three of the "respectable" minor parties now in his ministry, he could plausibly argue that his government constituted the sole democratic alternative to Communism. Such was also the opinion of the American Embassy. And the Church and Catholic Action quite naturally felt the same way. In the electoral campaign of 1948 the Church, the United States, and the vast majority of Italian anti-Communists fought in one solid phalanx. Even Italo-Americans were officially encouraged to join in and send letters to their relatives in Italy urging them to vote against the Communists. These were novelties in Italian politics—to have the Catholic priesthood and the diplomats of a foreign power taking an active part in an electoral campaign. For them—and for the bulk of Italian conservatives, who were far to the right of the Christian Democrats in their real political sentiments —the slogan was the same: an anti-Communist vote given to any other party than De Gasperi's was a vote wasted.

We shall never know whether there was any real danger that the "People's Bloc" of Communists and left-wing Socialists would win the election. At the time, many observers questioned it and argued that the leftist leaders were only bluffing when they threatened a post-election *coup d'état.* Yet we should remember that the election was fought under the shadow of the Communist seizure of power in Czechoslovakia, and that the fear of a repetition of similar events in Italy was widespread. In any case, the results of the anti-Communist campaign passed all expectations. For the first time in the recent history of Continental parliamentarism, a single party obtained an absolute majority in the Chamber of Deputies.

With 307 seats, the Christian Democrats far overtopped the People's Bloc, which had succeeded in electing 135 Communists and 51 left-wing Socialists. The minor parties associated with De Gasperi's government trailed way behind: the strongest of them, the Social Democrats, had obtained only 33 seats. For the next five years—the life-span of the new Chamber—the government was to be essentially a single-party affair.

3. THE PEACE TREATY

Seldom has an international document become outmoded in so short a time as the treaty signed between Italy and the wartime Allies in February 1947. Indeed, the premises on which it rested were already practically obsolete by the time the treaty was completed. Its territorial and economic clauses were based on the idea that Italy was a defeated enemy state, and on the concept of a Europe dominated by an understanding between the United States, Britain, and France, on the one hand, and the Soviet Union, on the other. But the year and a half that had elapsed since the end of the war had radically altered these preconceptions: Italy was already in fact, if not in theory, the ally of the Western powers in the cold war with the Soviet Union that was about to be declared. The signature of the treaty antedated by just one month the enunciation of the Truman Doctrine.

The terms of the treaty, then, disappointed De Gasperi and the other anti-Fascist Italians who had hoped that their country's record of co-belligerence after 1943 would wipe out the memory of Italy's three years of aggressive war at the side of Nazi Germany. It was a punitive document, whose harsher clauses reflected the Soviet point of view. The Western powers renounced any claim to reparations; but the Russians insisted on a bill of 100 million dollars, to which the treaty added 260 million more for Greece, Yugoslavia, Albania, and Ethiopia. Similarly, the British and Americans relinquished their right to a share of the Italian navy, while the Soviet Union maintained its claim to a specified quota of ships, including one old Italian battleship. Besides giving up the greater part of her navy, Italy was also obliged to reduce her army to 250,000 men, her air force to 25,000, and to renounce entirely the possession of certain offensive weapons like submarines and bombers.

On the territorial clauses of the treaty, disagreement among the wartime Allies was more open and intense. The French frontier proved comparatively easy to settle. Disavowing the annexationist activities of some of the more enthusiastic members of its resistance forces, the French government refrained from demanding the Val d'Aosta in Piedmont—where an extensive grant of local autonomy satisfied the requirements of the French-speaking population. France restricted herself to a demand for four small Alpine areas, important chiefly for their hydroelectric installations, to which the other powers readily agreed.

Similarly, the Austrian frontier raised no insuperable difficulties. In this case, where they were dealing with another former enemy, the Allied foreign ministers saw a good opportunity to conciliate the Italians: they left unchanged the Brenner border of 1919. Hence about a quarter of a million German-speaking Tyrolese remained in Italy. But here again, a grant of local autonomy assuaged the feelings of the local population. By a bilateral agreement concluded with the Austrian foreign minister in September 1946, De Gasperi undertook to establish a regional administration under which the German-speaking element would enjoy full equality of rights. This promise the Italian government faithfully carried out. The Austrians, however, made the valid criticism that the autonomous area should logically have been restricted to Bolzano province (or the Alto Adige), which was alone preponderantly German in speech; by including with it the heavily Italian-speaking Trentino, the autonomy statute assured an Italian majority in the regional assembly.

When they came to the questions of the colonies and the Yugoslav frontier, however, the victorious powers were soon hopelessly at odds. They could easily agree that Rhodes and the Dodecanese islands in the Aegean Sea should go to Greece and that the Empire of Ethiopia should recover its independence. But for the disposition of the three pre-Fascist African colonies of Libya, Eritrea, and Italian Somaliland, they found no neat solution. Wartime promises to native leaders and considerations of Mediterranean power politics embarrassed the discussions at every turn. Eventually the four foreign ministers confessed their inability to agree, and in the text of the treaty simply declared their intention of settling the problem within a year. Ultimately they found no recourse except to pass it on to the United Nations.

In this new forum, the colonial question proved equally perplexing. It was not until December 1949 that the General Assembly of the United Nations was able to vote the final disposition of the former Italian colonies. The solutions arrived at reflected less the wisdom than the desperation of the delegates. Libya was to receive its independence—an illogical and potentially explosive solution, since this was the least advanced country in North Africa, far less so than its neighbor Tunisia, which remained a French protectorate. Eritrea, on the basis of "consultation" with local opinion, was to have its choice of independence or federation with Ethiopia. Italian Somaliland alone, a depressingly barren stretch of coastline, was to remain under the administration of Italy as a trust territory; but within ten years it also was to be prepared for independence. These dispositions were subsequently carried out: Libya and Somalia became independent states, and Eritrea an independent territory federated with Ethiopia under the rule of the Emperor Haile Selassie.

On the problem of the Yugoslav frontier the powers disagreed most profoundly and reached their most questionable decision. Marshal Tito's Yugoslavia, strong with the prestige of its unparalleled record of Partisan activity against the Nazis, was claiming all of the Istrian peninsula including the city of Trieste. The Russians were supporting Tito's demands: Yugoslavia at this time ranked as their most reliable and aggressive satelite. The Western powers, with varying degrees of enthusiasm, were proposing a series of lines that would follow more closely the ethnic frontier between Italians and Yugoslavs. But such a frontier was extremely difficult to draw: while most of the Istrian hinterland was Slavic in speech, the coast, including the city of Trieste itself, was unquestionably Italian. Eventually the powers agreed on a frontier that gave the greater part of the peninsula to Yugoslavia. While this line approximated the ethnic border for the inland area, it left under Yugoslav control a number of coastal cities and towns of Italian speech and tradition. For Trieste itself, in another solution of desperation, the foreign ministers decided to establish a free territory under international supervision.

This was the last time, in the immediate post-war era, that the Western powers tried to conciliate the Soviet Union by making a dramatic concession. The establishment of the Free Territory of Trieste proved to be a compromise without substance—a constant source of irritation, nothing more. The other punitive clauses of the treaty soon ceased to operate: the reparations were either paid or canceled, and the Western nations by individual action lifted the provisions limiting the size of the Italian armed forces; with Italy a partner in the Atlantic alliance against the Soviet Union, it was considered absurd that her military contribution should still be kept down by a treaty whose severity had come about largely at Russian suggestion. These anomalies the Western powers could easily do away with. But they could not so quickly settle the problem of Trieste—the gravest legacy of the Italian treaty for the future peace of Europe.

The statute of the Free Territory never actually came into effect. Since the Western powers and the Soviet Union proved unable to agree on the selection of a neutral governor, the *de facto* situation of 1945 simply continued to exist. This situation was unsatisfactory to both Italy and Yugoslavia. Zone A, the smaller but more populous part of the territory, contiguous to Italy and including the city of Trieste itself, was under British and American military occupation. Zone B, the larger, more rural, southern portion, was occupied by the Yugoslavs. In this latter zone the Titoist forces after 1945 steadily extended the application of their own laws and economic arrangements until for all practical purposes it was being ruled as a part of Yugoslavia. In retaliation—and to conciliate Italian opinion—the British and Americans gradually permitted a nearly complete administrative fusion of Zone A with the Italian state.

In March 1948, a month before the Italian elections, the British, French, and Americans proposed that in view of the demonstrated unworkability of the peace treaty provisions, the whole Free Territory should be transferred to Italian sovereignty. This proposal occasioned jubilation in Italy and was not without its effect on the electoral victory of the pro-Western Christian Democrats. But then only ten weeks after the election an event occurred that upset all previous calculations—the break between Tito and the Cominform. If the British and Americans had once thought of unilaterally returning their own zone of the Free Territory to Italy, Yugoslavia's defection from the Soviet bloc effectively closed off this line of action.

For now Tito had become a potential friend of the West, to be courted away from a lingering loyalty to the cause of international Communism. This the Yugoslav leader early realized, and he used his bargaining position to good effect. For more than six years he proved immovable. Not until the autumn of 1954 were Italy and Yugoslavia able to agree on the rough but practicable solution of permitting each country—with one minor border rectification— to annex the zone of the Free Territory that it was currently administering. Thus at last the city of Trieste returned to Italy. But the rejoicing at this outcome was tempered by disappointment over the renunciation of Zone B and by concern for the substantial Italian population of that area: the final settlement of the Trieste question was far from being entirely satisfactory to the Italians. Yet it conferred one enormous benefit on Italian democracy. By depriving the extreme nationalists of their most reliable argument, it served to strengthen the government in its unremitting battle against the forces of political reaction.

4. THE INSTITUTIONAL SOLUTION

It is time now to pause and examine the institutional framework that the Constituent Assembly had given the country—the institutions under which the Italian state has been operating since the beginning of 1948.

The most important thing to notice about Italy's postwar constitution is how little of a change it represented from the old *Statuto* of 1848—or at least from how the earlier document had been interpreted since the foundation of united Italy. Certain obvious anomalies in the old constitution disappeared: the monarchy had already been abolished by the plebiscite of 1946; the royally nominated Senate likewise had to go. But even these institutions reappeared under another form. A president replaced the King: like constitutional monarchs elsewhere in Western Europe, he functions as the titular and ceremonial head of the state rather than its active executive. He lives in the old royal palace on the Quirinal, surrounded by much of the pomp traditionally attributed to the King. This was apparently against the personal wishes of the first incumbent, Luigi Einaudi, who would have preferred to live more simply; but he himself had been a monarchist before the plebiscite and presumably understood the arguments in favor of ceremonial continuity. Hence although the House of Savoy had gone, it was sometimes difficult to detect its absence. The new republic lacked content: it was a mere convenience rather than the symbol of a new Italy that had inspired the fighters of the resistance.

The Senate was restored as an elective body, chosen by universal suffrage on a different and more complex system than that by which the Chamber of Deputies is elected. Its term is one year longer than that of the Chamber—an inexplicably cumbersome arrangement which has usually been disregarded by holding elections at the same time—and in power the two bodies are coequal. In this latter respect, the Italian upper house resembles the American Senate more closely than it does the British House of Lords. Moreover—and this is where the first republican Senate began to look like its monarchical predecessor—it contained besides the 237 elected senators, over a hundred additional senators "by right," who were entitled to sit for life. These men held their seats solely by virtue of their individual records: the institution of senators by right was strictly a temporary expedient.* The roster of those entitled to such seats proved most complicated to work out: it was intended to include the political leaders who had either served the pre-Fascist state with unusual distinction or most firmly opposed Fascism itself. Hence the final list made bizarre reading: alongside the name of a distinguished elderly gentleman of conservative views who long ago had been embalmed between the covers of history books, one found a dedicated Marxian revolutionist, the veteran of a decade and a half of Mussolini's prisons. The result was to overweigh the Senate both on its Right and on its extreme Left and to leave the Christian Democrats without the majority that they had gained among the elective seats. For its first few years, then, the Senate looked like something of a hybrid—a museum of political antiquities grafted on to an elected body differing in composition scarcely at all from the Chamber of Deputies.

The Chamber under the republic is almost an exact replica of that same institution as it existed between the elections of 1919 and 1924. Its 600-odd members are chosen by universal suffrage under a pro-

---

* Except for the provision that each President of the Republic may nominate as senators for life five men of particular distinction in social and cultural fields, and that he himself, on the completion of his term of office, similarly becomes a life senator.

portional system that, as in 1919, is intended to discourage *trasfor-mismo* and the building up of local centers of personal power, but which in practice has accomplished little more than to strengthen the discipline of major party machines. The only great novelty is that the women vote—presumably a bonus to Christian Democracy in a country where women are far more religiously inclined than men; the Communists, however, also feel they have profited by the new arrangement. The Italian Chamber is impressively noisy and disorderly: the Communists can be relied on to provoke the supporters of the government at every turn, and the Christian Democrats frequently rise to the bait. Yet there is something grandly operatic about a stormy day in the Italian Chamber: it has more diapason and ground-swell than the mere petulance of other legislative bodies. And occasionally someone even gets hurt. On days when political passions are aflame, the ushers set up a kind of football wedge to keep the opposing parties separated and to protect the ministers making their reports from the government bench.

It is from this line of seats—which face the deputies under the chair of the presiding officer rather than being simply the front row of the assembly itself, as in France—that the prime minister and his colleagues defend their policies before the elected representatives of the country. The Italian ministry, like its pre-Fascist predecessors and the governments of Britain and France, is responsible to the legislature: it requires a parliamentary majority to support it, and the prime minister is selected by the President with that consideration in mind; in a situation dominated by large political parties, as at the present time, he will regularly be a leader of the strongest party. But in Italy, as opposed to Britain, the government is responsible to *both* chambers of Parliament rather than to a single popularly elected house.

Local government under the new constitution similarly returned to the pre-Fascist model. Centralization is still the rule. Mayors and municipal and provincial councils—which under Mussolini were appointed from the capital—are once again elective, but their powers are, as before, narrowly circumscribed. The prefect of the province, responsible solely to the Ministry of the Interior, is now, as under all the previous governments of united Italy, the supreme arbiter of local affairs. He has the power of removing recalcitrant mayors and dissolving uncooperative municipal councils—a power that the Christian Democrats have exerted more than once against locally elected Communist officials.

In the original discussions of what post-Fascist Italy would be like, there had been much talk of decentralizing. There was almost universal agreement among anti-Fascists that centralization had in the long run proved a dubious blessing—whatever its indispensability in the early days of the united kingdom—and had greatly aided Mussolini in consolidating his dictatorship. The Christian Democrats, like the *Popolari* before them, particularly insisted on the need for developing a new grass-roots democracy. But this, like so much else that once seemed important in the anti-Fascist movement, for the most part failed to materialize during the De Gasperi era.

The constitution of 1948 provided for the organization of regional governments, based roughly on the large subdivisions of the country —Tuscany, Calabria, and the rest—that had long existed as merely descriptive areas. Of these only five had come into existence by 1962. And all of them were for peripheral areas where agitation for separation from Italy, or, at the very least, local autonomy, had been a serious postwar problem—the small French-speaking Val d'Aosta in Piedmont, the partly German-speaking Trentino-Alto Adige, Venezia Friuli, bordering on Yugoslavia, and the islands of Sicily and Sardinia. In these areas, where concessions to local sentiment seemed urgent, three of the regional administrations had already been established before the vote of the constitution. In the main part of Italy, however, no such agitation existed, and the government found compelling reasons for proceeding with caution. The Christian Democrats were no longer the party of a Catholic opposition that felt itself outside the main current of public life in the Italian state. Under De Gasperi's leadership they became the very reverse—the majority party responsible for running that state. Once in power—quite like the Democrats in the United States —they turned into proponents of centralized control. In this new capacity, they were acutely aware of the danger that to proceed with the establishment of the regions provided for in the constitution might be to create a solid band of Communist-dominated governments across north-central Italy—the area of maximum Communist strength. Hence they simply refrained from taking any action at all: the constitutional provisions in question remained a dead letter.

Christian Democracy's position as the majority party likewise dictated the character of Church-state relations. In this sphere, however, it was the legacy of Fascism that predominated over that of the pre-1922 parliamentary monarchy. We have seen how—with the help of Communist votes—De Gasperi succeeded in getting the Concordat of 1929 incorporated *unaltered* in the new constitution. This has meant that the illiberal and anachronistic features of that document are still in force: the position of the Catholic Church as the "sole religion of the state"; the vexatious limitations on the religious activities of Protestants and Jews; the complete Catholic supervision of the institution of marriage—even such an odd provision as the denial of teaching rights to defrocked priests. These regulations, as under Mussolini, apply today. And in some ways they apply even more rigorously than they did under Fascism. For then the state was in the hands of godless men, who favored the Church for reasons of policy. Now it is run by believing Catholics, responsive to ecclesiastical authority. An examination of the record of Christian Democracy in power will suggest what this has signified in practice.

5. CHRISTIAN DEMOCRACY IN POWER

Since the election of 1948, Christian Democracy has been in power without interruption. And in all essentials, the party ruled the country singlehanded for fifteen years.

Originally, De Gasperi preferred to continue the governmental coalition that he had established just before the election with the three minor democratic parties—the Liberals, the Republicans, and the Social Democrats. And these parties, humbled by their mediocre showing at the polls, were glad to go along with him. The first year following the election was a period of truce within the government coalition. The minor parties were slow to criticize: the ministry was still on trial, and Christian Democracy's parliamentary allies were inclined to give it the benefit of the doubt. Moreover, the Christian Democrats were themselves proceeding cautiously in the practical application of their religious principles. They were concentrating on a more pressing task on whose overriding importance all the partners in the coalition could agree—the struggle against Communist-inspired disorder and economic sabotage.

In July 1948 and again the following autumn, the government successfully resisted a Communist offensive masked under the form of a general strike. On the first occasion, the shooting and severe wounding of Togliatti as he was coming out of the Chamber of Deputies—the act of an isolated fanatic for which, however, the Communists immediately blamed the government—unleashed a protest strike that in some northern cities like Genoa reached insurrectionary proportions. The government remained calm: for a day and a half it let the insurgents build their barricades and roam at liberty through the streets. Then by a simple threat of military action it dissolved the strike movement in a few hours. Similarly, a second autumn wave of strikes directed against the European Recovery Program was broken by severe police action. This time, the effects were permanent. After the autumn of 1948, the Communists presented no serious threat to public order.

This substantial consolidation of government authority coincided with two years of relative economic stabilization—the years of mounting production and level prices based on Marshall Plan aid. Here again the minor parties could find reason for satisfaction: the government's economic policy was bringing results. In the middle of 1950, however, the situation suddenly changed: the outbreak of the Korean War and its consequences—economic and international —again threw the country into a state of uncertainty; more and more Italians began to question the wisdom of De Gasperi's course. After 1950, the government was assailed on all sides. The charges against it were extremely varied, and some mutually contradictory. A number of them can best be dealt with in subsequent chapters— the government's delays and hesitations in undertaking economic reform, and its foreign policy of Western alliance and dependence on the United States. For the present, we shall restrict ourselves to examining the general character of Christian Democracy and the kind of administration it gave the country.

These were the things that made the three minor parties restive members of the government coalition—or even caused them to leave it entirely. Within two years of the 1948 electoral victory, two of the parties had withdrawn from De Gasperi's ministry. Ostensibly they departed because of disagreements on economic policy. The Liberals got out in early 1950 because they found the government's proposals for land reform too radical for their taste. The Social Democrats left a year later in protest against Christian Democratic conservatism. The Republicans alone elected to remain. This again was logical in terms of economic philosophy. As opposed to the conservative Liberals—who in general spoke for the employer classes—and the reform-minded Social Democrats, the Republicans held the middle ground among the three minor parties. Of all Italian parties, they were perhaps the closest to an American political philosophy. And their stand on foreign policy was similarly pro-American: their two most prominent representatives in the De Gasperi government, Count Carlo Sforza, foreign minister from 1947 to 1951, and Randolfo Pacciardi, the former commander of the Garibaldi Brigade in the Spanish Civil War and subsequently Italian Minister of Defense, were particularly associated with the policy of the Atlantic alliance and Western European integration.

Even the Republicans, however, were troubled by Christian Democratic clericalism. Despite the basic differences of economic philosophy that divided the three minor parties, they were united on one thing: defense of the pre–1922 tradition of the Italian lay state. Their gradual realization of what Christian Democracy was after was the deeper reason for the rupture of the post-election truce among the government parties. Whether or not the individual minor parties decided to stay in the ministry, they all had a common concern—the threat of clerical resurgence and the gradual establishment of a Christian Democratic "regime."

To an American the word "regime" used in this context proved rather puzzling. To him Prime Minister De Gasperi and his successors were the leaders of the great democratic party that was holding the line against Italian Communism. Christian Democracy's religious character seemed distinctly secondary and not particularly troubling. After all, both the Republican and the Democratic parties in the United States constantly paid their respects to religious values. To an Italian, however, the concept of a "regime"—even of a religious character—carried a threatening meaning; it recalled the factitious national harmony of the twenty years of Fascist rule. In contrast to parliamentary democracy—with its free competition of party ideologies and its alternation of party representatives in the government—a "regime" suggested the dominance of a single ideology. It might or might not mean dictatorship or the corporate state. As used in Italy in the 1950's, the word usually conveyed the narrower meaning of gradual reorientation of the directing public bodies—the administration, the police, the schools—to conform to the standards and demands of a rather special ideology, while the framework of political liberty remained intact.

Such was the process that Italians saw going on in their country after 1948, as Christian Democracy steadily extended its influence. This influence was at the same time pervasive and intangible. It was extremely difficult to pin down since Christian Democracy was both more and less than simply a Catholic party.

Like all such parties, it included a rainbow of social classes and tendencies. Italian Liberals or Communists stood for fairly well-defined class interests. Not so Christian Democracy. Like its pre-Fascist predecessor, the Popular party, it was a political movement both of great landowners and of poor peasants, of industrialists and of Catholic workers, and of all the different types of middle-class citizens. The only common tie that bound together these disparate elements was their Catholicism. Even democracy was not a completely shared value—since the various internal factions understood it in different ways, and on the party's extreme right wing the loyalty to anything that an American would call democracy was far from certain.

The pre-Fascist *Popolari* were true reformers. Or at least their "Center" leadership under Don Luigi Sturzo offered an advanced social program. This was less true after 1948: De Gasperi—originally Sturzo's faithful lieutenant—had become more conservative during the quarter century that had gone by. In the immediate post-Fascist period, the traditional left wing of the party associated with the Catholic trade unions had considerable authority and prestige. The temper of the time, as we have seen, was quasi-revolutionary, and Christian Democracy could hope to play a leading role only if it spoke the language of leftism. But after 1945, this older Christian Democratic Left lost much of its influence. Subsequently there appeared a new and more doctrinaire form of leftism advanced by a circle of intellectuals around Professor Giuseppe Dossetti. In 1951 this group also went into a decline; Dossetti resigned as vice-secretary of the party, and his ideological organ, *Cronache sociali,* ceased to exist. A year later, however, it revived in another form. The 1952 party congress was dominated by an organized tendency calling

itself "Democratic Initiative," which was particularly strong among
the rank and file and the party youth and which represented an
amalgam of Left and Center under the slogan of loyalty to the
"De Gasperi line." Its triumph was sealed in 1954 when its chief
spokesman, Amintore Fanfani, was chosen party secretary in succession to De Gasperi shortly before the latter's death.

Yet this was a Left of a special sort—an "academic" or "corporative" Left. Half contemptuously, half humorously, its members were
referred to by their adversaries as "little professors." (It was, in fact,
as a professor of economics that Fanfani originally made his reputation.) And there was something pedagogic about Fanfani and his
associates. They tended to be ascetic, hard-driving, humorless, and
to take a paternalistic attitude toward Italy's masses. They felt that
they knew what the country needed and were impatient with anything that stood in their path. In consequence their understanding of
the word "democracy" was often more authoritarian than that of
the older party leaders. Too young to have experienced pre-Fascist
parliamentary democracy—Fanfani was only fourteen when Mussolini came to power—they had a different political pedigree from
the former *Popolari*. They had come to maturity in a radically
altered atmosphere: a number of them, at least nominally, had been
members of the Fascist party.

Mario Scelba was only eight years older than Fanfani. But a gulf
of contrasting experience separated them. As the former secretary
of Don Luigi Sturzo and De Gasperi's political heir, Scelba represented both the old *Popolare* tradition and the party Center—
cautious, parliamentary in outlook, and committed to the ideal of
political liberty. To the right of him stood the party conservatives—
the "economic" Right, with its ties to big business, and the "clerical"
Right, attentive to the directives emanating from Catholic Action.
By the 1950's then, the party was torn between those who argued
that only a reform program could win the Italian masses away from
Communism, and those who contended that this was hopeless, that
the main problem facing Christian Democracy was electoral competition from the Right. Between these two positions the party hesitated—and suffered in consequence from the simultaneous accusa-
tions of reforming too little and reforming too much.

With so miscellaneous and divided a following, De Gasperi was
reduced to the role of political juggler. Externally Christian Democ-

racy was impressive in its bulk and discipline. Internally it was a maze of factions, personal and ideological, too complex and shifting for enumeration. It was De Gasperi's task to keep this restless mass of nearly 400 parliamentarians loyal to the government and reasonably happy. At the same time he was obliged to conciliate the contradictory interests that in turn were pressing on the deputies— industrial employers eager for government favors, impoverished clerical workers, and impatient peasants clamoring for land. To this work of conciliation, De Gasperi brought an unparalleled political finesse. For more than seven years, he managed to keep order within his motley following. But this achievement was at enormous cost. It meant the postponement of all organic reforms and a policy of drift and improvisation. For De Gasperi's method of governing was to concede where the demand was greatest—to grant a favor or a reform, and then, when the pressure had relaxed a bit, to delay and to reduce the practical application of what he had just granted. It was a policy of patchwork solutions and short-term reprieves. In this sense, De Gasperi was a new Giolitti. Unlike his famous predecessor, the Christian Democratic leader was not obliged to manufacture a majority from bits and pieces of political following. But he still felt it necessary to perform as a virtuoso majority-monger in order to keep together what he already had.

Hence it was not surprising that the government consistently showed vigor only in those two areas where the Christian Democrats were in substantial agreement—the police and the interests of the Church. At the Ministry of the Interior Mario Scelba kept the police at an enviable level of alertness and efficiency; if the forces of public order were not always overscrupulous in respecting the rights of individuals, there were few within the majority party who raised their voices in criticism. The advancement of Catholic interests came in slower and more subtle fashion. It took the form of government sponsorship of pilgrimages and processions; intervention by the clergy in questions of public administration; and the beginnings of moral legislation and even of press censorship. These last were alien both to the Italian tradition of good-humored tolerance and to the general Western respect for personal liberty. They were what Italians primarily had in mind when they talked of a drift toward a Christian Democratic "regime."

They were also thinking of the spoils system. In this respect

Christian Democracy behaved with less restraint than any of Italy's parliamentary rulers of the past. Everywhere it replaced the adherents of other parties with its own stalwarts. By the 1950's Christian Democracy had taken over virtually the whole internal administration of the country. High and low—and not only in the government itself, but also in the parastatal economic bodies* and the organs of cultural life—Christian Democrats occupied the influential and remunerative posts. Obviously this practice further demoralized a civil service already weakened by three decades of Fascism, internal disorder, and economic hardship. And similarly it lowered the intellectual caliber of the Italian public service: in respect of personal talent, Christian Democracy had less to offer than the minor democratic parties. In the field of education, for example, the intrusion of Christian Democratic appointees brought a gradual change from a spirit of free inquiry to a mentality of narrow and routine loyalty to party and Church. Finally—and most serious—these subordinate appointees displayed more zeal and less discretion than their superiors. While the Christian Democratic government itself nearly always respected the accepted standards of democratic procedure, the lower officials—il sottogoverno—began to apply principles reminiscent of intellectual alignment and single-party rule.

Again the American might think that the fears of liberal-minded Italians were exaggerated. Surely, the civic attitude of a practicing Catholic and the public morality of the spoils system had nothing in common? But in mid-century Italy they did meet in the baffling, equivocal phenomenon of Christian Democracy. Here they actually reinforced each other. They had in common a spirit of forgive and forget, of an indulgence derived from long experience of human nature. Toward Fascism, for example, the attitude was much the same. In both cases, the tendency was to be distrustful of political militancy and to leave things as they were. Hence the Christian Democrats did not tamper as much as might have been expected with the legacy of Fascism—whether in laws, institutions, or human beings. At the beginning of 1948, after the adjournment of the Constituent Assembly, De Gasperi terminated the purge of Fascist officials; nearly all suspended civil servants were restored to their

* IRI, Finsider, Finmeccanica, etc. (see Chapter 8).

former positions. At the time this was probably a good thing. The purge in Italy, as almost everywhere else in Europe, had been badly handled, and hordes of minor Fascists had suffered excessively through it. But during the next five years the reparation for past wrongs overshot the mark. Not only the small Fascists regained their jobs. The larger figures in Mussolini's party—all except the greatest hierarchs—returned in full force and began to occupy leading positions in the administration and in private economic activity. And they, unlike the small fry, were mostly unrepentant.

Christian charity and political expediency met, then, on a common ground of civic indulgence. It was in this that critics descried the "anti-Risorgimento" character of Christian Democratic rule.* Yet we should not close the discussion on too harsh a note. Even the critics of Christian Democracy—if they were honest with themselves —recognized the benefits it had conferred on the country. It had restored public order without sacrificing the essentials of Western freedom. It had stabilized the currency. It had made a start toward agrarian reform. And it had brought Italy into the Atlantic community as a respected and equal partner. At the very least, the government of Christian Democracy was preferable to the only alternatives available.

6. THE DISLOYAL OPPOSITION

The alternatives were Neo-Fascism and Communism. These were the mutually antagonistic poles of a disloyal opposition that maintained an unrelenting attack against the very existence of political democracy in Italy. Both were disloyal in the sense that they enjoyed the advantages of parliamentary activity under the constitution of 1948 while at the same time working for the subversion of the whole constitutional system.

Between them the two blocs in the 1953 election commanded about 48 per cent of the popular vote. This impressive total explained why they were not balanced by a loyal or constitutional opposition —why there was no real alternative to the government of Christian Democracy. And it revealed the radical difference between Italian

* For example, Arturo Carlo Jemolo, *Chiesa e Stato in Italia negli ultimi cento anni* (Turin, 1949), pp. 715–724.

political life on the one hand and British or American on the other. In Britain or the United States, the vast majority of the electorate accepted the existing constitutional arrangements, the whole tradition of fair play and minority rights implicit in the Western democratic tradition: in the English-speaking countries elections did not call in question the very existence of constitutional government; they concerned differing interpretations of a commonly accepted tradition—the greater or lesser extent of government interference in economic life and the social pressures, whether of labor or of business, that would exert most influence on the new administration. Hence for Britain or the United States the alternation in power of two large, democratically minded parties appeared the normal form of political activity. Not so for Italy at mid-century. In a country where only a little more than half the electorate accepted the Western constitutional tradition, to split the democratic vote between two great parties meant to invite disaster. Under such circumstances, a loyal, constitutional opposition remained a luxury that Italy could not afford.

This was a hard truth to which many democratically minded Italians assented only with the greatest reluctance—if at all. They argued quite correctly that Italy required a great laical party to balance the growing influence of Christian Democratic clericalism. And they frequently proposed the launching of such a political movement through an alliance among the three minor democratic parties already in existence—the Liberals, the Republicans, and the Social Democrats. But this alliance proved extremely difficult to achieve. The two larger of the parties—the Liberals and the Social Democrats—were poles apart in their economic philosophies. Moreover—and far more serious—no one of them had an adequate electoral following. Foreigners traveling in literary and intellectual circles got the impression that nearly everybody belonged to one of the minor parties. And this impression was substantially correct: the fact that Italy's greatest intellectual figures could be found in their ranks was both the pride and the fatal weakness of these parties. By the frank admission of their leaders, they, like the Party of Action during the war years, were elite formations without substantial popular followings. Even when lumped together, they commanded less than 10 per cent of the electorate.

The Liberals could appeal to the businessmen and landowners and to the more prosperous members of the middle class—but these were neither very numerous nor solidly Liberal in allegiance; for them authoritarian conservatism offered competing attractions. The Republicans continued to command a loyal following in certain traditional strongholds like the Romagna, but they lacked an economic program clearly directed at any one group in the population, and their Mazzinian slogans began to lose their point when Italy became a republic. Finally the Social Democrats, the largest of the minor parties and the one with the widest potential appeal, disappointed the expectations of its founders. The courageous decision of Saragat and his colleagues to break away from Italian Socialism's philo-Communist majority failed to bring its electoral reward. The new party received several accretions of strength from subsequent Socialist secessions. But these were again mostly of leaders without followers. Hence the Social Democrats proved unable to capitalize on the undoubted attractions of their program—a program combining economic reform with an insistence on personal liberty. They remained a party of the intellectuals and of a substantial section of the lower middle class. Among organized labor and the peasantry, they made only modest gains.

In 1947, a group of Mussolini's former adherents founded a new party, the MSI (*Movimento sociale italiano*), that was frankly neo-Fascist where the *Uomo qualunque* had been only potentially so. The MSI participated in the election of 1948 but made a poor showing: in that year, the conservative, anti-Communist vote went almost solidly to Christian Democracy. It was not until two years later that the new neo-Fascist movement began to make substantial inroads among supporters of De Gasperi's ministry.

For purposes of popular oratory, the internationalist foreign policy of the government in general and the Trieste issue in particular provided the most rewarding campaign themes. But among the rank-and-file Neo-Fascists the argument that counted was—to use the American equivalent—the charge of official "softness" toward Communism. For it was anti-Communism alone that gave the MSI strength and cohesion. The Fascism of 1950, like Mussolini's movement, was a welter of contradictory tendencies, held together by their common conviction that strong methods were required to break the hold of Communism on the Italian masses. The moderate wing of the Party was scarcely distinguishable from Monarchism. The dominant tendency was only slightly less conservative, reflecting the ideas and personalities of a number of unreconstructed Fascist "hierarchs" left over from the period of Mussolini's glory: for them corporatism provided a convenient ideological tent, combining a solicitude for the interests of the large producers with the appearance of a social policy directed at the welfare of the working classes. The youth of the party were generally content to go along with this politic equivocation: like the postwar generation of other countries they were more conformist than anything else. But for those in their thirties—the veterans of Mussolini's bloody Republic of Salò—such a course looked like cowardice and treason to the memory of the Fascist dead: fanatically republican and even socialist in their platform vocabulary, uncompromisingly hostile to the Atlantic alliance, this radical wing, which originally gave the MSI its characteristic color, subsequently became an embarrassment and a danger to the responsible leaders of the party.

Although it was hard to discern at the time, Neo-Fascism had no future before it. It was Communism, rather, which had won an apparently unshakable allegiance among the Italian masses. This had not always been the case. The Italian Communist party that in the De Gasperi era—either directly or through its allies—controlled roughly one third the electorate, was originally far from being a mass movement. The group that walked out of the Socialist congress at Leghorn in January 1921 to found the Italian Communist party was little more than a core of convinced revolutionists. Its trade-union backing did not extend much beyond Turin, which had been the testing-ground of the new party. Turin was the headquarters of one wing of Italian Communism—the "Piedmontese" wing led by Antonio Gramsci. This branch of the party possessed leaders of unusual intellectual stature who at the same time enjoyed the confidence of the skilled metalworkers, the elite of the Italian labor force. The other major wing, the "Neapolitans" led by Amedeo Bordiga, were revolutionists of an older type, emotional and undisciplined. In organizational and tactical skill, they lagged far behind the Piedmontese.

In 1926, at a congress held in France, Gramsci's northerners gained control of the party. Gramsci himself was soon to be sent to prison

—from which he emerged only to die—but his lieutenant Palmiro Togliatti carried on in the course the older leader had marked out. For nearly four decades Togliatti remained the undisputed chief of Italian Communism.

Togliatti, a trained intellectual like Gramsci, combined a singularly subtle mind with an irreproachable orthodoxy in essential matters. His long residence in Moscow, where he passed nearly the whole of the Fascist period, made him a reliable interpreter of directives from the Kremlin. But unlike the cruder type of Communist leader, Togliatti had learned to gauge with accuracy the extent to which he could modify the Moscow line to fit Italian conditions; he had a sure sense for the permitted deviation that fell just short of heresy. This was one reason why Italian Communism did not suffer the losses in following which so many other Communist parties experienced after 1948.

The high intellectual level of its leadership was, then, one of the most important distinguishing features of Italian Communism. This tendency was strengthened in the thirties and early forties, when, as we have already seen, a large number of university students clandestinely joined the party. A decade later these recruits formed an influential element among the younger Communist leadership. In a country like Italy, where educational levels varied radically from class to class and where illiteracy had not yet entirely disappeared, the intellectual in politics enjoyed a high prestige. Even a leftist party—or perhaps particularly a leftist party—took pride in the intellectual distinction of its leadership.

The real acquisition of a mass base by the Italian Communist party, however, came only with its assumption of control over the trade-union movement. This was a sudden and comparatively late development. We have noted how during the Fascist years the Communists gradually gained strength and prestige by their courage in organizing clandestine cells, their sponsorship of Popular Fronts, and their military activities during the Spanish Civil War. All this assured them a position of organizational pre-eminence; but it could not give them a mass following. Their central core of trade-union strength they acquired only in the years after 1941. In the autumn of that year, spurred on by the Soviet entry into the war and the signs of approaching Fascist collapse, the Communists launched a mighty clandestine effort. They sent into the factories of the major northern cities a flying squadron of party organizers to spread defeatist propaganda and enroll the workers in secret Communist cells. These efforts were amply rewarded. Their success was suddenly revealed in the spring of 1943 with the great strike movement that touched off the series of events leading to Mussolini's fall.

As the instigators of the first major strikes of the war period, the Communists could plausibly lay claim to being the chosen representatives of the Italian industrial workers. Hence when it came time to dissolve the nationwide "syndical" organizations established under Fascism, the Communists were let in on a share of the inheritance. As early as the Forty-Five Days, Badoglio's post-Fascist ministry took the first steps in setting up a new labor confederation. To this body the government turned over the funds and the membership cards of the defunct syndical organization. The new anti-Fascist directorate was spared the trouble of a recruiting campaign: the workers simply continued to send in their union dues through the familiar channels.

Virtually from the start the CGIL* was tripartite in direction: representatives of the Christian Democratic, Socialist, and Communist parties exercised joint authority on its governing board. But soon the Communist member gained the predominant influence. A veteran of the International Brigades in the Spanish Civil War, Giuseppe Di Vittorio was both a vigorous popular leader and a skillful organizer; he early established a personal ascendancy over his Socialist colleague, thereby isolating the Christian Democratic member of the triumvirate. Meantime other Communists were gaining similar positions of dominance as local labor secretaries: month by month they drew workers away from their traditional Socialist allegiance. By 1947 it had become obvious that CGIL had been transformed into a dependency of the Communist party; the strikes of that year against the Marshall Plan demonstrated that the Communists could mobilize the bulk of the Italian workers to support a political campaign that had no semblance of economic argument behind it.

The result was a series of secessions from the CGIL of unions loyal to the Christian Democratic, Social Democratic, and Repub-

* *Confederazione generale italiana del lavoro.*

lican parties. These secessions, which were backed by moral and financial support from American union representatives, deprived the CGIL of perhaps a third of its membership. And in 1950 most of the independent unions united to form a new confederation in opposition to the CGIL. This development encouraged the supporters of trade-union liberty in Italy. And they were also heartened by evidence that the Communists could no longer count on the membership of the CGIL for a purely political strike; the failure of their campaign to prevent the unloading of military supplies from the United States revealed the limits of Communist control over the Italian trade-union movement. It was unquestionable that the years 1948–1953 saw a loss of influence for the extreme Left. But in more tenuous form the Communists retained the allegiance of the bulk of organized labor: most of their dramatic gains from the early and mid-1940's were intact.

Labor remained the core of Communist electoral and organizational strength. It accounted for a substantial share of the two and a half million members that made the Italian party the largest in the non-Communist world. The figure of something over two million stayed fairly stable after 1946. Losses were balanced out by systematic recruiting campaigns. More particularly, a steady growth of Communist influence among the peasantry compensated for the reduction of following among industrial labor Simultaneously the party was extending its influence in the South—an area to which neither of the leftist parties had formerly paid much attention. In the election of 1948 the "People's Bloc" of left-wing Socialists and Communists polled about 40 per cent of the vote in the North, 50 per cent in the Center, and between 20 and 25 per cent in the South and the islands. Five years later these percentages had increased everywhere—but most dramatically in the South, where the Left raised its vote by nearly a third.

Without their Socialist allies, the Communists would have lost a quarter to a third of their potential following. The Communist leadership knew this very well and handled the Socialists with consummate tact. The phenomenon of left-wing (or majority) Socialism was difficult for an American to understand: its *raison d'être* escaped him and he usually dismissed it as a feckless movement of blind fellow-travelers. It was true that under Nenni's leadership the party that was once the strongest in Italy became little more than an electoral and trade-union annex to Communism. With the departure of their right wing (or Social Democrats), the Italian Socialists lost nearly every vestige of tactical indpendence. On the majority of issues they followed the Communist line. But the more astute observers of Italian affairs refused to write off the Socialists entirely: they pointed out that in certain northern cities like Milan the latter retained their traditional hold on the loyalties of skilled workers, and that on international issues they frequently deviated from the Communist position; as opposed to a strictly pro-Soviet line, they advocated a policy of neutralism between Russia and America. This intermediate stand made Socialism attractive to many Italians who would have hesitated to cast a Communist vote.

The tenacity and resilience of the left opposition baffled foreign observers. Each year the Communist positions seemed about to crumble, and each year the heralded collapse failed to materialize. In 1949 a papal excommunication of party members threatened to shatter the Communist cadres; but the leadership worked out techniques for circumventing the ecclesiastical ban and lulling to rest the disturbed consciences of its Catholic followers. Two years later deputies Magnani and Cucchi launched a dissident Communist movement that looked capable of winning over large sections of the party from their Soviet allegiance; again the Communist ranks held firm. At the end of the De Gasperi era, despite its transparent subservience to Moscow and the unpopular courses that its Soviet masters had obliged it to pursue—notably in opposing the European Recovery Program—Italian Communism still commanded a potent following. Nevertheless a net reduction in strength was apparent: the *active* force that the party could mobilize in an emergency was almost certainly less in 1948; only its *electoral* following continued to grow.

To seek the reasons for this continuing appeal we must leave the sphere of party politics. The explanation for the hold of Communism on the Italian masses lay in the very nature of the country's economy and social structure—in the oligarchic character of the social groups that wielded decisive economic power.

8

Economic Recovery and Land Reform

1. THE STRUCTURE OF THE ITALIAN ECONOMY

WITH THE FALL of Fascism, the elaborate corporative structure built up during the preceding two decades was dismantled piece by piece. It was not too hard a task to eliminate the formal structure of corporatism. But it was something else to change the habits of nearly twenty years. Corporative procedures and the corporative mentality remained.

This persistence of corporative attitudes was partly attributable to the fact of Christian Democratic rule. Originally Christian Democracy, like most Catholic parties, favored a limited amount of corporative representation in the organs of government. In the debates on the 1948 constitution the party proposed that the upper house of the legislature should consist in part of representatives of organized economic interests. But in view of the determined opposition of the other parties, the Christian Democrats abandoned this proposal and gradually dropped the corporative theme from their official propaganda.

In less explicit form, however, Christian Democracy continued to favor corporative procedures. In its passive, live-and-let-live fashion, the government permitted the various economic interests to carry on in the old routines. Indeed in economic policy more than in any other field, the Christian Democrats revealed their tendency to leave unchanged a surprising number of the laws and institutions inherited from Fascism. As in the other areas of government, it yielded to the strongest pressures, to the best organized interests.

And these interests were strongly corporative in orientation. About the employers there was not much room for doubt. They were roughly the same people who ran the economic activity of the country under Fascism, and they continued to operate in similar fashion. The employers' organization of industrialists, the *Confindustria*, was virtually the same body that existed under Fascism as an officially recognized confederation; after 1945 it simply returned to being the private organization that it had been before 1926. As under Mussolini, it enjoyed a near monopoly of employer representation in negotiating with organized labor.

What was more surprising, however, was that labor itself operated in a similarly corporative fashion. This was particularly the case before 1948, when the Italian trade unions were still grouped in a single confederation: a monopolistic employers' organization and a monopolistic labor representation could meet each other across the bargaining table as near-equals. And, drastically opposed as they were in their articulate political ideologies, they could still agree on a number of policies of mutual benefit—and usually of detriment to the other classes of the population. Thus Communist union leaders and ultra-conservative employers were at one in pressing on the government the necessity of maintaining a fixed quota of workers in the factories, whether or not they actually had anything to do. To the workers, this guaranteed the retention of their jobs; to the employers, the continuation of government subsidies.

After the anti-Communist secessions from the CGIL in 1948 and 1949, and the unfreezing of fixed job quotas in 1950, the corporative monopoly of organized labor was broken. But the corporative attitude persisted. In a country like Italy, where jobs were scarce and unemployment a continuing nightmare, it was too much to expect of the trade unions that they should show great concern for the welfare of the country as a whole. With the needs of their constituents in mind—with the desperate pressure to hold on to the existing jobs at all costs—the leaders of Italian labor were naturally distrustful of any efforts to alter or rationalize the expensive, top-heavy structure of Italian industry.

Thus Italian labor, like Italian capital, had a vested interest in the maintenance of Italian industry as it was. And the very structure of industry lent itself to corporative attitudes. Not only was it territorially concentrated in the northwestern portion of the country, particularly the triangle Milan-Turin-Genoa; in addition, most branches of industry were characterized by the predominance of very large or very small enterprises, with medium-sized business less well represented: the small size of the national market frequently allowed room for only one large producer. And it was naturally the giant industrial concerns that ran the affairs of the *Confindustria*. In chemicals the Montecatini company had a virtual monopoly. Pirelli had a similar monopoly in rubber, and in the metallurgical and automotive industries, concerns like Ansaldo of Genoa and FIAT of Turin dominated the field.

Moreover, these monopolistic companies had grown up under a regime of government favors. Since the 1880's Italian industry had been accustomed to the protection of a high tariff. And under Mussolini's program of self-sufficiency and preparation for war, the stimulus of government orders expanded the heavy mechanical industry beyond all reasonable bounds. In the depression of the thirties, many of these concerns went bankrupt. But the government came to their rescue through the IRI program of official loans to insolvent corporations. After the fall of Fascism, IRI continued to exist. It held a controlling interest in most of the large heavy industry plants, with the significant exception of FIAT.* The result, however, was in no sense the nationalization or socialization of these industries. The government did nothing with its controlling interest: it left management in private hands.

This was characteristic of De Gasperi's economic policy. Most of the time the government left the initiative to the representatives of organized industry, and followed policies that the latter recommended—or, more usually, refrained from adopting measures that industry opposed. Hence, in practice, corporatism still operated: the employers' organization, under De Gasperi as under Mussolini, brought its massive pressure to bear directly on the government, and generally with decisive effect. In fact, its pressure was perhaps less overpowering when it was officially recognized and canalized through the appropriate corporative bodies.

---

* The *Finsider* subsidiary of IRI produced 60.5 per cent of Italy's pig iron and 43 per cent of its steel. The *Finmeccanica* subsidiary controlled 80 per cent of the country's shipyard capacity.

In general, then, large industry was left free to pursue its traditional policy of restricting output in order to maintain high prices. Such practices were obviously against the interests of the country as a whole: only by expanding industrial production and making the existing establishments more efficient could Italy hope to raise her standard of living to the level of other Western nations. But to pursue the latter policy required a vision and coherence of purpose that the government displayed only in limited areas—notably in the fields of land improvement and foreign trade. Elsewhere it tended to follow the line of least resistance—to live by improvisations. Under De Gasperi as under Mussolini, the basic problems of Italian economic life were not faced. But whereas under Fascism they were masked by the stately façade of corporatism, after the fall of Mussolini they reappeared, unadorned and insistent, in all their stark immediacy.

2. THE STAGES OF ECONOMIC RECOVERY

In the devastation inflicted by the war, Italy suffered more heavily than any Western nation except Germany. And in Italy the privations endured by the civilian population were even more severe than those undergone by the Germans. From 1943 to 1946, the Italian people passed through the hardest trial of their history as a united nation.

Yet even in the midst of homelessness, undernourishment, and anxiety about the future, the Italians enjoyed certain advantages over their neighbors. The fact that they had always been poor, that they had known hardship as their normal lot, gave them a special kind of experience and fortitude to face the deepened misery of wartime. They knew how to cope with want and devastation in a way that the populations of France and Germany, accustomed to a higher standard of living, were unable to match. The Italians did not simply look at their ruined houses in helpless despair: they went to work to rebuild them with their own hands.

Moreover, the devastation of war did not cripple the productive facilities of the country as severely as had been expected. The regions of maximum destruction lay across the two belts of military stalemate during the successive winters of 1943-44 and 1944-45—the towns and villages between Naples and Rome, and between Florence and Bologna. Neither of these areas contained any of the great commercial or industrial cities of Italy. Hence the major cities of the central part of the country—Rome and Florence—survived the war virtually intact. In the North the industrial centers suffered severely from Allied bombardment; but they were spared the ravages of artillery barrage and ground fighting, or of systematic sabotage by the retreating Germans. The Italian Partisans, by their decisive action in liberating these cities before the arrival of the Anglo-American armies, succeeded in preserving the main factories from any further war damage.

Shortly after the conclusion of the war, then, Italian industry was in shape to resume production on a large scale. The international market was favorable, with consumer goods in short supply everywhere and foreign buyers eager for Italian products. In 1946 and early 1947, Italian industry, particularly the textile industry, experienced a brief and eccentric boom. To superficial observers, it suggested that the country's economic recovery was much farther advanced than was actually the case.

In reality, the bases of this apparent prosperity were extremely shaky. Prosperity was shared in only by the industrial proprietors and the workers who actually were employed—the ostensibly antagonistic partners in the corporative legacy from Fascism. Moreover, it rested on a monetary inflation that made long-term productive planning impossible and reduced the mass of the population to want and insecurity. The inflation—and the black market that accompanied it—were entirely out of control. From Allied military government the Italian postwar ministries not only had inherited a depreciated currency (even at the official rate, the occupation lira was quoted at one hundred to the dollar, where the prewar rate had been about twenty); they also had taken over a nearly worthless collection of economic controls. At the best, price controls are difficult to enforce: in postwar Italy they became a cruel joke.

Against this potentially explosive situation, the government took no clear line. The tripartite ministry of Christian Democrats, Communists, and Socialists was in no position to pursue a coherent policy —divided as it was between theoretical Marxists and advocates of a free enterprise system. It was not until June 1947, when De Gasperi formed a new ministry without the Communists and left-wing Socialists, that the government could confront its economic problems with some hope of success.

As his Minister of the Budget, with the rank of vice-premier and a general supervisory authority over economic affairs, De Gasperi appointed Luigi Einaudi. A universally respected economist associated with the Liberal party, Einaudi was a persuasive advocate of economic freedom and financial orthodoxy. Here at last was a coherent policy. Einaudi offered a simple, straightforward program that all could understand: the stabilization of the currency and the end of the controls inherited from the war period. In essence, the new Minister of the Budget told the country that the black market had become the real market and should be recognized as such, and that there was no hope of stabilizing prices until the government's income and expenditure had come somewhere near into balance.

During the summer and autumn of 1947, as we have seen, Einaudi's policy brought results. Prices began to hold even, as the lira was stabilized at roughly one-fiftieth of its prewar buying power —a level that it maintained, with only slight increases, for years thereafter. This in itself was a noteworthy achievement. Italian economists were nearly unanimous in applauding Einaudi's deflationary policy as exactly what the country required. But they also noted that its social results were more questionable. The application of orthodox economics placed the bulk of the Italian people in a stationary situation of well-ordered misery.

Moreover, the deflationary policy checked the productive momentum of Italian industry; on the earlier industrial boom there followed a period of quasi-stagnation. This was where the European Recovery Program was intended to impinge on the Italian economy. The promise of American aid had been an essential element in Einaudi's success: the prospect of the early arrival of Marshall Plan shipments gave the needed lift to public confidence. But, still more important, the European Recovery Program supplied the indispensable complement to economic stabilization—a way to raise the general standard of living by increasing Italy's productive output. The basic concept of the plan was that the United States should furnish the raw materials and capital equipment that would enable Italian industry to expand production far above prewar levels.

Technically, during the four years that the European Recovery Program was in effect, this goal was attained. By the middle of 1952 the index of industrial production stood at 140 per cent of the 1938 level. This was an encouraging figure and was rightly pointed to as proof that Italian economic recovery had virtually been completed. But the program of industrial expansion had not gone as far as the architects of the Marshall Plan had hoped. Relative to the increase of population that had taken place since the outbreak of the Second World War, the level of production was actually about 25 per cent above that of 1938—which was by no means a year of prosperity. Moreover, as the Marshall Plan economists themselves complained, the program had not resulted in as high a level of investment as they had originally intended.

The European Recovery Program, then, saved Italy from economic deterioration and social unrest. But it did not alter the basic structure of the Italian economy nor bring its crying problems any closer to solution. That this did not happen was at least as much the responsibility of the Italians themselves as of their American advisers. It was the Italians, rather than the Americans, who insisted on maintaining financial stability as against increasing the rate of capital investment. After the election of 1948, when Einaudi was chosen first President of the Republic under the new constitution, De Gasperi could find no successor of similar stature to direct the government's economic policy. Einaudi's heirs—now, significantly enough, drawn from the Christian Democratic party—were men of little imagination who followed his own program to the letter without adapting it to changed circumstances. Throughout the De Gasperi era what Italy lacked above all was a long-range plan of the type Jean Monnet had given France, to inspire and canalize its constructive efforts.

Yet on the periphery of the main industrial problem there were certain dynamic and encouraging features in the Italian economy. Perhaps the most important was the exploitation of the country's newly discovered resources of natural gas. For a nation lacking coal and whose hydroelectric resources were being used nearly to capacity, the location of deposits of natural gas in the Po valley was a tremendous windfall. It meant not only cheap fuel but also an abundant source of raw material for the chemical industry. By the summer of 1952 a pipeline, the largest in Europe, was bringing gas to the factories of Turin. The still more recent discovery of extensive oil fields held out similar prospects for a farther future.

Finally we should note that Italy's economic assets were by no means limited to industry and agriculture. For decades she had relied on the three invisible items of maritime freights, tourist expenditures, and emigrants' remittances. The first two of these soon returned to the prewar norm. Italian foreign trade recovered rapidly after the war, and a gratifying percentage of it was carried in Italian ships. The Italian merchant marine, 90 per cent of whose tonnage was destroyed during the war, by the end of 1952 had reached its prewar strength. Meantime the tourist trade had surpassed its prewar high. The failure of the third of these items—emigrants' remittances—to return to its old level formed part of the larger problem of Italian overpopulation that will occupy us shortly.

3. FISCAL REFORM AND THE BUREAUCRATIC STATE

Contrasting with the government's usual caution and conservatism in economic matters, were two areas in which it demonstrated reforming vigor—tax policy and the problem of large landed estates.

In the first of these areas reform was particularly urgent. The tax structure which the postwar Italian governments inherited from their predecessors was antiquated in the extreme. It consisted of a bewildering variety of levies, both local and national, in which indirect taxes accounted for four-fifths of the total. Such tax burdens were an anomaly in a modern democratic state, since they weighed more heavily on the poor than on the wealthy.

Italy also had an income tax. But it accounted for only 11 per cent of the national revenue—as opposed to about 80 per cent in the United States. This low return reflected grave faults in the method of collection. The tax rate itself was frequently high—but at the same time the tax payers were not obliged to declare their true incomes. It was the bureaucracy of the finance ministry, rather, that drew up estimates of each individual's income, to be negotiated later with the interested parties. Under such a system, it was no wonder that tax evasion was nearly universal. The Latin peoples have traditionally enjoyed a poor reputation in matters of fiscal morality. But in

Italy the very method of collection encouraged fraud and dishonesty.

In the autumn of 1951, the government inaugurated a new system based on American precedent and backed by encouragement from the United States. On October 10, Italians were obliged for the first time to make written and signed declarations of their income, itemized as in the United States, and subject to judicial penalties for false statements. Nearly four million citizens made declarations; more than a million reported incomes exceeding the tax-free minimum of 240,000 lire ($384) plus 50,000 lire ($80) for each dependent.

To encourage cooperation by the tax payer, the Ministry of Finance purposely set the rates low; 50 per cent was fixed as the maximum. Hence even under the new system, although receipts rose, the income tax accounted for only a modest portion of the national revenue. Critics were quick to point out the methods of evasion that sprang up to circumvent the new regulations (some of them, like the formation of dummy corporations, already familiar in the United States). It was also true that the penalties for evasion were too mild; no defrauder went to prison. Italians certainly did not become model tax payers overnight. Yet the fairest verdict on the reform, in the words of one of its more judicious critics, was to call it a long-range project for "fiscal education and the formation of a tax-paying conscience" among the Italian people.*

Throughout the Italian administration, the same problem of personal probity existed in acute form. No reform can be better than the individuals that carry it out. In Italy, every reform project came up against one basic difficulty—the character of the bureaucracy.

As a highly centralized state, Italy always had too large a bureaucracy for its financial resources. From early in the history of the united kingdom, a career in public administration was eagerly sought after by young men of education who found meager outlets in the professions of law or teaching; for impoverished southern families in particular, Rome became the goal of their more ambitious sons who hoped by dint of education and hard work to move up one tier in the social layer-cake. Under Mussolini, these earlier tendencies were greatly strengthened. The central bureaucracy expanded enormously, and the comparative contentment of the South under

---

* Giovanni Ravagli, "I principi democratici della riforma Vanoni," *Il Ponte,* 7: 365 (April 1951).

Mussolini's rule was partly due to the career outlets the new regime provided.

With the fall of Fascism, the bureaucracy should normally have contracted in size. Certain departments, like the Ministry of Corporations or of "Italian Africa," had either ceased to exist or had lost nearly all their functions. Moreover, in the desperate circumstances of the immediate postwar period, strict economy in the public services would have been logical. Yet virtually no civil servants were discharged. Even when they had nothing to do, they were kept on the payroll. Their pay, it was true, was inadequate to live on. Hence many of them would simply turn up in their offices for an hour or two in the morning and then, having satisfied the letter of the regulations, go off to more remunerative pursuits—as likely as not in the black market.

The scandal of the bureaucrats with time on their hands evoked a storm of criticism.* Yet what could the government do? To discharge these men would be to condemn them and their families to privation and despair. In Italy to lose one's job was the ultimate, the unspeakable misfortune. And to discharge a man with a family ranked as a grave offense against human charity. As family men and good Christians, the members of the government could not face so terrible a decision. Once again, the arguments of personal charity outweighed the ethics of civic responsibility.

So the excess civil servants stayed on. By 1950, the worst scandals had been eliminated. The bureaucracy had, as the Italians put it, been "systematized." Yet the basic problem remained. Overstaffed as it was, the Italian administration was necessarily underpaid. The average Italian civil servant could not support his family on his salary alone: he was virtually driven to seek outside sources of income. Underwork and underpay reinforced each other to produce slovenliness and demoralization; their logical corollaries were inefficiency and a punctilious adherence to vexatious procedures. What wonder, then, that so many Italian civil servants alternated between the two equally repugnant attitudes of petty domineering and of servility and the outstretched palm.

---

* Notably in the brilliant articles by the economist Ernesto Rossi that first appeared in the journal *Italia socialista* and later were published in book form under the title *Banderillas* (Ivrea, 1947).

4. THE STANDARD OF LIVING

The problem of the bureaucracy was only part of the larger social dilemma of postwar Italy. On the surface the situation did not appear as grave as it actually was. By 1950, the per capita income of the Italian people had regained the level of 1938; the standard of living and the situation of the various social classes seemed about what they had been in the latter years of Fascism. In the eyes of the casual observer, the country had returned to "normal."

Yet changes had occurred, some fairly obvious, some obscure. About the situation of the rich, there was no particular secret: every day it was heartlessly flaunted in the streets of Rome. The postwar display of luxury against a background of bitter poverty was a novelty in the social manners of the Italian constitutional state: before 1922, even in periods of prosperity, it was considered poor taste to show off one's wealth. The unprecedented lack of restraint in these matters was partly the result of the rise of a new class of profiteers, which had been a feature of European life in postwar periods. Yet what was still more striking in Italy—as opposed to Britain or even France—was the extent to which the rich of the mid-century were the same people who had been wealthy a decade or two earlier. In contrast to France or Britain, in Italy no national-ization of basic industry had occurred: the leading industrial fami-lies retained their former holdings. Moreover, as opposed to the salaried or *rentier* classes, the industrialists, as the owners of tangible assets, did not suffer in the inflation of the years 1943–47. The same was true of landed proprietors. These, in fact, profited from the postwar boom in agricultural prices. The great estate-holders of Italy, many of whom bore princely titles, kept their former social and economic pre-eminence.

For the classes that lived on salaries and other fixed incomes the situation was just the reverse. The Italian middle classes suffered in the 1940's from the same kind of difficulties that plagued them under Mussolini—but in intensified form. Once again a postwar inflation had brought them ruin. After the First World War, the lira lost roughly four-fifths of its value; in 1950 it was worth less than one-fiftieth of what it was worth in 1938. As a practical matter, the savings of the middle class were totally destroyed: government bonds, insurance policies, pensions, and saving-banks accounts became practically worthless. Nor did salaries keep up with the post-war rise in the cost of living: the real wages of civil servants, for example, were far below what they had been in 1938.

The social effects of these changes were tragic in the extreme. Hundreds of thousands of families that before the war lived simply, but with dignity and self-respect, had been reduced to privation and near-squalor. Widows and old people could see no way out of their difficulties. Young people, even more than before the war, found little encouragement in the over-crowded professions of law, teaching, or the public service: the intellectual proletariat grew larger than ever before. These people felt that all their traditional props had been pulled out from under them: they lost faith in their government and their society. But only a small minority of them turned to Communism: they still felt themselves superior to manual workers—even when their economic status was lower. It was Neo-Fascism, rather, that for them had a special and very personal appeal.

The clerical middle class was at least partially organized in trade-unions: both civil servants and clerical workers in the metallurgical, textile, and chemical industries were represented by major labor federations. But in the trade-union movement as a whole the manual workers predominated. They alone had an adequate corporative organization. This corporative strength explained why Italian industrial workers enjoyed a favored position which—while not remotely comparable to that of the rich—still contrasted with the situation of the mass of the people. *Employed* industrial workers were better off under De Gasperi than under Mussolini: by 1951 real wages had reached a level more than 20 per cent above that of 1938.

There were, however, certain new conditions that sharply limited the comparatively favorable level of real wages. In the first place, the difference between the pay of skilled and unskilled labor had narrowed. Most of the postwar wage increases that were constantly being given to meet the inflation were simply of flat sums across the board regardless of skill. Moreover, a worker's basic wage often formed only a small part of his take-home pay: the rest was made up of family allowances, cost-of-living allowances, and the like. In the immediate postwar period, these allowances were likewise being steadily raised. Hence in two simultaneous developments, the part of the worker's pay in which skill differentials applied came to figure as a less and less important part of his total earnings. Ironically enough, it was frequently the skilled workers, angered at the loss of their favored position, who became the most enthusiastic Communists.

A more serious change, and one that virtually nullified industrial labor's postwar gains, was the rise in unemployment. At mid-century Italy had nearly two million unemployed—more than twice the prewar figure and the equivalent of 10 per cent of the total labor force. An undetermined number of additional workers were underemployed or partially employed. And—most serious of all—it was the youth of Italy that was increasingly suffering from the job shortage: there were simply not enough new positions to absorb the thousands of young people entering the job market each year. With plenty of trained workers available, employers preferred to fill their rare vacancies with older men laid off from other jobs.

In the desperation of the unemployed, Communist organizers found a receptive audience. And not only in the cities—for unemployment was at least as much an agrarian as an industrial problem. This was one among the many reasons why in the late 1940's Italy's rural classes began to shake off their age-old apathy.

5. POPULATION PRESSURE AND AGRARIAN TENURE

In an absolute sense, Italy might not be an overpopulated country; sociologists and demographers insist that overpopulation is a relative concept. Several European countries—both England and Belgium, for example—in 1950 were far more densely populated than Italy. But England and Belgium were highly industrialized nations, with abundant natural resources, either at home or in the colonies. Hence these two countries could support a density of population about twice that of Italy. In England, only slightly over 6 per cent of the people derived their livelihood from the soil: in Italy the figure was nearly one-half. Italy, in absolute terms, did not have too many people—but she had too many on the land.

Before the First World War, emigration provided a safety valve. The mass emigration of the late nineteenth and early twentieth centuries drained off the excess agrarian population. In the decade 1901-11 Italy suffered—or rather, enjoyed—a net loss through emigration of more than a million and a half people. These departures did not merely keep the population from growing too fast. They had the more positively beneficial effects of reducing the competition for farm laborers' jobs, thereby raising agricultural wages, and of increasing the number of emigrants who might send money home. In the peak year of 1907 these remittances totaled about 100 million dollars—a touching proof of the excesses of self-denial to which the emigrants customarily forced themselves in order to aid their families in the old country. In short, emigration helped produce the national prosperity associated with the "happy" decade of Giolitti's rule.

Much of the emigration was only temporary. Italian workers, despairing of jobs in their own country, would go abroad for a season or a number of years without taking their families along. Such was particularly the case with those who left northern Italy for such neighboring countries as France or Switzerland. Overseas emigration was more likely to be permanent. And in this latter category southerners predominated. Indeed, for Sicilians or Neapolitans, the countries of the New World came to seem more familiar and psychologically closer than the European nations only a few hundred miles to the north of them, to which they rarely thought of going.

Before 1900, the preponderance of Italian overseas emigration went to South America, particularly to Brazil. After the turn of the century, the United States was the more usual goal. Here, after prolonged and discouraging rebuffs, the Italian immigrants eventually found acceptance. In the period between the two World Wars, they broke through the barriers that had confined them to manual labor and to a limited number of trades popularly associated with Italians. But as opposed to their situation in the old country, most of them had become city-dwellers rather than agriculturists. Only in the vineyards of California did Italians constitute a sizeable element in the American rural population.

Meantime, however, the quota acts of 1921 and 1924 had virtually cut off new immigration to the United States. And in the same interwar period, other nations that had received the surplus population of Italy—Argentina, Brazil, Uruguay, Australia, and New Zealand—began to limit the influx of Italians. Mussolini's reaction was characteristic. Instead of doing his best by tactful persuasion to reopen the barriers, he made a virtue of necessity and proclaimed his will that good Italians should remain at home. Nor did he limit himself to measures restricting emigration. He also instituted a "Battle of the Births" to increase the number of Italian children, including such a very practical provision as a tax on bachelors. These latter measures, at least, failed of their effect: the national birth rate steadily fell, and the population continued to increase only because the death rate was falling still faster.

Here again, as with so many of Mussolini's other policies, the gravity of the problem was concealed under a smoke screen of nationalist propaganda—in this case, under the specious argument that the new empire conquered by the Duce in Africa would absorb the excess Italian population. The war's end revealed the true situation. Italy's colonial empire had been lost, and at home the pressure of population had become more overpowering than ever. From 1936 to 1951, despite the war losses, both military and civilian, that Italy had suffered, her population increased from just over 42 million to more than 47 million. And it was currently growing at a rate of nearly half a million a year.

In postwar international planning for large-scale resettlement, priority went to finding new homes for refugees or displaced persons from central and eastern Europe. This was a new and dramatic problem which forced itself on the attention of both statesmen and the public. In comparison, the old and familiar question of Italy's surplus population semed less urgent. The Italian government was left to find foreign outlets for its excess people as best it could by individual negotiation with the various European and American countries.

For the most part, these negotiations brought disappointing results. France, as in the past, proved the most reliably hospitable of all foreign nations. With no domestic unemployment to worry about and an actual shortage of labor in certain sectors of the economy, France was able to absorb a steady flow of Italian workers. The same was true to a lesser extent of Britain and Belgium. But the countries of the New World, which alone were in a position to receive a massive influx of Italians, responded less warmly. The United States did not budge from its established quota policy. And Argentina and Brazil proved only slightly more receptive.

Thus Italy succeeded in finding homes abroad for nowhere near the half million people annually whose departure would at least have kept its population from growing any further. The figure in the early 1950's averaged only about 150,000.* Nor were internal migrations a substitute solution. Initially, there was talk of settling a large number of peninsular Italians on the island of Sardinia, the least densely populated area of the country. The success of a four-year campaign to wipe out the malaria that had made Sardinia so uninviting a place to live in, encouraged expectations of large-scale resettlement. But only small groups of miners, fishermen, and war refugees actually moved to the island. Population movements, either abroad or at home, proved inadequate to meet the problem of Italy's rural surplus. By very necessity the Italian government was driven to re-examine the structure of landholding and to advance reform proposals to relieve the pressure of agrarian discontent.

By no means the whole of the Italian countryside was over-populated. Densities of settlement varied greatly from region to region, and it was not necessarily the most heavily populated areas that presented the most serious social problems. The greater or lesser extent of population pressure derived partly from the relative fertility of the soil, partly from methods of cultivation, partly from the system of land tenure. Similarly, large landholding in itself was not necessarily a social evil. Nor was peasant proprietorship synonymous with contentment and prosperity. Some of the areas of Italy where the peasants owned the land they cultivated were among the most miserable in the country. And other areas where large ownership prevailed ranked among the most prosperous.

The Po valley fell in the latter category. In this, the richest agricultural region of Italy, a concentration of landholding in comparatively few hands—and even absentee ownership, ordinarily considered a grave social danger—seemed to fit the character of the land. The prosperity of the Po valley depended on systematic ir-

---

* A figure arrived at by taking the overseas total of about 140,000, subtracting the number of those who did not remain permanently abroad, and adding an estimate for emigration to European countries, for which no exact statistics were kept.

rigation, which, combined with the raising of commercial crops, encouraged large-scale cultivation. Hence the medium-sized or large farm became the usual agricultural unit. These, however, although they might approach the great estates of the South in size, differed markedly from them in character. They were cultivated on modern scientific principles as a unit rather than parceled out among a number of peasant cultivators. And a great many of them were farms in the English rather than the American sense—that is, they were leased from their owners by tenant farmers who were solely responsible for their cultivation. These cash tenants were usually enterprising, well-trained men, experts at getting a maximum yield from the soil. Although they did not own the land they cultivated, they ranked in the social scale far above most peasant proprietors. It was natural, then, that Mussolini should have grouped them with the possessing classes in his "syndical" organization of Italian agriculture.

The characteristic form of tenure in central Italy—*mezzadria* or share tenancy—was more difficult to generalize about. In the first place, it did not fall clearly into the category of either small or large landholding. The individual farms cultivated under the *mezzadria* system were fairly small: a single peasant and his family, perhaps with the help of one or two hired hands, usually managed them alone. But a number of these farms might be owned by one landlord, so that on a map showing the comparative size of Italian agricultural holdings, Tuscany—the classic home of *mezzadria*—appeared as the region of the highest concentration in land ownership. Moreover, the social effects of *mezzadria* were equivocal. From some standpoints, this system of tenure was a source of social stability. Peasant families who had cultivated the same plot of land for centuries, under a share-tenancy contract hallowed by tradition, might have a feeling of attachment to their land more firmly rooted than that of the average peasant proprietor. This was presumably what Mussolini had in mind when he encouraged the spread of *mezzadria* tenure.

But the stabilizing effects of share tenancy belonged to an earlier era. After the Second World War, the drawbacks of *mezzadria* predominated over its advantages. Under the share-tenancy system, neither the owner nor the tenant had any direct interest in improving the land. And the tenant was virtually driven to cheating the land-lord when it came time to divide up the year's crop. Hence that sly, ironic attitude of peasants toward landowners that travelers fre-quently noted in the Tuscan countryside. We have seen how during the Fascist period *mezzadria* contracts were generally interpreted in favor of the owners. After the war, the terms of these contracts again changed, this time in favor of the tenants. Under a provisional award made by Prime Minister De Gasperi in 1946, the peasants' share of the crop was raised in most cases well above the traditional one-half. But the share tenants remained dissatisfied. Theirs was not the black, unforgiving anger of the peasantry of the South—an explosion of the pent-up grievances of centuries. In central Italy, the resentment was quiet and contained. Nevertheless the share tenants of Tuscany and the Romagna refused to be reconciled to the existing order: they continued to vote Communist.

In a few areas of central Italy such as Latium and the Tuscan Maremma, there existed *latifondi* on the southern model. And the South itself was by no means entirely dominated by the *latifondo*. In the coastal areas around such cities as Naples, Palermo, and Catania, and along the Adriatic shore between Barletta and Lecce, prosperous small farms devoted to the cultivation of fruit and other specialized crops were the rule. Although these favored regions constituted only one-tenth the area of the South, they produced one-third of the value of its agricultural output. Moreover, through-out the South, there were occasional large estates cultivated as single units by resident owners on modern scientific principles. Yet it was the *latifondo* that gave such regions as Calabria and Sicily their tragic character as depressed areas. The *latifondo* was not merely a type of land tenure—it was the symbol of a whole social situation.

A discerning student of Italian rural society has argued that the concept of the *latifondo* should not be limited to the neglected great estate rented out in scattered parcels to impoverished peasants. It should also include the average southern area of small peasant ownership. Both were equally "latifundistic" in character. In both cases, the unit of cultivation was small—usually too small to support a family. In both cases, the peasant generally cultivated a number of scattered strips—a situation that practically forced him to live in a bleak, overcrowded town in the middle of a desolate country-side. And in both cases, he was virtually at the mercy of a large landowner—the dominant figure in the society, the politics, and the land and labor market of the whole area. In social terms it mattered little whether the peasant was technically the owner of his land or whether he rented it from the local agrarian potentate. Sometimes he did both at the same time. But in neither case did he cultivate what could properly be called a farm. He was "only man alone, face to face with a hostile land."*

It was natural, then, that Italian agrarian reformers should have concentrated their attention on the *latifondi*. These and the neighboring areas of tiny peasant holdings were the critical centers of agrarian overpopulation. Dwarf holders and the tenants of the *latifondo* constituted two of the three depressed classes of southern rural society. The third—the lowest element in the social scale —were the landless agricultural workers. These laborers might be of several types. The more fortunate worked on regular contracts, by the season or by the year, or even, in some cases, for a set number of years. The majority, however, who numbered nearly a quarter of the Italian rural population, were simply day laborers. They were called *braccianti*—a name suggesting the grim truth that their only resource was the strength of their own arms. The *braccianti* led a life of extreme insecurity: they could never be sure of employment from one day to the next, and they were frequntly jobless for more than half the year. Under Mussolini, as we have seen, landless farm laborers forfeited most of the gains they had made in the period 1919–22. After the fall of Fascism, their legal situation improved. Technically they enjoyed a wide range of social security benefits. In practice, however, these benefits amounted to very little. The real index of the situation of agrarian labor was not so much the current wage rate—which was well above that of 1938—as the number of people bidding for the available jobs. The steady growth of the population produced such a labor surplus that landowners could safely offer wages far below the rates specified in the standard labor contracts, while rural unemployment greatly exceeded the official figures.

* Mario Einaudi, "The Italian Land: Men, Nature, and Government," *Social Research*, 17: 19–20 (March 1950).

The problem of agrarian labor was not confined to the South. Such northern areas as the Po valley, with its capitalistically operated farms, naturally had large concentrations of landless workers. But here farm laborers more frequently worked on regular contracts than was the case in the South, and the excess of available workers was smaller. It was primarily for the South, where the rural misery was greatest and the pressure of population most intense, that the Italian government, in the spring of 1950, at last made concrete proposals for agrarian reform.

6. THE PROGRESS OF LAND REFORM

When casual observers considered the problem of agrarian reform in Italy, they usually thought of it in terms of a mere redistribution of the land—of splitting up the great estates. Land redistribution was actually only one of four main aspects of the problem. The other three were the reform of farm-tenancy contracts, regulating the wages and working conditions of landless laborers, and the reclamation and improvement of undeveloped areas.*

In the first two fields, the Italian government made little progress. The status of landless labor was not altered, and on tenancy contracts, no change took place after the provisional award made by De Gasperi in 1946. A bill granting virtually permanent tenure to holders of *mezzadria* contracts, presented by the then Minister of Agriculture, Antonio Segni, one of the few convinced reformers among the higher leadership of Christian Democracy, remained buried in the Senate. Both the government and the Parliament seemed reluctant to push it through. And this reluctance was understandable in terms of what a permanent revision of tenancy contracts would have meant. Thousands of middle-class Italians owned a farm or two that they rented out on a *mezzadria* or cash-tenancy basis. For the owners, the revenue from this patch of land represented the difference between straitened circumstances and a comfortable standard of living. Hence a substantial revision of the traditional tenancy arrangements would not simply have reduced

---

* Howard R. Cottam, Robert A. Brand, Victor B. Sullam, "Land Redistribution: One Aspect of Agrarian Reform in Italy," *Foreign Agriculture* (issued by the U.S. Department of Agriculture), 13: 219 (October 1949).

the surplus income of a few hundred families, as in the case of land redistribution: it would have struck at the vital interests of a large segment of the Italian bourgeoisie.

A cautious government, then, limited its concrete reform measures to land redistribution and land improvement. This, at least, was what finally resulted from the tortuous history of land reform under De Gasperi. In the electoral campaign of 1948, the Christian Democrats made a number of reform pledges. But after their victory at the polls, they let a year go by without doing anything. Then in April 1949, on the anniversary of the election, De Gasperi at last came forth with a specific plan. He proposed the redistribution, in peasant holdings averaging twelve acres apiece, of 3.7 million acres of neglected farmland—a total amounting to about 5.5 per cent of the agricultural land of the country.

The government's proposal went to an interministerial commission for further study. Here, for the next few months, it was subjected to the skirmishing attacks of the *Confagricoltura,* the corporative employers' organization in the agricultural field. Meantime, in a number of southern areas, the peasants, who had gotten wind of the planned reform, began to grow impatient. First in the Sila area of Calabria, later in Apulia and the Roman Campagna, they resorted to direct action. From October—the time of the autumn sowing—to the following March, they "occupied" neglected tracts of land. These occupations were frequently more symbolic than real: the peasants would simply march in procession to the land—in at least one case, under the leadership of their parish priest—and formally take possession. In other cases, however, they set up primitive cooperatives and actually began cultivation. At all events, the agitation was sufficiently serious and widespread to prod the government into action. De Gasperi pacified the peasants by bringing in a special law for the Sila area, to be enacted on a rush basis, and by laying before the Chamber the final version of the main law— a full two years after the original electoral pledge had been given.

The proposed bill provided for the expropriation of from 10 to 95 per cent of the acreage of large estates, on a scale varying inversely with the intensity of cultivation, to be gauged by yield per acre. Hence in effect the measure fell heavily on the neglected *latifondi* of the South, while practically exempting from its provisions the scientifically managed farms of the Po valley. Besides this blanket premium for good management, the bill also specified a complicated series of additional exemptions, for example, to protect the interests of landowners with more than one son. Experts calculated that in no case would the law reduce an estate to smaller than 74 acres, or leave it larger than 2470. The peasants were to acquire title to the land by paying installments over a period of thirty years, and the owners were to receive indemnities, partly in cash, partly in government securities.

As postwar land reform measures went, this was a moderate proposal. It would have deprived no one of his birthright, and the provisions for compensation to the owners were commendably generous. But few people are ever ready to give up their property without protest, and the *Confagricoltura* was a highly conservative, well-knit body, resolved to fight the reform at every turn. Hence the law in practice proved to be less extensive than as originally proposed. The large landowners not only worked out a number of dodges for evading its terms—such as giving land to their relatives or making dummy sales to peasants; they also succeeded in reducing the scope of the law itself.

As originally presented, the land redistribution was set up in three stages. To the Sila area, where the gravest peasant disturbances had occurred, it was to be applied immediately. For a selected number of other regions, where reform appeared to be of comparable urgency, an advance installment of the main law—the "slice" or *Stralcio*—was to be voted earlier than the rest. Finally, there was to be the full law to cover the remainder of the country. Two of these stages were completed roughly on schedule. By May 1950, the Sila law had been enacted. The following October, the Parliament voted the *Stralcio,* and in December a special law for Sicily was passed by the regional assembly. But then, with something at last to show its peasant constituents, the government quietly allowed the main law to drop. Less than one-half of the land originally scheduled for redistribution actually went to the peasants.

For each main area, the government established an autonomous *opera* (works administration) or *ente* (public corporation). After this organization had been set up and the agricultural experts were on the spot, the first order of business was to make an exact census of landholding—a complicated matter, since the registers were usually out of date and the proprietors not always cooperative. Then came the selection of the portions of land to be expropriated. When the final list had been established, it was posted in the towns concerned, and the experts proceeded to the most difficult task of all, the delimitation of the peasant plots. Here the problem was to balance size against fertility and accessibility so as to come out with farms that were as nearly as possible equally desirable. Of course not everyone could be satisfied and complaints were frequent, particularly in areas where existing peasant leaseholds were to be amalgamated so as to convert a number of scattered strips into a compact farm. The final act was the assignment of the land itself.

Beyond the assignment of the land lay the further tasks of supplying the peasants with cattle and building houses on the individual plots. And beyond that loomed the question of reclamation and improvement—the fourth aspect of agrarian reform as a whole and the other area in which the De Gasperi government made substantial progress. This latter entailed a large number of public works projects such as dams and aqueducts to harness the undependable southern watercourses. The greater part of the funds for such improvement were assigned to the *Cassa per il Mezzogiorno* (Southern Italy Fund), originally established in 1950, with an initial annual appropriation of 110 billion lire, which was later substantially increased.

By the end of its first eight years of operation, the land reform had resulted in the redistribution of a million and three-quarters acres, nearly two-thirds of which were located in the South and the Islands. Newly-established farms had averaged twenty-two acres in size, while more than half of those who received them had been former agricultural laborers and another two-fifths share or cash tenants. Despite the deep-rooted traditions of favoritism, deceit, and suspicion of the government characteristic of Italy's depressed areas, the local organizations in charge of land redistribution had operated with relative honesty and efficiency. The *Cassa per il Mezzogiorno* had not become the gigantic pork barrel that the government's critics had predicted. Taken all together, this was a most impressive achievement, which in effect had broken the power of the great landowners and given a wholly unprecedented social mobility to wide areas of the Italian South. Yet those whom the reform had benefited were only slightly more numerous than the net annual increase in population; in terms of Italy's demographic situation of the mid-1950's, there simply was not enough land to go around. It was still too early to predict the great social change of the next decade—the move of nearly three million southerners northward—that was to bring relief both to the problem of Italy's population surplus and to the plight of its underemployed agrarian labor.

Moreover, in terms of moral attitudes and creating a new sense of local responsibility, the reform had largely failed of its effect. Its Christian Democratic administrators had operated in paternalistic fashion without any significant participation by the peasants themselves. And the directives they carried out had been correspondingly uniform. True to their original ideology, the Christian Democrats had conceived the reform as the creation of individual farmsteads; they intended that the new rural proprietors should actually live on their land like American farmers or the peasants of the happier regions of Italy to the north of Rome. This was not only the most expensive type of land redistribution—far more expensive than establishing some kind of village co-operative—it was also unsuited to several of the crucial zones affected by the reform.

In the Po delta, the Tuscan Maremma, and the irrigable level regions of the South—totaling perhaps 40 per cent of the area subject to land reform—the creation of 12- to 35-acre farms had produced good results. In the poorer regions of the South and Sicily, however, in the back country and the clay-soil uplands, the reform had worked in a capricious and disorderly fashion. The existing village complexes had been broken up, as only part of the peasants who dwelt there had received land and been moved away from their previous homes. Critics of this process suggested that it would have been better to have left the old villages in being—to have foregone the expensive job of transplanting a portion of their inhabitants— and instead to have devoted the funds available to raising the technical level of the whole countryside.*

* For this line of criticism, see Manlio Rossi-Doria, *Dieci anni di politica agraria nel Mezzogiorno* (Bari, 1958).

Finally, in terms of the long-range needs of the Italian South, both land redistribution and the improvement schemes administered by the *Cassa per il Mezzoqiorno* marked only a beginning. Logically they could be thought of as little more than a pre-industrialization program. For the problem of the South was not merely one of dividing up the land or raising the peasants' standard of living. It was a question of breaking a whole vicious pattern—of making a new start where the old ways of doing things had dragged the area farther and farther back in the unequal race to keep up with the North. It was a question of "soldering together" the North and the South—of closing the gap between them. It involved ending the exploitation of southerners by northerners—breaking the industrial monopoly of the northwestern triangle of cities and spreading industrial activity over the whole country. It meant evening out the discrepancies of economy and manners that placed one-half of the country alongside the advanced modern nations like France or Britain, while the other half remained back with Spain or the Balkans. It was a problem of fusing two societies which existed simultaneously and in tragic disequilibrium—the static, stratified society of an agrarian regime that had outlived its usefulness, and the advanced society of a modern industrial state which was itself damaged by the possibilities of exploitation the other society afforded.* Without such a fusion political democracy in Italy threatened to remain abstract, precarious, and incomplete.

This problem—virtually insoluble in the early 1950's—could be approached with some degree of hope only after the events of the next half decade had drastically shaken up both Italy's politics and the balance of forces within the Italian economy.

* Francesco Compagna, *La lotta politica italiana nel secondo dopoguerra e il Mezzogiorno* (Bari, 1950), pp. 48, 137–138.

9

The Heirs of De Gasperi and
the "Opening to the Left"

THE TWO decades after the fall of Mussolini divide into four clearly-marked political periods of five years each. The first half decade, from 1943 to 1948, was by far the most eventful—the period of war, resistance, and liberation, the growing challenge of Communism, and the gradual displacement of the militant anti-Fascists by the more moderate and compromising Christian Democrats led by Alcide De Gasperi. The second period—from the election of 1948 to that of 1953—was the era in which De Gasperi governed as unchallenged master of the country and in which the cold war dominated the international scene. There followed a half decade of uncertainty: while no alternative to Christian Democratic rule emerged, the bases of this rule became shaky, as profound changes both in the Italian economy and in the world ideological alignment discredited the old political formulas. By the election of 1958 it was apparent that something new was stirring among the Italian parties and the Italian electorate. The fourth half decade was to be dominated by the search for a fresh political formula—which gradually revealed itself as the inescapable imperative of an "opening to the Left."

1. THE FALL OF DE GASPERI

The provincial elections of 1951 and 1952 had demonstrated that after seven years of rule De Gasperi's hold on the electorate was slipping. Both of the disloyal oppositions had made gains, but what was particularly disquieting was the progress of the Neo-Fascists and the Monarchists in the South. The four democratic parties together had polled no more than a bare majority of the vote.

The narrowness of this democratic margin came as a warning that in the elections to the Chamber of Deputies scheduled for 1953, the government would have an exceedingly close call. Almost immediately the leaders of Christian Democracy began to cast about for new electoral devices that might strengthen the democratic parties. After a summer and autumn of involved debate, they emerged with a scheme which seemed well fitted to turn the trick —an electoral bonus of 85 seats to the coalition of parties that should poll at least 50.01 per cent of the popular vote. In effect, the new law was calculated to raise a bare majority in the Chamber to a comfortable working majority of 65 per cent that would give Christian Democracy and its allies sufficient elbowroom in which to govern.

Some such electoral change was almost unavoidable, and De Gasperi saw no alternative but to demand it. In form, however, the proposal was unfortunate: it recalled too closely the Acerbo Law of 1923 by which Mussolini had similarly sought to assure himself a safe majority. Hence the minor democratic parties were not particularly happy about it. They knew that their weakness condemned them to follow where the Christian Democrats led and that they had no choice but to participate in the proposed Center coalition. But they would have liked the bonus of seats to have been smaller: they feared that under the new law Christian Democracy *as a party* would retain the absolute majority in the Chamber which it had won in 1948 and that after the election, as before, it would be able to dispense with the support of its minor allies.

Nevertheless, nearly all the Social Democrats, Republicans, and Liberals went along with the Christian Democrats in voting the new law, which, after scenes of parliamentary violence and an unparalleled filibuster on the part of the leftist bloc, was passed by the Chamber in January 1953. Only a handful of Social Democrats broke party discipline and voted against it. Duly expelled from the party, they established an "autonomist" electoral list independent of both the Center coalition and the parties of the Left. This autonomist current—later strengthened by two or three notable figures such as former Prime Minister Parri—offered the first great surprise of the electoral campaign.

The second was the rough going the new measure encountered in the Senate. Here, where passage had been anticipated as easier than in the Chamber, the Left repeated the same obstructive tactics. It was only at the end of March, in a scene of total pandemonium, that the electoral law slipped through. Disgusted with the indiscipline of the Senate, De Gasperi determined on a bold course. He persuaded President Einaudi to dissolve the Senate along with the Chamber—although the former's term had still a year to run. This meant not only that the institution of senators by right automatically lapsed: it meant that the government parties were risking their Senate majority in an appeal to the electorate held simultaneously with the Chamber elections and one in which the new law just voted with such difficulty would not apply. The polling date was set for June 7.

The result was an election from which no one emerged as the victor. In some respects the campaign was a repetition of that of 1948: the Church, Catholic Action, and the American Embassy repeated their transparently veiled admonitions. Again De Gasperi pleaded for unity in support of the government bloc. But this time it was not simply the Communists he was attacking: he turned at least as much of his fire on the Neo-Fascists. The crowds, however, seemed less interested than in 1948. The voters remained apathetic, and it came as a surprise when an unprecedented 93 per cent of the electorate went to the polls.

Everywhere the "swindle law" was the main target of the opposition, whether from the Right or from the Left. But these two oppositions were less united than before. On both sides, the left-wing Socialists and the Communists, the Monarchists and the Neo-Fascists, ran separate lists. This was partly through electoral calculation: both extremes knew that they had no chance of winning the bonus provided for in the new law, and that they would do better if they underlined their opposition to it by refraining from forming coalitions. There was also a deeper reason. The two less extreme parties, the Socialists and the Monarchists, were growing restive with their allies. They wished to emphasize their moderation—and with it their possible usefulness to a future government whose majority might be either non-existent or precariously slim.

And indeed this second calculation proved correct. By the narrowest of margins, the democratic coalition failed to qualify for the electoral bonus. (If they had had the vote of the "autonomists," they would have made it.) But—since the workings of proportional representation are only approximate—they obtained a 16-seat majority in the Chamber, and one of 13 seats in the Senate. For the minor democratic parties, and particularly for the Social Democrats and Republicans, the election proved a near debacle. The Christian Democrats, on the other hand, did rather better than expected: with 40.1 per cent of the popular vote, they regained more than a third of the support they had lost between 1948 and 1952. The Communists and Neo-Fascists made moderate advances. The greatest gainers, however, were the left-wing Socialists and Monarchists.

The former, whose leader Nenni had been making vague motions toward independence from the Communists ever since a trip he had taken to Prague in 1951, raised their representation in the Chamber from 52 to 75 seats. If the Socialists should choose to break with the Communists, they were now in a position to bring the government a precious accretion of strength. Similar vistas gleamed before the Monarchists. This party, which before had ranked as an amorphous collection of anti-democratic traditionalists, held together by the money of the Neapolitan shipowner Achille Lauro, now emerged as a parliamentary force in its own right. With 40 Chamber seats (11 more than the MSI) the Monarchists might be able to offer De Gasperi exactly the extra support he needed—and at less of a risk to the government than an understanding with Nenni. Both of the new pivotal parties demanded their price. And with the Monarchists this meant a slowing down of the agrarian reform.

It was on the Right, then, that the election had produced the most serious contender for a share in governmental responsibility. During the succeeding years the Monarchist bid for power was continually advanced; it replaced Neo-Fascism as the "clear and present" danger to Italian democracy. In itself the Monarchist party did not amount to much—a disparate gathering of southern demagogues with a constituency of politically illiterate peasants and a superstitious Neapolitan plebs. It had no clear principles—its royalism was merely for show—and it stood for little but the defense of the established order camouflaged by the vacuous slogans of traditional nationalism. Yet as a symptom of an attitude, organized Monarchism epitomized what was most disquieting in Italian political life. This De Gasperi realized as he sought to organize his eighth successive ministry.

Weary and downcast after his electoral exertions, the man who had been prime minister for seven and a half years and master of his country for five, set about the unrewarding task of pulling together his reduced and demoralized parliamentary following. He soon ruled out both of the two suggested enlargements of the four-party coalition. With the Monarchists he refused to traffic: as a man who had undergone prison and political extinction in the defense of democracy, he would have denied his whole past if he had consented to do business with a party that scarcely bothered to pay lip service to democratic principles. "Operation Nenni," as the Italians called the alternative, proved equally impossible; the leader of the left-wing Socialists, while broadly hinting at his independence from Communist direction, refused to make any statement clearly dissociating himself from the party with which he had worked in alliance for nearly twenty years.

This meant that the Social Democrats must also be counted out as active participants in the government: to enter the ministry without Nenni's support, Saragat felt, would be to give open recognition to what was in fact the case—that Social Democracy could no longer claim to speak for any substantial segment of the Italian working classes. Inevitably, then, the government would have to represent a minority of the Chamber. De Gasperi's problem reduced itself to one of organizing a minority government sufficiently satisfactory to the lesser parties to command their passive support on a vote of confidence.

It was not until July 21, more than six weeks after the election, that he was at last ready to present his new ministry, consisting solely of Christian Democrats, to the Italian Parliament. Both Senate and Chamber received his declaration with frosty reserve. Day after day, through the burning discomfort of a Roman heat wave, the Prime Minister sat listening to the oratory, looking ever paler and sadder as his chances dimmed and finally flickered out. On July 28, he rose to reply to his critics. The verdict was already certain. The galleries were overflowing with the select of journalism and society: even the pretty girls had come back from the beaches to watch the old man fall. The Romans have been noted through several thousand years of history for their special form of cruelty. And they showed it to the full in the way they treated the man who claimed with some justice to have saved the country from Communism. Before a hostile, gloating audience, De Gasperi made his last address as prime minister. With his back to the wall, he tried for one more time the old parliamentary tricks: in a feeble, pathetic gesture of appeasement he sought to win abstention from the Monarchists. But his speech changed not a single vote. All three minor parties abstained; the Monarchists voted against. The final tally was 282–263.

The fall of De Gasperi was a climactic event in Italian parliamentary history. Depending on whether one was Italian or American, the reaction to it was notably different. The American Embassy was sunk in gloom: an air of stern disquiet reigned, as the staff speculated on the uncertain future of the alliance they had nurtured. Most Italians were far less worried—many actually jubilant. The myth of De Gasperi's indispensability had been exploded, and Italy was on its own.

2. THE SEARCH FOR A POLITICAL FORMULA

The long-range effects of De Gasperi's fall were not immediately apparent. Where the old Prime Minister had failed in July to convince the newly-elected deputies of the virtues of a single-party, minority government, another Christian Democrat, Giuseppe Pella, succeeded a month later. But the Pella ministry rested on a grave equivocation. Its initial declaration had been so skillfully phrased as to raise hopes in nearly every quarter of the Chamber. Only as the autumn wore on did it become clear that what Pella was after was a gigantic act of *trasformismo*—a complete refashioning of his government (and, in the process, of the Christian Democratic party) to suit the wishes of both the economic and the clerical Right. Eventually Pella's own party brought him down. A similar fate overcame

Fanfani after a mere two weeks in office. By February 1954, when Scelba became prime minister, Italian political life seemed to have returned to normal.

In fact, with De Gasperi's retirement and his death a year later, the Christian Democratic party entered on five years of hesitation and flux: neither party nor country found a political formula to replace the "De Gasperi line." Inevitably all the prime ministers were Christian Democrats. Although the party had lost its parliamentary majority, it still commanded something over forty per cent of the popular vote, and it was the only political grouping capable of governing the country. But it was far from clear *what sort* of Christian Democratic government there should be. Was it to be a coalition of Christian Democracy with its small laical allies, such as De Gasperi himself had preferred? Or was it to be a *monocolore* government of the leading party alone? And of the various factions within Christian Democracy, which was to provide the prime minister?

In the third era of Italy's post-Fascist history, neither of these questions was satisfactorily settled. Among the successors of De Gasperi leaders of the Right (Pella), of the Center (Scelba), and of the Left (Segni) of Christian Democracy all had a chance to be prime minister, but none was able to give the party a definitive political orientation. Nor did the most powerful figure within the Christian Democratic hierarchy, its general secretary and manager of its electoral machine, Amintore Fanfani, ever himself succeed in forming a viable government. Moreover, the final prime minister of the half-decade, Adone Zoli, was an honest nonentity of uncertain political views running a stopgap ministry intended only to get the country through to the elections. Similarly with respect to the government's party composition, both of the two possible formulas were tried, with no conclusive results: of the post-De Gasperi ministries, two (those of Pella and Zoli) were single-party affairs, while two others (Scelba and Segni) revived De Gasperi's quadripartite formula. Yet neither type worked in any permanently satisfactory fashion. The *monocolore* was dependent on the benevolent neutrality of at least one other party of reasonable size—which in practice usually proved to be the Monarchists—while in the four-party government, the minor participants gradually lost patience with a dominant coalition partner that quite obviously had no intention of respecting their wishes. By the time of Segni's fall, in May of 1957, the quadripartite formula had just about lost its meaning.

Yet one of the successive ministries had had a substantial record of accomplishment and had inaugurated programs that gave an imaginative guide to the next half-decade of Italy's social development. The government of Antonio Segni was the longest-lived of the post-De Gasperi ministries; it was the richest in talent; and it was the first to put the country's economic needs in the center of its program. De Gasperi himself had been bored by economics: he had tended to settle issues of this sort in the way he settled so many other matters—by giving in to the pressure group that at the moment seemed to have the strongest political claim. His immediate successors—Pella and Scelba—had led ministries too short-lived and too unsure of their parliamentary base to engage in long-term economic planning. With Segni, however, there opened a new era in Christian Democratic policy: with a representative of the party's reform-minded Left for the first time providing the prime minister, the way was opened to constructive statesmanship. And besides being a professor and the original architect of the land reform program, the new head of the government was a Sardinian—that is, a man who from his earliest youth had known the misery of Italy's neglected and impoverished provinces.

The appointment of Segni ended the stagnation that had descended upon Italian politics with the liquidation of its outstanding postwar issues—the reacquisition of Trieste and the completion of the agrarian reform. Or, more precisely, Segni's nomination to the prime ministership came as the logical consequence of a related event of two months earlier which had initially broken the political impasse—the election of Giovanni Gronchi, in May of 1955, to the presidency of the Republic.

Gronchi's election was the first of a series of major surprises that were to enliven the Italian scene for the next two years. For Gronchi, although a Christian Democrat himself, was not the choice of the party's political machine, which had advanced a conservative non-party candidate. To its intense chagrin, it found itself outvoted by an impromptu coalition of Communists, Socialists, and Christian Democratic dissidents. Gronchi, like Segni, was an elderly leader of the Christian Democratic Left; he had a reputation for neutralist leanings and for being "soft" toward Communism; as president of the Chamber of Deputies for more than seven years he had displayed a firmness and impartiality that had won him respect in all political camps. And in his new role as President of the Republic he set out to strengthen his office and to make it an effective force in the national life. Hence one of his first acts was to call on a leader of similar temper to head a new ministry.

And so in the first year of the Gronchi-Segni era, from mid-1955 to mid-1956, Italian political life once more began to move. Most notably, there was finally established the Constitutional Court that had been promised eight years before when the new republican constitution had come into effect. The earlier Christian Democratic governments had shown no enthusiasm for setting up such an insti- tution—which, in manifest imitation of the United States Supreme Court, was to pass on the constitutionality of legislative acts. De Gasperi and his immediate successors had preferred to leave things as they were, to keep their own authority untrammeled, and to take advantage of the Fascist security laws that remained on the statute books. By the time the Segni government at last established the new court, Italian constitutional law experts had almost given up hope that it would ever materialize. And the latters' expectations—as well as the forebodings of Christian Democratic conservatives—were immediately confirmed by the vigorous fashion in which the court, under the presidency of Enrico De Nicola, set about sweeping away the accumulated debris of Fascist administrative practice.

Almost equally important were two of the Segni government's economic measures. The law on subsoil deposits (oil and natural gas) regulated a potentially explosive situation by striking a compro- mise between the pressure of concession-hungry American com- panies and the already existing rights of the Italian parastatal monopoly. And with the implementation of the Vanoni Plan (which had originated under the previous ministry), Italy attained another long-standing programmatic goal*

In its second year the record of the Segni government was less inspiring. Defeatism and weariness set in as the Prime Minister began to appease the conservative and the routine-minded among the Christian Democratic leadership by backing away from one controverted issue after another. First he ran into difficulties with

* See Chapter 10.

the Constitutional Court: his Minister of the Interior had refused to carry out the court's rulings on the unconstitutionality of certain provisions of the Fascist Public Security Law—indeed, had defended in the Chamber the Fascist institution of *confino;* Segni supported his minister in this and subsequent disputes, and eventually "Chief Justice" De Nicola resigned. Similarly, in another controversy involving a legacy from the Fascist past, Segni took the safe and unimaginative course. For years the Christian Democratic Left had been demanding a rationalization of the IRI industrial holdings. The *Confindustria* wanted to leave things as they were. In the showdown, Segni succumbed to *Confindustria* pressure and appointed as his minister for IRI affairs a Christian Democratic leader with excellent connections in organized industry.

When in May of 1957, after a record twenty-two months in office, the Segni government fell, it had long ago spent its reforming zeal. And the occasion of its fall was symptomatic—an intricate parliamentary tangle over the draft law regulating agrarian tenancy, an issue capable of splitting Italian society from top to bottom, and a touchstone of reform that had brought grief to nearly every Italian government for half a generation. After Segni's fall, there was no logical candidate to take his place. In the previous four years, all possible ministerial formulas had been tried: Left, Right, and Center in the Christian Democratic leadership had had their chance, and the party had juggled its parliamentary alliances in every conceivable fashion. Under the circumstances the appointment of Zoli's caretaker government to muddle its way through the remaining pre-electoral year seemed the only expedient available.

3. THE ELECTION OF 1958

On the surface little happened during Zoli's tenure of office. But just below the level of interest of the American press, a whole series of developments were in progress that were to alter profoundly the alignment of forces in the coming election. And the more significant of these had had their origin in that year of transition 1955–1956 when so much in Italian politics seemed to be on the move.

On the Right there had occurred both a regrouping of forces and an overall loss of strength. The two years preceding the election had seen a slow but cumulative exodus from the old conservative parties.

Already public opinion surveys made after the 1953 balloting had demonstrated that these movements had little appeal for Italian youth. The Monarchists had split into two factions: both the more orthodox (or "national") branch of Italian Monarchism and the Neo-Fascists (MSI) approached the 1958 election in a state of demoralization, disorganization, and a pitiable shortage of funds. Of the rightist parties only the Liberals and the dissident (or "popular") Monarchists went to the polls with any confidence.

The first of these had almost more money than it needed or could respectably digest. Ever since its talented general secretary, Giovanni Francesco Malagodi, had converted it into an unabashed mouthpiece for the *Confindustria* and other organized business interests, the Liberal party had enjoyed more funds per capita and more press support than any other Italian political group. But the nature of its program restricted its electoral appeal to a narrow segment of the population. In contrast, Popular Monarchism was more amorphous and plebeian. The personal emanation of Achille Lauro, it had seceded in 1954 from the main body of the Monarchists in protest against the latters' pedantic opposition to the government of Christian Democracy. What Lauro quite obviously wanted was to make himself indispensable to the governing party.

As the electoral campaign opened, Lauro began to change the character of his own party to give it a wider appeal: its monarchist label he quietly dropped, and for it he substituted a *qualunquista* or "know-nothing" program. With the tricks that had already proved their worth in Neapolitan city politics—personal showmanship, grandiloquent promises, and *largesse* on a massive scale—Lauro set out to win the vote of the politically retrograde southern constituency. Thus he made his party a vehicle for the miscellaneous (and often contradictory) grievances of the South: he tried to appeal to all elements in its population—and, in addition, to those displaced southerners who had been migrating in a steady stream to the northern industrial cities. To protest against discriminatory treatment by the North, to defend the interests of the South against outside exploitation—this became the new rationale of Popular Monarchism. As an incoherent protest on the part of the economically backward, it recalled the movement of small shopkeepers that Pierre Poujade had led in France a few years earlier.

Lauro himself defined his party as "an opposition . . . that goes along with the dominant forces." By the very illogic of this characterization he betrayed what he was really after. In the new parliament, Lauro's seats would be up for sale, and it was his purpose to show the Christian Democrats that of all the possible alliances offered, his would be the most satisfactory. This argument took on particular plausibility from the fact that Christian Democracy's earlier allies—the three small democratic parties of the Center— were all for one reason or another in a state of crisis or change.

Thus the Liberals, by their transmutation into a frank interest-group, had become so conservative, in economic and social terms, as to offer few political attractions. Similarly the Republicans— although reinforced by the more truly liberal element from the former party—no longer had any substantial constituency: they had been reduced to little more than a last refuge of anti-clerical protest. And the Social Democrats had been caught in the repercussions of a series of explosions on the Italian Left.

The chain of events that rocked both the Communist and the Socialist constituencies began with the address of February 1956 in which Khrushchev detailed to an astounded party congress the crimes of the defunct Stalin. The first effect on the Italian Communists was one of liberation and relief: with the Soviet leaders apparently giving the cue for ideological latitude at home and for more tolerant "guidance" abroad, the Italian party undertook its own liberalizing experiments. And its leader—Palmiro Togliatti—since Stalin's death the senior figure, in prestige and experience, among European Communists, began to send out feelers of a "polycentrist" variety. Through the cautious wording of his public statements gleamed the ambition of establishing Italy as a rival center in Communist influence to those already existing in Russia, in China, and in Yugoslavia.

The autumn brought a brutal end to these illusions. With the suppression of the Hungarian revolution, the Soviet leadership swung sharply back toward orthodoxy. And Togliatti—always a master of ideological modulation—himself began to make an involuted return to safer channels. But his "re-Stalinization" of the Italian Communist party was effected at a terrible price. For the first time in postwar history, the party congress of December 1956 saw a vociferous opposition to the official leadership. In the person of the young Antonio Giolitti—the grandson of Italy's leading statesman of the early twentieth century—the newly-discovered "liberalism" within the Italian Communist party found eloquent expression.

Subsequently Giolitti left the party. And with him—or shortly thereafter—went a large group of the writers and intellectuals who had given Italian Communism its unparalleled distinction of talent. Overall—and according to Togliatti's own admission—by 1957 the party had lost at least 700 thousand of the two and a half million members it had claimed six years earlier. And of these the post-1956 loss of forty thousand had largely consisted of the party elite, of intellectuals and skilled workers. As the election of 1958 approached, Italian Communism seemed to have retained most of its voting strength. But it had lost its driving power. With so much of its intelligence and its moral fervor gone, it ran the deadly danger of being reduced to a protest party of the economically desperate and the "sub-proletariat"—the unemployed, the pensioners, and agrarian labor.

On the Socialist side, the post-1956 crisis had been even more complex. For Pietro Nenni the dethronement of Stalin seemed to offer the long-awaited opportunity for his party's deliverance from Communist bondage. In the spring of 1956, Nenni declared his independence. And the following summer he entered into negotiations with his earlier enemy, Giuseppe Saragat, for the reunion of his own majority Socialists with the smaller Social Democratic party whose secession Saragat had led nine years before. In these discussions, Nenni went a long way to satisfy the Social Democratic demands. He agreed to break his unity of action pact with the Communists and to accept the Atlantic alliance as the basis of Italian foreign policy. But he would not comply with Saragat's broader requirement that he recognize in effect that the latter had been right all along and convert to the Social Democratic formula. This, Nenni suspected, might entail the ruin of his party. For it meant giving up his vision of Italian Socialism as something different from the other European movements which bore that name—a party that would combine democratic method with revolutionary militancy as none of them had been able to do—and his wider aspiration of eventually leading into his fold a large portion both of the Communists and of the Christian Democratic Left. Nenni further saw that so long as his own party followers and the Communists shared the same trade-union organization, he ran the danger of repeating Saragat's performance of a decade earlier. At all costs he wished to avoid the fate that had befallen Italian Social Democracy—of being reduced to a clique of leaders with only fragments of working-class support.

Thus by the beginning of 1957 it became apparent that no immediate reunion of the two Socialist parties would occur. And the electoral campaign of the following year found them in an intense competition for the marginal voter. On the Social Democratic side, Saragat could point to the purity of his own ideological past. But Nenni offered more—a new perspective and an opportunity to break the stalemate in Italian politics that had confined effective power to the Christian Democrats and their allies, on the one side, and the Communists and their dependents, on the other. Although burdened with a lifetime of political mistakes, Pietro Nenni approached the electorate with a rough and good-humored candor. From a democratic standpoint, he still left much to be desired: his party machine refused to break all its local ties with the Communists. Yet to intellectuals and others tired of casting a protest vote for a minor party that stood no real chance, Nenni offered a welcome alternative. Now for the first time since 1946, the independent voter had a chance to support democracy without endorsing—either directly or through the electoral alliance system—the claims of the Christian Democrats. Nenni might be far from blameless; but his new-found independence had at least restored fluidity to the Italian electoral process. It was significant for the attitude of this sort of voter that at the end of 1957 *Unità Popolare,* the tiny group of "autonomist" intellectuals that had successfully combatted the "swindle law" of 1953, should have decided to affiliate with Nenni's Italian Socialist Party.

As for Christian Democracy, a democratic alternative was the last thing its leadership wanted to confront. Once again, as in 1948 and 1953, the governing party sought to run on the claims of its own indispensability: Fanfani's machine aimed to repeat the performance of ten years earlier and win an absolute majority in the

Chamber of Deputies. Shoving the old party "notables" into the background, the hard-driving party secretary turned the election of 1958 into a kind of personal plebiscite. Its verdict was to be read both within and outside the Christian Democratic ranks as an endorsement or rejection of his political management. The time had long passed when Fanfani had emerged as the young, aspiring, ascetic candidate of the new or corporative Left within Christian Democracy. Now he had been transmuted into the thorough politician, flexible in ideology though ruthless in decision, with all his energies directed to a single goal. Nothing less than an absolute majority would satisfy him—nothing less than irrefutable proof that Christian Democracy, and Christian Democracy alone, was capable of governing the country.

In this hope Fanfani was disappointed. The electorate refused to be bullied and tended to vote as personal preferences suggested. In retrospect, the election of 1958 proved the "freest" consultation of the Italian people that had occurred since the war's end. For now for the first time there was no *arrière pensée,* no national obsession to deflect the normal expression of political sentiments. In 1946, the overriding issue had been monarchy against republic; in 1948, there had been the Communist danger; in 1953, the "swindle law" had threatened to distort the pattern of preferences. In the election of May 25, 1958, such extraneous issues were lacking. With the political pressure notably lowered, the voters were free to make the choices that interest or ideology prompted.

The result was a catastrophe for all the parties of the Right. Together they polled no more than 9.5 per cent of the vote. Lauro's clownish tactics had failed; so had the free spending of the *Confindustria.* With the election of 1958, authoritarian conservatism ceased to be a popular force in Italy, although its continuing hold on a powerful segment of the political class was to be manifested repeatedly during the next two years.

In contrast, the parties of the Left either gained or held their own. The Communists stayed about at their previous level—22.7 per cent —which in view of the troubles they had undergone since 1956 was a remarkable achievement. Both Socialist parties made advances— Nenni's, with 14.2 per cent, rather more than Saragat's; among the new Socialist deputies was Antonio Giolitti, who had successfully opposed his former Communist comrades in his native Piedmont. The election of 1958 put the Italian Socialist party, for the first time since the rupture with Saragat eleven years earlier, in a position of decisive influence; already the "opening to the Left" was beginning to appear an outside possibility.

Yet the Christian Democrats still dominated the political horizon. On balance, the election strengthened them, if it did not quite prove their indispensability in the way Fanfani had hoped. With 42.2 per cent of the vote, the Christian Democrats regained some of the following they had lost in 1953. No doubt the nearly simultaneous advent of De Gaulle in France had helped them. For the argument from French experience worked both ways: to advocates of strong authority, it suggested a precedent worthy of imitation; to those fearful for the future of European democracy, it gave warning of what might happen in the absence of stable government under Christian Democratic leadership.

Thus, though the electoral results failed to reach the plebiscitary proportions at which Fanfani had aimed, they amounted to an endorsement of continued Christian Democratic rule. The new Socialist independence and the Socialist electoral gains foreshadowed an alternative—but its realization was to be delayed for four more years. In the meantime, the only sensible course, and the one that President Gronchi chose, was to give Fanfani a chance to govern. Fanfani likewise had been kept in the wings for four years; now at last he could put together the ministry of social and economic reform which he had so long advocated.

4. THE TAMBRONI "ADVENTURE"

Again and again in the history of democratic politics, the man who has waited his chance too long proves a disappointment in office. (Once more from French experience, we may recall Gambetta and Paul Reynaud.) So it was with Fanfani in the summer and autumn of 1958. He brought the Social Democrats into his government; his program of "progress without adventures" both stimulated and reassured; specifically, he proposed to raise educational expenditures by more than a third over a ten-year period. Yet despite his brave beginnings, Fanfani skirted the prickly questions that his country's economic expansion was thrusting into prominence. On the central issue of industrial planning, the Christian Democratic left wing—now ostensibly in power—betrayed its lack of a coherent economic philosophy. Nor did Fanfani take adequate precautions against the enemies within his own party—the old "notables," the clericals, the economic conservatives—who began to snipe at him quite openly as the autumn wore on. Eventually, at the beginning of 1959, the attacks of these "sharpshooters" brought Fanfani down. The punishment he had so often dealt his predecessors now fell on his own head. Outsiders may well be puzzled at a political system in which the dominant party regularly destroys the prime ministers who have emanated from its ranks.

What to do next? Again, as in the case of Pella and Zoli, a *monocolore* seemed the only choice. And again, the old force of *trasformismo* was apparent in the leader assigned this uninspiring task. Antonio Segni had earlier been a reformer; his first and highly promising ministry had bogged down during its second year in inertia and appeasement of the vested interests; now, in February 1959, he returned to power—with President Gronchi's blessing—as the avowed candidate of Christian Democracy's right wing. The two party notables had evolved together: the President and the Prime Minister who had once represented the reforming element among Christian Democracy's senior leadership had wearily adapted to the status quo.

If the *monocolore* was a well-tried Christian Democratic device, the way Segni interpreted this reliable formula was a startling novelty. For the first time such a minority government lasted a full year: what had previously been thought an anomaly or stopgap now began to seem perfectly normal. And the manner in which the second Segni ministry managed to survive was also novel: the Prime Minister and his colleagues gratefully accepted the support of Monarchist votes—which had earlier been considered a shameful under-the-table transaction. Five of these colleagues were openly favorable to the *Confindustria*, including the key minister responsible for IRI and the other "state participations."

Thus for all its feebleness the Segni government of 1959 made one decisive contribution to Italy's political development. It clarified the ambiguities of "center" rule. It ended the equivocations of a formula of government that in practice was far more conservative than it purported to be. For the first time since the fall of Parri fourteen years earlier, the democratic Left and Right in Italian politics were brought into sharp confrontation. Christian Democracy could no longer evade the choice: it had to decide in which direction it was going to move—toward Socialism or the *Confindustria*, toward economic planning or continued boom and drift.

The logical next step, then, when Segni finally wore out his mandate, was an "opening to the Left"—an understanding with Nenni. This was what Fanfani proposed in March 1960. He was met with the stinging rebuke of a double veto—by the *Confindustria*, of course, but also, and more troublingly, by the Vatican itself through the columns of the *Osservatore Romano*. And this latter veto was all the more painful since it seemed in conflict with the character and personality of the new Pope. A year and a half earlier, on the death of Pius XII, Angelo Giuseppe Roncalli, the simple-mannered and profoundly human Patriarch of Venice, had acceded to the papal throne under the name of John XXIII. He was known to be sympathetic to reform, both in public policy and in religious doctrine. But he was not yet fully master in the Vatican: a "pentarchy" of elderly, conservative cardinals hemmed him in, and the dramatic innovations of his final two years were still in the future. The opening to the Left had to wait until 1962.

And so once more, after Fanfani's trial balloon had been shot down, the long-established protocol of Christian Democratic maneuver dictated a move to the Right. But this time, with President Gronchi's evident connivence, the swing went so far as to seem to threaten Italian democracy itself. The new prime minister, Fernando Tambroni, was a relative unknown; although he appeared reluctant to take on the job, he still accepted neo-Fascist support to win his vote of confidence. This further—and still more dubious—political innovation gave the cue for what was to follow. Tambroni's tolerance toward neo-Fascist agitation scandalized the democratic Left, and quite predictably, the Communists also. Exactly what Tambroni was after has never become clear. Neo-Fascism was by now a spent force, and the realistic danger to democracy from that quarter was minimal. But the authoritarian tendency within the Christian Democratic party was still potent, and Tambroni's conduct in office aroused widespread suspicion that he was laying the groundwork for a Salazar-type "regime"—the nightmare that had haunted Italian politics for more than a decade.

By the end of June such suspicions had reached the proportions of mass obsession. A minor event—something that in America would have gone unnoticed—was enough to set off an explosion of political indignation. The government had given permission for the neo-Fascist MSI to hold a congress in Genoa; the Communist-dominated CGIL replied with a large popular demonstration which ended in a riot. Unquestionably, the first move against Tambroni came from the Communists, but the American press was quite wrong in describing the subsequent agitation as exclusively or even primarily Communist in inspiration and leadership. As strikes and street demonstrations spread from Genoa to Rome, Reggio Emilia, and a number of other cities, it became apparent that the democratic Left was also deeply involved. Indeed, for a few days the fraternity of the wartime Resistance seemed to have been restored and the bitter antagonisms of the succeeding fifteen years buried in the face of a shared danger.

The *Fatti di Luglio*—the events of July—as these riots and protest meetings came to be called, made Tambroni's continuance in office impossible. The ever-available Fanfani took over with a quadripartite government that included five former prime ministers. The aim was to present a front of solidarity in defense of the constitution and democracy; this time, even Nenni's Socialists abstained on the vote of confidence rather than performing their customary ritual of ideological negation. But the third Fanfani government was not a restored quadripartite in De Gasperi's and Scelba's sense. Too much had happened: the Liberals and the Social Democrats had followed opposite courses for too long to cooperate on anything more than a crisis basis. The formula was rather one of "convergence"—a pooling of democratic talents, with each party keeping its own freedom of maneuver. After the Tambroni "adventure," Italian politics could never be quite the same: the alternative on the Right had been tried and had ended in disaster; there remained only a move to the Left —with all its perplexities and all its dangers.

5. THE "OPENING TO THE LEFT"

The new era in Italian politics began with the municipal elections of November 1960. Quite logically, in view of what had happened the previous summer, the Left made substantial gains. And with these the Socialists felt emboldened to go a step further in their disentanglement from Communist alliances. Earlier, the two major parties of the Left had usually cooperated on the municipal level in the election of the *giunta* (executive committee) and mayor from the city council. The result had been Communist administration of a number of important northern and north-central municipalities. After the local elections of 1960, the Socialists began to shift allies: in Milan, in Genoa, in Florence, and in Palermo, they formed new *giunte* in coalition with the Christian Democrats. Both Communists and clericals denounced this reversal of alliances as politically immoral—yet silence in the Vatican suggested assent. The new city administrations of early 1961, established in the teeth of angry denunciations from all sides, proved the feasability of local cooperation between Christian Democrats and Socialists; there remained the more difficult task of extending such cooperation to the national level.

For a few months, the formation of the urban *giunte* had no sequel, and the whole experiment seemed in danger of becoming mired in the familiar inertia to which Italian reform initiatives periodically succumb. At this point the rank and file of the two mutually-suspicious parties began their own push in the same direction. The spring congress of the Socialists found Nenni once more locked in combat with the pro-Communists among his own following; yet out of the complex motions and counter-motions of the party factions there emerged a solid 55 per cent in support of Nenni's "autonomous" stand—and by implication in favor of further trafficking with Christian Democracy. A similar battle was fought out when the Christian Democratic congress met in Naples the following January. For months the party leadership had been tacking and veering in a final futile effort to avoid a choice. But Amintore Fanfani had long ago made up his mind: before resigning as party secretary, he had had time to raise to local leadership a new generation of activists committed to reform and economic planning—the party faction known as the *base,* or "grass roots." The *base* was the strongest single current within the party. Yet it lacked experience and well-known leaders. The turning point of the Naples congress, as of Christian Democracy's whole post-De Gasperi evolution, came when Fanfani's successor as party secretary, Aldo Moro, launched a five-hour harangue directed at the hesitant center factions which looked to him for guidance; with an overpowering combination of implacable logic and a torrent of words, Moro persuaded the party Center to align itself with the *base* and the Left. When the congress of 1962 adjourned, Christian Democracy had declared for a cautious approach toward Nenni and Italian Socialism.

This verdict gave Fanfani the cue for which he had been waiting. In March he obtained a vote of confidence for a new ministry, with the Liberals absent, the Social Democrats in a key role, and the Socialists committed to support the government in its reforming measures. This time there was no veto from the Vatican: on the contrary, there were unmistakable indications that Pope John approved. The first stage in the national opening to the Left had been successfully accomplished.

With a parliamentary election due the following year, the new Center-Left ministry was necessarily tentative and experimental. The Socialists were not yet ready to join the government, and the Christian Democratic mandate for an approach in their direction had stressed the need for caution. Hence the ministry's program did not go much beyond what Fanfani and his friends had been urging all along. The stress was as before on education and on economic planning, more particularly for the South.* The ministry's one major controversial decision was to proceed with the nationalization of the electrical industry—an action symbolic of its determination to curb the great monopolies. The nationalization of electricity only slightly altered the structure of the Italian economy; nor did the government ever mean to go on to a program of wholesale collectivization. The measure served rather as a warning to the major public utilities—in this case the Edison Company—and to the parastatal enterprises that in the future the government intended to have them administered in the interests of the Italian consumer and the economy as a whole.

* See Chapter 10.

Yet the impetus toward economic reform had begun, and now there was to be no stopping it. When the electoral campaign of 1963 was launched, it became apparent to everyone that the results would be read as a verdict on the opening to the Left. They would also be studied for what they showed about the changes that had been occurring in Italian society and in the Catholic Church itself. For the election of April 28, 1963, came at the culmination of the pontificate of John XXIII. During the previous two years the Pope had challenged the Italian episcopate and the conservatives in the Vatican with a series of bold innovations. In the summer of 1961 the encyclical *Mater et Magistra* had defined a concern for world poverty that transcended ideological differences; the next year had seen the convocation of the Vatican Council; finally, on April 10, 1963, less than three weeks before the election, the Pope's last great message, *Pacem in Terris,* had pleaded for international conciliation across the boundaries drawn by the cold war. The endorsement of the new tendencies in Italian politics could scarcely have been more explicit; Pope John seemed to be saying that the unbridgeable separation between Catholicism and Marxism, Pius XII's excommunication of the Communists, and the old injunction against voting Socialist, perhaps the very ideological division of the world, were being relegated to an unhappy past. This at least was how Italian conservatives interpreted his appeal when they denounced him as the "red" Pope. Those who applauded his stand differed only in the stress they laid on the promise rather than on the dangers of the new course. On all sides there was agreement that just as the Italian Socialists—and, to a lesser extent, the Communists also—had been evolving toward democracy, so the Church and the Christian Democratic party were advancing to meet them.

All this might have been expected to add a note of excitement to the electoral campaign. Quite the contrary. Despite the fact that the campaign was longer than customary and was the first in which television played a major part, the electoral activity seemed quieter than in the past and the public less interested in listening to the speechmaking. It was as though the voters had already made up their minds—or perhaps that circumstances had so thoroughly dictated the opening to the Left that little remained but to register the accomplished fact.

Yet the endorsement of what Fanfani and Moro, Saragat and Nenni, had been trying to accomplish, came in such a paradoxical form that both press and public were at a loss to explain it. The great gainers seemed to be the Communists, who with 25.3 per cent of the vote—the highest they had ever attained—surprised even themselves. On the other wing of the opposition, the Liberals, profiting from conservative disillusionment with Christian Democracy, doubled their poll of five years earlier. Both of the two main partners in the opening to the Left lost votes—the Christian Democrats by 4 percentage points, the Socialists by .4; among the Center-Left parties, the Social Democrats alone made gains.

That the Christian Democrats and Socialists should have been disappointed was only natural. But their chagrin obscured the long-range implications of the balloting. The electorate as a whole had taken a further step to the Left—that is, toward the sort of policy that these two parties had of late been sponsoring. Still more important, the four parties sympathetic to the opening to the Left had together polled 60 per cent of the vote. What they had lost had been constituents opposed to the new policy: just as Fanfani and Moro had alienated the economic and the clerical Right, so Nenni had outraged the philo-Communists in his own party. Both the Christian Democrats and the Socialists emerged from the election more solidly democratic than they had been before.

To understand the full range of these implications, we should turn now to examine the changes, economic and cultural, that made the Italy of 1963 so very different from what it had been at De Gasperi's fall from power ten years before.

10

Economic Expansion and Planning

IN THE mid-1950's the Italian economy began a great spurt forward. This formed part of a larger European change, which had begun in West Germany and later spread to France. Indeed, Italy was the last of the major Western nations to be hit by the wave of general prosperity. In view of the country's limited resources and long-standing economic underdevelopment, such a lag was only to be expected. What was noteworthy, rather, was the rate at which Italy began to catch up with its richer neighbors and the scale of its industrial expansion. Of the series of economic "miracles" which followed the mid-century, the Italian was the most dramatic —for here the need was greatest and the contrast between the old situation and the new stood out most sharply.

Among the national assets that contributed to the change, the most important was Italy's reservoir of skilled and hard-working manpower, particularly in the northern cities. The South also had a vast backlog of human energies which were only waiting to be tapped. Beyond these, at a few key points, Italy already possessed a developed technology, which could serve as a model to the rest of the economy, and which had been strengthened during the immediate postwar era. Those same years had seen a number of other preparatory changes, including the discovery of oil and natural gas reserves and the lifting of restrictions on foreign trade. Simultaneously Italy's rulers had redirected their national goals: they had turned away from foreign adventure to concentrate on politics and social problems at home; freed from the burden of colonies and of large military expenditures, the Italians were at last in a position to deploy their talents and their resources where these would count the most.

Yet in the first decade of the new prosperity, such assets were never fully mobilized. To be sure, the period from the mid-1950's to 1965 was marked by a series of striking innovations—the beginnings of national planning, Italy's membership in the European Common Market, and major expansion in the role of parastatal enterprise. These novel economic devices were indispensable for controlling the social changes that industrial expansion was unleashing and for diverting some of the new prosperity to the general welfare. But they were never adequate: for the most part the boom took its own course, and its benefits were unevenly spread among the Italian population. The old disparities between rich and poor, North and South, were not eliminated: in some respects they were even intensified. The new consumption patterns, the new social fluidity, that prosperity introduced did not affect the whole of Italian society: enormous pockets of backwardness and misery remained. The steady advance in the Communist vote was not the only sign of danger in the mid-1960's; there was also an inflation that the government had barely succeeded in stemming.

1. PLANNING AND THE COMMON MARKET

By 1955, as we have seen, the first Segni ministry was prepared to make economic planning a major policy goal. In this decision, it was following British and French, rather than German, precedent. Partly through the force of circumstances, partly through conscious choice, Italy began to accept as normal a mixed economy in which the power of large private enterprise was balanced by the authority of the state, but with this authority exerted indirectly and without resort to major structural reforms.

Such were the economic proposals drawn up by Ezio Vanoni and continued under his name after his death in 1956. The Vanoni Plan was sometimes criticized for not being a true plan at all. Certainly it was not the sort of tight, detailed blueprint familiar from Soviet experience. It offered no more than a general framework, with flexible goals, conceived within the existing social structure and with a clear preference for private over public initiative.

The Vanoni Plan aimed at an annual rise of 5 per cent in the national income, amounting to an overall increase of 63 per cent in the ten-year period for which it was devised. It emphasized investment over consumption and the need for the economy of the South to catch up with that of the North. More specifically, it designated industry, housing, and such "impulse sectors" as electric power, roads, and reclamation projects as the major targets for investment. Through these means the planners hoped by 1964 to reduce unemployment to 4 per cent—a rate comparable to that in the United States; for the South alone, the goal was a million new jobs. Here the national income was intended to rise at a rate of 8 per cent— twice that in the North—and industry to expand by 163 per cent, as opposed to 61 per cent in the North.

But to make such projections for the future—and in the absence of means for ensuring that individual businessmen followed the plan —was to reckon without the dynamics of the Europe-wide boom which was just beginning to affect the Italian economy. Prosperity among Italy's neighbors naturally fed into those areas which were best equipped to profit by it; foreign companies placed their orders where advanced technology already existed—in the North. The result was almost the reverse of what Vanoni and his colleagues had intended. By 1959 unemployment had begun to fall off sharply, but not at the rate the planners had specified, and the annual rise in income had come in just the pattern that they had hoped to eliminate. For the whole period of the 1950's, it amounted in the North to 5.7 per cent—considerably more than had been intended— and in the South to 4 per cent, which was only half the Vanoni goal. Or, to put the change in terms of per capita income, the rise for the decade had been 80 per cent in the North, and 70 per cent in the South. While the South had made more economic progress than in any previous ten-year period, it was still way behind the North. Far from catching up with the more advanced part of the country, in comparative terms it had lost ground rather than gained. Where per capita income in the South had formerly been about half that in the North, at the beginning of the 1960's it stood at 46 per cent.

Hence the immediate imperative arising from the perplexing results of the Vanoni Plan's first half decade was the industrialization of the South. The planners were agreed that this was the only way to combat the economic inequities that had marred the extraordinary progress of the 1950's. In practice, the task devolved on the larger companies and more particularly on the parastatal organizations. It formed part of the increasing role that these were playing in the national economy as a whole. In the present context it may suffice to note that the South possessed unsuspected assets in the push for industrialization.

We are already familiar with southern liabilities—locational handicaps, inadequate savings, and the lack of a strong entrepreneurial tradition. What is less well known is that the South had long enjoyed an infrastructure in basic equipment that was underutilized and disproportionate to its current needs. As compared with non-European areas of economic backwardness, the Italian South was extraordinarily well supplied with communications and public buildings. The legacy of a century of public-works programs, the southerners' tangible assets in good roads and impressive municipal structures reflected the guilty conscience or electoral calculation of the people in Rome. For three generations the rulers of united Italy had tried to appease the South by giving it the outward paraphernalia of modernity; Mussolini in particular had seen to it that the southerners received more than their normal share of public works contracts. The result was the imposing façade that so often misled those unfamiliar with the poverty lying behind it. It was at the same time an investment for the future which meant that when the moment came for full-fledged modernization southern Italy had laid the groundwork and was ready to go.

The Italian South likewise possessed the only substantial reservoir of unused manpower within the European six-nation community. Elsewhere in the first postwar decade nearly full employment had become the norm; in southern Italy alone there were great untapped human resources. This asset had earlier been of negligible importance; indeed, underemployment had usually figured alongside the region's many economic burdens. But with the signing of the Treaty of Rome in 1957 and the launching of the Common Market the following January, southern labor began to find new outlets and a new mobility. Among the many benefits accruing to Italy from the Common Market, not the least was the hope that it brought to the South. The strengthened economic ties with nations north of the Alps—with France, Germany, and the Low Countries—meant that Italy had at last been fully drawn into the advanced European society in which it had previously shared only in part. And as the least developed region within the new community, the Italian South was the one that in the long run had the most to gain from the change.

Initially, however, it was once more the North which profited. By 1962, when customs duties on industrial products within the six nations were reduced by one half, Italian large industry was ready and eager for the change. At first a number of Italy's industrial leaders had feared that their concerns would be unable to stand up against French and German competition, but as the 1950's wore on, they became increasingly confident. These expectations proved correct: by the end of 1961 Italian trade within the Common Market had risen in just three years by 80 per cent, and with iron ore now cheaper than it had ever been before, Italy had achieved the highest rate of growth in steel production of any major nation.

The danger, then, was that in the euphoria engendered by such astounding advances, the needs of Italy's less favored sectors might be forgotten. In the mid-1960's it was far from clear that the South would derive its full potential profit from the new economic unity of Western Europe. But there was one very hopeful sign: for a full decade the Italian government had been committed to planning —tentatively and pragmatically, to be sure, but with growing conviction. It was significant that within the councils of the Common Market the Italians tended to vote with the plan-minded French and Dutch rather than with the *laissez-faire* Germans. Planning in Italy had come to stay: it remained to be seen how thoroughgoing it would be in the years of further economic expansion that lay ahead.

2. *THE ROLE OF PARASTATAL ENTERPRISE*

We have seen how in 1956 the first Segni government persuaded the Italian parliament to pass a general law regulating the exploitation of gas and oil. The need for such legislation was urgent. American companies were coming into conflict with the existing Italian monopoly, and the rights of the latter remained undefined. The law compromised the issue by giving the Italian company a predominant position on the mainland, more particularly in the

Po valley, while granting foreign capital wider scope on the island of Sicily, which was now under its own regional government.

The activities of ENI*—the national corporation for liquid fuels —already figured as one of the most dynamic features in the Italian economy. And in the next decade ENI offered the outstanding example of the new prominence of parastatal enterprise or public corporations. Its origins went back to 1926, when the Fascist regime established a prospecting company to look for gas and oil—with an eventual success that made necessary the organization of a number of affiliates. In 1953 these were grouped together under the general control of ENI, whose director, Enrico Mattei, was to become the single most powerful individual in Italian economic life.

Under Mattei's lead, ENI expanded Italy's natural gas production eightfold; the output of petroleum went up from a prewar figure of zero to nearly two million tons in 1960. A network of pipelines was laid and refineries established in Italy's major ports, as well as an industrial complex at Ravenna for the manufacture of a wide variety of synthetics. This enormuos expansion did not free Italy entirely from its dependence on imports from abroad; but it reduced that dependence while providing the country with inexpensive fuel—indeed, in the early 1960's Italian natural gas was rated the cheapest fuel in Europe.

If this were all he had done, Mattei would have deserved nothing but gratitude from his own people. But Mattei was too restless and adventurous to restrict himself to the role of a conventional public servant. He played politics: he was the friend and backer of President Gronchi and was reputed to exert an occult (and possibly beneficent) influence in the councils of Christian Democracy. He gave only a sketchy public accounting of his far-reaching activities. Still more, he branched out into the foreign field until he became a decisive force in the politics of Middle Eastern oil. It was Mattei who stepped in when the British and Iranian governments were deadlocked; by offering to exploit Iranian oil on the revolutionary basis of only 25 per cent royalties for the foreign company, with 75 per cent going to the Iranians themselves, Mattei permanently shifted the international negotiating balance in the Middle East. Subsequently he signed similar contracts for Morocco and the

* *Ente Nazionale Idrocarburi.*

Sinai peninsula. When Mattei died in 1962, he seemed to be running a foreign policy in his own right, parallel (and sometimes contradictory) to that of the Italian foreign office.

After Mattei's death, ENI returned to more orthodox courses. And on balance the verdict was favorable on his decade of management. Few questioned the need of a public corporation to manage Italy's exploitation of gas and oil; the alternative would not have been free competition but private monopoly, with whose drawbacks Italians were only too familiar. The critics of ENI had nothing against its public character; they asked rather whether its policies were sufficiently directed toward the general interest—whether it contributed enough to the national treasury, whether it depended too heavily on the private money market and had too much capital tied up in speculative ventures. Questions such as these were unavoidable; the political opening to the Left had given them a new urgency; and they became still more pressing in the case of IRI, ENI's older and larger sister, which controlled roughly 30 per cent of Italian industry.

Again and again in the politics of the 1950's the rationalization of the IRI industrial holdings had loomed up as one of the major reefs on which ministries foundered. As a start, this meant drawing a sharp separation between the concerns in IRI that were fully owned by the state (such as Alitalia and the television system) and those that were predominantly in private hands. In theory such a regrouping seemed only logical; but it ran up against a multitude of entrenched interests. Even the reform-minded among the successive Ministers of State Participations—men like Ugo La Malfa— were able to make only minor changes in the ramifying IRI structure.

At the same time, once the government had committed itself to planning, IRI was necessarily drawn into the process. Particularly in those sectors of the economy in which IRI dwarfed private enterprise, the parastatal combines became the national pacesetters. Such was notably the case with shipbuilding, with ferrous metals, and with the industrialization of the South.

In shipbuilding, IRI's subsidiary *Fincantieri* (which had split off in 1959 from *Finmeccanica*) by the early 1960's was accounting for three-quarters of the total Italian production. In metallurgy, the IRI holdings—grouped under *Finsider*— were turning out 54 per cent of the country's steel. Most of these, of course, were located in the North and Center. It was at Cornigliano, near Genoa, that Italy's most modern steel plant had been constructed in the period of the Marshall Plan. In 1961, Cornigliano merged with ILVA— another *Finsider* holding—to form a new company, *Italsider,* which by itself produced more than a third of Italian steel. Taken together these regroupings suggested both the pace of industrial expansion under IRI's auspices and the beginning of a more positive attitude toward planned economic growth.

Of far greater significance for the future, however, were IRI's projects for southern industrialization. In 1960, the South had less than 9 per cent of Italian steel capacity; this figure the planners hoped to triple by 1965. Already *Italsider* had set up new plants at Taranto and at Bagnoli near Naples. Under the terms of a law passed in 1957, IRI was obliged to place two-fifths of its yearly investments in the South, even though regard for immediate profits might dictate otherwise. The result was the establishment of a series of new industries, concentrating on such basic commodities as steel, cement, and synthetics rather than on the production of finished consumer goods.

The rationale behind this emphasis was that a large plant for basic production would act as a point of attraction for secondary industry and exert a spreading effect throughout the southern economy. Similar considerations applied in the case of private capital which sought to take advantage of new tax privileges favoring industrial investment in the South. Characteristically such investment meant establishing a southern branch of an already successful northern concern—most notably the Olivetti typewriter plant set up at Pozzuoli north of Naples. Olivetti's experience at Pozzuoli gave a heartening example to those who argued for the feasibility of southern industrialization. For within a short time skills and production costs at the recently-established plant equaled those of the parent factory at Ivrea in Piedmont. The advocates of this form of industrialization contended that in the Italian South it was possible to reverse the usual historical process: instead of modern industry growing up in places where a trained artisan class was already in existence, a raw labor force trained on the spot could become the vanguard of a new industrial society.

Yet skeptics remained. These argued that the government's policy was attracting capital-intensive industries at the expense of labor-intensive industries—that is, those requiring large quantities of capital rather than those providing a great many new jobs; it was unwise, they maintained, to risk "large amounts of investments in basic industries . . . and . . . it would have been more prudent to have established simpler industries for which the unskilled labor of the South would have been better adapted and which local entrepreneurs might have been able to run."* The force of such an argument was undeniable. But given the structure of the Italian economy in the 1950's and 1960's, it was more than doubtful that the alternative policy of favoring small or labor-intensive industry would have worked. The most curious feature of the vast anomaly of IRI in Italian economic life was the way it partook of both past and future—the way it belonged to the old system of quasi-monopolistic private enterprise on the one hand, and on the other to the new world of planning under state auspices. IRI had a foot in both camps, and until this contradiction was resolved, official favor was almost bound to go to the larger firms—some within the IRI complex and some outside—which were in the best position to exploit the new opportunities that government planning opened up.

3. POPULATION SHIFTS AND SOCIAL STRESSES

In terms of simple statistics, the Italian economic achievement in the 1950's and 1960's was unquestionably impressive. Even more than Germany, Italy deserved the much-abused word "miracle" for what it had accomplished. From 1950 to 1960, its economy had grown at a rate of almost 6 per cent, as compared with a Western European average of 4.5 per cent. In the single year 1960, after a perceptible recession during the previous two years, industrial production had risen by an unprecedented 11 per cent. Similarly during the 1950's the volume of Italy's imports had more than doubled, while exports nearly trebled, as the country for the first time in modern history became a major exporter of manufactured goods.

* Shepard B. Clough, *The Economic History of Modern Italy* (New York, 1964), pp. 349–350.

Industry, then, had led the economic boom, with a vastly expanded production geared both for export and for the domestic market. From 1953 to 1960 such production had risen 85 per cent, paced by the mechanical industry, which by itself accounted for just under 30 per cent of the net national product. Within the mechanical field the greatest expansion was in typewriters and business machines, but it was the production of automobiles that most dramatically caught public attention. Here the eight-year growth from 1953 to 1961 was more than four-fold—with FIAT producing almost 90 per cent of the cars for civilian use; in addition, FIAT climbed to second place in auto production among European companies and fifth in the entire world. A single figure may suggest what this growth meant for domestic consumption: in the year 1963 alone car sales in Italy rose by 45 per cent.

While the ordinary Italian shared in the new prosperity, more than half of the expansion in national product went to investment rather than to current consumption. This was only natural in view of Italy's capital equipment needs. What was more troubling was that so much of the consumer's share came in the form of luxury or semi-luxury items like automobiles rather than in more basic things such as public housing. A great deal of the output for consumption purposes was showy and speculative; new luxury dwellings were far more visible than government-financed apartments. Moreover, the real estate men were as ruthless as their American counterparts in the way they bulldozed parks and open fields, pleasant seasides and historic urban quarters, until Italy's cities and resorts threatened to succumb to the expensive sprawl and squalor that is so depressing a feature of our own landscape. Most of such building was totally unplanned, and much was both ugly and irrational—like the construction of a skyscraper by an open beach. Italian builders apparently adored concrete; in the new urban quarters there was scarcely a tree to be seen. Under the realtors' onslaught, municipal councils (which were chronically short of funds) stood helpless, while those who fought to save Italy's artistic heritage found to their dismay that they lacked legal weapons. Meantime the giddy rise in car ownership was producing some of the worst traffic jams in the Western world. For poorer Italians, who profited little if at all from the business boom, its chief effect might simply be to make life more noisy, smelly, and inconvenient.

The influx of cars, of buildings, and above all of people into the cities was the most dramatic of the social changes and stresses that economic growth entailed. From the mid-forties to the mid-sixties such cities as Rome, Milan, and Turin nearly doubled their populations. In the year 1961 the old Fascist law that had tried to check the movement of peasants to the great urban centers was finally abrogated. The result was to reveal how many people had been living in the cities with a technically illegal status—in Rome alone there were more than a quarter million. In the preceding decade, in fact, two million Italians from the countryside had swollen the urban population, as the agricultural element among the people as a whole had fallen twelve percentage points to a figure of 30 per cent. The movement had been a double one: its more prominent aspect was the fact that for the first time in history southerners in large numbers were going to the northern industrial cities; less noticeable was the gradual move of land-hungry peasants from the South to the farms of northerners who were selling out and seeking urban employment. Up to 1963, two and three-quarter million southerners had moved to the North—300,000 in that year alone.

In the long-term view, these changes were undoubtedly for Italy's benefit. Taken together, they meant that the country had finally crossed the decisive social watershed—that the majority of its people were now living in modern industrial conditions and deriving their livelihood from urban pursuits rather than from the land. The fall in rural population—both in absolute and in relative terms—was only what was to be expected and desired; the experience of one Western country after another had shown that this was the key to a rise in the general standard of living. Moreover, the cultural effect of such migrations, combined with the rapid spread of television, was to reduce provincialism and increase the number of those who spoke standard Italian in preference to a dialect. All this was to the good. But in Italy the change came in a particularly fast and uncontrolled fashion; in the social as opposed to the productive sphere, governmental planning was almost entirely absent.

Thus there was no comprehensive housing scheme or facilities for finding dwellings for the new arrivals; in the large cities of the North and Center social services proved totally inadequate to accommodate so large an influx. Southern families poured off the trains bewildered and frightened; often they could scarcely make themselves understood—Calabrian and Piedmontese, for example, are at opposite poles among Italian dialects—and the strangeness of their ways aroused resentment in those among whom they settled. Neither municipal officials nor the Church seemed able to cope with their plight. In the absence of any other form of welcome, the Communist party and its trade-union affiliate stepped in. One did not have to look any farther to explain Communism's advances in the northern industrial cities in the election of 1963. "The Communist vote of the emigrants to the North" was the "reckoning" that the Italian people had to pay for "having delayed for at least a decade . . . a policy of global planning . . . So disproportionate and uncontrolled a transformation of society and the economy . . . could not fail to bear this political fruit."*

"Disproportionate" and "uncontrolled"—such were the dominant attributes of Italy's new prosperity. They suggested a typically "affluent" situation in which some sectors and classes were making a big profit, from which others felt shut out almost entirely, and from which the majority were deriving just enough benefit to wish it were much more. In terms of real wages, Italy's workers in 1960 were only about 25 per cent better off than they had been in 1948. The political results were apparent in the way the Communist vote inched up and the Communist-dominated CGIL—after a crisis of defections and self-criticism in the late 1950's—regained its nerve and held on to its position as the most influential of the Italian trade-union federations. The discontents of the 1960's were incomparably less dangerous than they had been two decades earlier; their revolutionary potential had disappeared entirely. But they were real and deeply felt: they pointed to the enormous backlog of unfinished business confronting the Italian government as it made its dramatic turn toward the Left.

4. UNFINISHED BUSINESS

Some of this business was of long standing and stood no chance of being settled in the near future. Such were the related problems of rationalizing IRI and curbing the power of the *Confindustria*.

* Marco Cesarini, "Il voto comunista, la grossa calamità," *Il Mondo,* May 14, 1963, p. 3.

To meet these two issues head-on meant to challenge at its strongest point the "economic" Right, which remained a potent force within the Christian Democratic party. Similarly, in the agrarian field, what had started out more than a generation before as the Italian version of a rural cooperative movement—the *Federconsorzi*—had become a semi-monopolistic organization for price-fixing and marketing with a bloc of two score deputies under its control. Any program for the modernization of the Italian countryside would be sure to encounter the entrenched opposition of the *Federconsorzi* and its affiliates.

With the mid-century exodus from southern dwarf holdings and *latifondi*, it had become possible for the first time in Italian history to think in terms of an agriculture which would no longer be limited to providing a bare livelihood to an excess reservoir of human beings but would be directed in a rational fashion toward maintaining the food supply of a predominantly urban population. This was the first and perhaps the greatest of the economic tasks which the government saw some realistic possibility of accomplishing—to raise the productivity of Italian agriculture to a level commensurate with that of other advanced Western nations. Italian industry was already proving its competitive efficiency within the Common Market; the rural sector was lagging behind. In 1963, with 27 per cent of Italy's labor force, agriculture was accounting for only 16 per cent of the gross national product; per capita its output was just over one half that of the other sectors of the economy. Although the twelve years 1950 to 1962 had seen a 40 per cent increase in production—and with a labor force reduced by a third—farm prices had not kept up with those of other goods and services; real income from agriculture had risen a mere 1.5 per cent.

It was with problems such as these in mind that the parliament voted the government's "Green Plan" in 1960. This plan and the subsequent reports and legislation designed to put it into effect drew a basic distinction between the progressive and the static areas of Italian agriculture. The former, they specified, included not only such a long-established region of advanced agricultural technique as the Po valley but also areas like the Tuscan Maremma and the Po delta where the reforms of the previous decade had worked particularly well. The latter, besides the familiar regions of southern misery, embraced wide stretches of central Italy where share tenancy predominated. Among the striking novelties of the agrarian planning of the 1960's was the firm stand it took against *mezzadria;* the question of regulating tenancy contracts—which had ranked as the bête noire of a long succession of ministries—seemed about to be faced at last. Legislation introduced in early 1964 aimed at the virtual elimination of *mezzadria:* while raising the sharecroppers' part in the annual division of output to 58 per cent and giving them the right to make all working decisions on the farm, the draft law forbade the signature of new contracts and offered share tenants forty-year loans at one per cent interest to enable them to buy up their holdings; it was anticipated that existing *mezzadria* contracts would gradually run out over a twenty-year period.

The eventual aim of such legislation was intensively-cultivated farms on the American or Western European model. The rural labor force, it was estimated, would continue to fall by about 3 per cent annually, while the farm workers who remained would become steadily more efficient. In addition, the Green Plan and its successors proposed a shift from grain-raising to the production of high-quality foods such as meat. The newly-affluent Italian consumer was already turning in this direction; meat consumption was going up by 4.5 per cent a year, while production was increasing at only just over half that figure. On balance, the planners hoped to encourage two main types of Italian agriculture—the medium to large-sized "industrially" managed holdings that had long been characteristic of the Po valley, and small farms, at least ten acres in size, grouped together where possible in co-operative associations. This emphasis on agricultural co-operation was the most imaginative feature of rural planning in the 1960's; it was also the aspect that was likely to run up against the greatest conservative resistance.

The Green Plan antedated the political opening to the Left. But it formed a logical part of the intensified emphasis on planning that began in 1962. The ministerial patron of such planning was Ugo La Malfa of the Republican party, already known for his effort to bring order into the IRI holdings and for his measures liberalizing foreign trade in the early 1950's. The chief technical planner was Pasquale Saraceno, a former colleague of Vanoni, who had made

a reputation as an economic adviser for southern development and
for the regional governments of Sicily and Sardinia. Shortly before
the 1963 election, La Malfa and Saraceno announced a five- and a
ten-year plan to run concurrently with the next two parliaments. In
political terms, their aim was to mediate between the collectivist
tendencies of the Socialists and the *laissez-faire* preferences of an
influential wing within Christian Democracy; in terms of economic
growth, they proposed to maintain a rate just under that of the
1950's (4 rather than 5 or 6 per cent), while correcting the grave
imbalances in development that had become increasingly apparent.

In order to make such corrections, a decentralization of planning
appeared essential. And this involved the establishment of regional
governments, as provided for in the constitution of 1948. Only by
delegating initiative and responsibility to local bodies—particularly
in the South—could adequate provision be made for the special
needs of those parts of the country that had failed to derive their
share of profit from the general prosperity. This was a second area
of unfinished business in which major reform had at last become
feasible. With the opening to the Left, the old political objection to
decentralization had lapsed. There was no longer the danger of a
swathe of Communist-dominated governments extending across
the north-central part of the country. Since the Socialists were now
cooperating with Christian Democracy on the national level, it was
possible and even probable that these two parties could together
set up regional administrations, as they had done with the municipal
giunte following the local elections of 1960. Yet even so apparently
uncontroversial a reform had its hidden hazards. The boundaries of
Italy's fourteen "ordinary" regions (as opposed to the five special
regions in which local government already existed) had been drawn
a century earlier; in a number of cases they no longer corresponded
to contemporary economic reality. Moreover there was the danger
that staffing the new administrations would further expand the
country's already swollen bureaucracy. Or, if specified departments
and individuals should be transferred to the new regional capitals
—as the government proposed—it might be only the mediocrities
that would go, since the more talented would have sufficient
political influence to enable them to stay in Rome. Once more, the

central problem was one of personnel: decentralized economic planning would become a reality only if able and devoted administrators were found to make it work.

The control of urban growth was a third area where the government saw hope of enacting a long-delayed reform. The earlier history of city planning had been extremely discouraging. A law of 1962 directed against real estate speculation had largely failed of its effect, since it had neglected to provide funds from the national treasury to pay compensation for expropriated land, and only a very few municipalities, including Turin, had been able to avail themselves of its provisions. The following year a more comprehensive law became caught up in electoral polemics between Christian Democrats and Liberals. Although the measure's ministerial sponsor was one of Christian Democracy's younger reformers, it aroused such opposition among the real estate lobby that his own party colleagues forced him to drop it and subsequently blamed him for having cost them three-quarters of a million votes. Yet with the formation of the Moro ministry in late 1963 the government returned to the attack. Moro's Minister of Public Works—this time a Socialist—offered a new urban development bill that had been drafted with the assistance of a number of leading architects, economists, and city planners. Besides offering the services of such specialists to municipalities requesting them, the draft law provided financial assistance for expropriation, for low-cost housing, and for housing cooperatives. As before, its opponents directed their fire at the bill's expropriation provisions, which they stigmatized as an assault on private property. But its supporters retorted with the incontrovertible argument that Italy's cities would not survive much longer unless the government were given legal weapons with which to defend them.

Finally, in the field of education the opening to the Left focused attention on a depressing backlog of urgent requirements. Already in 1962 Fanfani's revamped ministry had put aid to education in the center of its program. Two years later Moro was prepared to go still farther. For here the need was desperate: school buildings were antiquated and overcrowded, teachers' salaries pitiful and their number inadequate—in higher education the ratio of professors to students was one to forty.* Not until 1962 had public schooling been made available up to the age of fourteen; at the same time it was officially reported that 200,000 more classrooms were needed, that 850,000 children between six and fourteen were attending no school at all, and that 8 per cent of the population was still illiterate. Meantime Church education seemed to be the only kind that was making progress; encouraged by government financial support— which in itself was a constant source of conflict between Christian Democrats and Socialists—attendance at Catholic institutions had gone up from 5 per cent of the total school population in 1957 to 10 per cent six years later.

Under the circumstances, it was no wonder that dissatisfaction was widespread and that strikes among students (and even professors) were not uncommon occurrences. The crisis in Italian education was deep-seated; there was grave doubt whether any government—however reform-minded—would be able to provide funds sufficient to meet the need. It was the major blot on a cultural scene that in so many other respects gave solid grounds for self-congratulation.

* Arturo Colombo, *Rapporto sull'università italiana* (Milan, 1962), pp. 50, 57.

11

The Cultural "Renaissance"

IT HAS BECOME a cliché to speak of a post-Fascist cultural renaissance in Italy. The cinema has been its most obvious manifestation and the one most easily accessible to Americans—but those better versed in things Italian have expressed a similar appreciation for the novel, for painting, and for the work of an internationally-renowned architect like Pier Luigi Nervi. The more specialized may even be familiar with contemporary Italian music or post-Crocean social thought. All of these cultural products have not been of equal distinction; debate has continued to rage on the merits of an individual film or novel, and some critics have dismissed the whole idea of a renaissance as an unwarranted inflation of second-rate work. What is undeniable, however, is that for the first time in centuries Italy's artists and writers have commanded respectful attention in a wide variety of fields; they have no longer felt themselves isolated in a European backwater or limited to a single realm of expression such as music or social criticism. After a generation of nearly total eclipse —and a much longer period of subordinate status—since the fall of Fascism Italy has once more been in the main stream or even in the forefront of Western cultural life.

To assess the nature and extent of this revival in brief compass is a perplexing task. Perhaps the best way to approach it is to focus on those cultural manifestations which have dealt directly with the realities of contemporary Italian life—social criticism in the widest sense and the successive phases of expression in the novels and in the films.

1. POST-CROCEAN SOCIAL CRITICISM

The most curious feature of Italy's cultural atmosphere in the immediate aftermath of liberation was its conservatism and even complacency. At a time when political life was torn asunder by the struggle between militant and quiet anti-Fascism, on the question of basic cultural values there reigned a surprising unanimity of thought. Here the forces of "restoration" were not arrayed against those of "revolution"—as they were in the political parties, the trade-unions, and the public administration. In the cultural field there was no corresponding debate over whether Italy should return to the pre-Fascist *status quo ante* or go on to devise new forms and new institutions. And this for the simple reason that "the problem of restoration or revolution . . . seemed to have no point, since during the years of Fascism culture had followed its own independent path." All that appeared necessary was to tidy things up, to expunge a few unfortunate "verbal practices," and deflate some undeserved reputations. The almost uniform conviction was that Italian cultural life was basically healthy, that it had come through the Fascist experience intact, and that there was no question either of restoring or of recasting this tradition but rather one of "linking up with a past which . . . had never undergone profound shocks or a true collapse."*

Such was the view even of the Communist leader Palmiro Togliatti. And the fact that he felt this way revealed a great deal about Italian education and the Italian political class. Like Italy's more conservative political leaders, Togliatti had been classically trained and simply assumed the virtues of a cultural tradition that was primarily literary and rhetorical. In terms of *this* tradition, Italy had indeed emerged from the two decades of Fascism in amazingly good shape. Although the country's experience of authoritarian rule had been nearly twice as long as Germany's, its cultural life had been far less profoundly upset and corrupted. The great majority of its artists and writers had remained untouched by Fascist influence, and a distinguished minority had resolutely opposed it. The

* Mario Sansone, "La cultura," *Dieci anni dopo 1945–1955: Saggi sulla vita democratica italiana* (Bari, 1955), p. 519.

most prominent of these, of course, was Benedetto Croce, and Croce's final triumph in his protracted philosophical duel with Mussolini seemed to epitomize all that was sound in Italy's cultural heritage.

The immediate effect of Mussolini's fall, then, was to strengthen the hold of Croceanism on Italian literature and social thought; the position of pre-eminence that the Neapolitan philosopher had achieved in the past forty years seemed only to be confirmed by the destruction of the Fascist tyranny. Yet this leadership was more precarious than it appeared: in most cases it rested on vague respect rather than on true understanding, and Croce was by now too old to adapt to the new Italy that was emerging from the ruins of war. Moreover, competitors were lacking: younger talents had not yet won recognition; the returning exiles were finding it difficult to make themselves understood in a country from which they had been so long absent; and there was no group of modern Catholic writers —such as played so distinguished a role in France—to lift to the level of philosophical abstraction the new prestige of the Church in Italian public life. Thus Croceanism in the immediate post-Fascist era exerted an influence almost diametrically opposed to what it had stood for a generation earlier. In the first two decades of the twentieth century Croce's historical and literary idealism had come as a breath of renewal; in the 1940's it figured as a solidly-established cult whose aesthetic formulations masked rather than illuminated the harsher features of contemporary Italian life. It was only a question of time before some new approach to reality would shake up Italy's intellectual world and almost over night release it from Croce's hypnotic spell.

That the challenge came from Marxism was not surprising in view of the Communists' and Socialists' contribution to Italy's liberation and the revolutionary current in post-Fascist Italian politics. But the form in which it came gave it particular prestige. The revolt against Croce—and with it the effort to define new and more relevant criteria of social criticism—was inaugurated in 1947 with the posthumous publication of Antonio Gramsci's prison writings. Gramsci had been Togliatti's friend and his predecessor as leader of the Italian Communist party; he had passed in Mussolini's prisons the last decade of his career until his death in the mid-1930's.

This circumstance not only made him a Marxist martyr; it also kept him out of the squalid struggles of party factions in the Stalinist era and imposed on him a detachment and an enforced leisure to reflect on the nature of Italian culture and the reasons why the country had fallen so easily into Mussolini's grasp.

Gramsci's prison reflections suggested a way to resolve the apparent paradox of a nation whose cultural tradition had remained uncorrupted but which nevertheless had succumbed to Fascism. As a Sardinian Gramsci had known poverty and backwardness at first hand. And despite the fact that he had later studied in Turin and acquired an impressive cultural equipment of his own, he never lost his sense for the realities of Italian popular life. Indeed, he was almost unique among Italian social observers in keeping touch with the simple beginnings from which he had sprung. The official —the literary and rhetorical—culture of Italy, Gramsci concluded, bore almost no relation to the life of the peasant masses; it was a veneer—the property of a restricted elite—hardly more. Hence the anti-Fascism of a writer like Croce could find little popular echo: his urbanity and his skepticism, his wealth and his scholarly pursuits, were in a world almost totally removed from the emotional universe of the Italian people—a universe of blood-honor, a simple Catholic faith, and brutal, crushing toil.

Those who read Gramsci's letters and fragmentary prison writings found in them far more common humanity than Marxist dogma; the letters to his wife and children in particular evoked a warm response among the wider reading public. In addition, when they did deal with dogmatic issues, these writings conducted the debate with a notable breadth of view and on a high level of intellectual sophistication. As such, they provided a rare and precious model for subsequent Marxist—and more particularly Communist—writers. The result was a paradoxical "sub-renaissance" within the wider reawakening of Italian cultural life, a revival of Marxist thinking on Italian soil just at the point when in the rest of the Western world it was going into its final decline. The explanation lay partly, of course, in cultural lag: the Fascist dictatorship had deprived Italy of the more usual experience of Marxist resurgence in the 1930's. But Gramsci's personal example was also decisive: it both reflected and reinforced the intellectual acumen and relative tolerance of dissent which gave the Italian Communist party its perennial attraction for artists and intellectuals.

The subjects which Gramsci's writings suggested—the study of small communities, social structure and social classes, the problem of the South—were to be systematically pursued by Marxist scholars during the late 1940's and 1950's. Such studies were in part "objective"; a number of them still posed ideal issues in Crocean terms and won the respect of the more conventional economists and historians. Beyond that, they filled a vacuum in Italian intellectual life. For in the realm of social studies, as in so much else, the twenty-year hiatus of Fascism had taken Italy out of circulation precisely during the decades when in other countries such disciplines as sociology, social psychology, and economic history were developing their contemporary formulations. With "bourgeois" social science almost totally lacking, Marxist scholars found a free field before them.

This Marxist pre-emption of the social studies that dealt realistically with Italy's poverty, economic backwardness, and class stratification often made it difficult for non-Marxists to gain an intellectual foothold. The universities were also inhospitable to such studies: the faculties were dominated by the literary folk and the methodologically conservative, and chairs of social science were in extremely short supply. Not until the late 1950's did a considerable group of non-Marxists begin to make their mark as social science students and critics. And they did so most often by dealing in polemical vein with the same issues that their Communist or near-Communist counterparts had first raised. In such polemics, American theories of economic development took a prominent place: as the 1950's wore on, and the attention of economists focused on the underdeveloped world of Asia and Africa, Italians began to discover that they too lived in an underdeveloped country—or at least one whose southern half lagged far behind the Western European norm. Still more, some Italian scholars began to see in their own late nineteenth-century history a preview of the struggle for economic "catching-up" that obsessed the non-European world in the third quarter of the twentieth century. Marxist theory had been elaborated in an earlier age and in an exclusively European context; outside Europe its formulations most of the time proved inappropriate or misleading. In this respect, the economic development theories of Western European and American scholars were both more up to date and more specifically devised for the issues at hand. They gave the younger non-Marxist economists and sociologists indispensable reinforcement in their efforts to digest a generation's work in social science that Italy had missed and in the process to beat the Marxist critics at their own game.

The problem of poverty in its widest sense remained the major theme of both schools. And this was true also of the less systematic social critics who captured the public imagination. Among the older generation, Arturo Carlo Jemolo exemplified a new view of Italian social reality beyond the warfare of ideologies. A meticulous scholar of history and law, yet profoundly committed to the struggle for social justice; a devout Catholic, yet independent in thought and unsparing in his criticism of clerical influence on Italian public life; a passionate defender of the constitution and liberal ideas, yet convinced that only government action could curb the monopolists and lead the Italian people to a better life—Jemolo suggested in his life and writings an Italy that was both Catholic and social-minded, bold in reform while remaining true to what was still valid in its nineteenth-century tradition of parliamentary liberalism. Jemolo's writings on Church-state relations, his pitiless exposure of Christian Democratic hypocrisy, his defense of the rights of Protestants before the Constitutional Court—this medley of scholarship, litigation, and polemic might strike the unsympathetic observer as merely quixotic. But to those who knew Italy's plight at first hand, it offered the possibility of a new ideological synthesis. Such a synthesis had been implicit in the astounding innovations of Pope John's last two years; it had found concrete political expression in the experiment of an opening to the Left.

Some younger Italians, neither scholars nor political leaders yet eager to understand and to remedy their countrymen's woes, found Italy's gradual evolution toward reform too slow for their taste. Such was Danilo Dolci, an architect from the North who chose to settle in the impoverished Sicilian town of Partinico and there to teach by example. Dolci tried to rouse the peasants from their stubborn and unchanging lethargy; his writings infuriated the conventional-minded by blurting out the full truth about waste and corruption and heartlessness in the government of Sicily; he organized non-violent protest on the model of Gandhi or Martin Luther King; he urged his followers not to wait for official action that never came but to start building highways and dams with their own hands. After a few years of this sort of thing, he found both the *mafia* and the public authorities arrayed against him. Dolci was obsessive, single-minded, humorless. His admirers themselves frequently found him hard to deal with. Yet a more conciliatory man might have gotten nowhere; even Dolci made only a minor dent in the unyielding stuff of Sicilian society. His achievement was less a work of construction than a desperate appeal to be heard. For this was what Marxists and non-Marxists, scholars and direct-actionists, had in common: they were outraged at the intolerable conditions in which so many Italians—and a majority of those in the South—were still living at a time when the Western world as a whole was advancing to new heights of economic abundance. And this was also the subject matter of the creative artists, the novelists and the film directors, who for more than a decade had been trying to stir the public conscience with a scrupulously honest depiction of what Italians had suffered during the war and were still suffering in the years that followed.

2. THE UNIVERSE OF NEOREALISM

For the Italian creative imagination, the fall of Fascism came as the sudden bursting of a dam. The energies, the talent, that had been thwarted for more than twenty years gushed forth in a flood of tumultuous expression. And the first imperative was to tell the truth about the war and Fascism and human misery, to tear away the veil of lies with which Mussolini's regime had tried to conceal the bitter realities of Italian life. Such was the very simple origin of what came to be called neorealism. Neorealism was not an organized or fully self-conscious aesthetic school. Indeed, most of those who were regarded as its representatives denied the label entirely; the name was attached after the fact and did no more than call attention to something that was already in existence. Neorealism was a temper and an attitude that faithfully mirrored Italy's actual situation in the war and immediate postwar years.

Its origins went back to the 1930's when a handful of younger writers began to gather in cafés, to publish little magazines, and to express their distaste for Fascism by writing in a style that was more honest and direct than the inflated official rhetoric. As models these young men had the writings of the "hermetic" poets—Giuseppe Ungaretti, Eugenio Montale, and Salvatore Quasimodo (who received the Nobel Prize for literature in 1960)—and of such American novelists as Faulkner and Hemingway. Yet it was not just a new authenticity of style that Italians beginning their literary careers found in the American novel. In the 1930's an interest in the United States was itself an act of political protest, a token of admiration for a free and dynamic society and at the same time of an uneasy awareness of the violence below the surface of American life. This, of course, was particularly true of the American South, and if Hemingway was to be the master of a spare, stripped style for the young Italians, it was from Faulkner's novels that they learned to see in a new light the terror and emotional frustrations of their own South, which was likewise the national stepchild and a region of perennial defeat. The translations from "the American" (as the Italians persist in calling our language) which writers like Cesare Pavese and Elio Vittorini produced just before and during the war gave them their apprenticeship in literary integrity and a new sense of fiction as an exacting craft.

They also had an Italian forebear—the slightly older novelist Alberto Moravia. As early as 1929, the twenty-two-year-old Moravia had scored a *succès de scandale* with his first novel, *The Time of Indifference*. This was in no direct sense a political or anti-Fascist book, but it was emphatically non-Fascist, and in its depiction of the empty lives of the Roman bourgeoisie it laid bare the cynicism behind the lip service that the rich and the wellborn paid to Fascist "ideals." Such were to be Moravia's abiding themes throughout the generation and more that he figured as Italy's most prominent novelist. A natural storyteller, with a fluent if negligent pen, Moravia shared the neorealists' honesty while lacking their lyricism and political conviction. Not until 1951, with *The Conformist,* did Moravia publish his first explicitly ideological novel.

The note of political and social urgency in neorealism came, rather, from the experience of the wartime resistance. Around this time, most of these young writers became Communists or near-Communists. Some subsequently broke with the party; one of the most promising, Pavese, committed suicide in 1950; the majority were never Marxists in any dogmatic or doctrinaire sense. They simply wanted to express their solidarity with the poor and the oppressed, and in the Italy of the 1940's to become a Communist seemed the most appropriate way of doing so.

It is difficult to select a typical neorealist novel or to define with exactitude the guiding characteristics of this kind of writing. Certainly the book that won the widest acclaim in the United States—Vittorini's *In Sicily,* originally published in 1941—could scarcely be called realist in any sense: it was more a series of impressions, of emotional encounters, of hallucinations, in the few days that a Sicilian worker, heartsick at the hollowness of his life in the North, spends with his mother in the scenes of his childhood; even the political references (note the date of publication) are fragmentary and allusive. Perhaps the novel that can best stand for the movement as a whole is Vasco Pratolini's *A Tale of Poor Lovers* (1947). Here the setting is Florentine rather than Sicilian; but this is of no crucial importance—in neorealism, as opposed to late nineteenth-century realistic writing, folklore and local color are not significant for their own sake and figure as little more than a backdrop against which is played out a drama of common human emotion. Moreover, the novelist makes none of the pretense of scientific objectivity toward his characters that was a source of pride to realism in its earlier phases. He takes their part, rather, and argues their case against their oppressors. Thus, in *A Tale of Poor Lovers* Pratolini conducts the reader to a narrow, densely-populated Florentine street just behind the Palazzo Vecchio and sympathetically introduces a vast cast of characters one by one; they are little folk—artisans for the most part—and few have any deep political convictions; their chief concern seems to be for the complex net of love relationships that link a dozen or more of their young people; yet the Fascist terror is advancing—the date is the mid-1920's—they are forced to take sides, and in the end political tyranny overwhelms them all.

Pratolini's book is directly felt and sentimental almost to a fault; it deals with simple people and is written in a style and tone attuned to the ordinary reader. For such was the aesthetic goal of neorealism: it aimed at a popular literature, politically engaged and alive with contemporary passion, a literature that would present in all their abjectness the squalid lives of the Italian poor and then lift them to a new type of beauty and faith in the future. This was the achievement of neorealism, and this was its fatal weakness. Once it had had its say—once it had burst through the hated limitations imposed by Fascism, and the emotional impetus of the resistance had spent itself in the disappointments of the postwar years—the neorealist manner proved too thin. Something less topical and aesthetically more sophisticated was required to sustain Italian literature into the next generation.

The same may be said for the cinema, which during the middle and late 1940's played a counterpoint to the neorealist novel. In this case once again, the aesthetic rationale came after the fact. The great films of the era—Roberto Rossellini's *Open City* and *Paisà*, Vittorio De Sica's *Shoe-Shine* and *Bicycle Thief*—reflected actual conditions both in theme and in technique. The last years of Mussolini's regime had produced a new crop of talented film directors —some of them trained in the Experimental Center which was one of that regime's few genuine gifts to Italian culture—men who had seen the war at first hand and felt that they knew how to film it. But they were poor like the characters they put on the screen, and they did their best with what they had. So in the absence of studios they worked outdoors; they frequently used as actors the ordinary people whom they found on the streets; and some—particularly Rossellini—improvised their scripts as they went along.

For a half decade, Italy seemed to be producing the most original motion pictures in the Western world. But the neorealist films were never popular with the Italian public, which preferred Hollywood's frothier wares (one may feel some sympathy for their complaint that having experienced all this suffering themselves, they objected to seeing it once more on the screen). Nor did the government and the Church appreciate the work of men like Rossellini and De Sica: officialdom found that their films displayed too many shameful features of Italian life; the clericals were scandalized that priests were almost invariably depicted as unsympathetic or at best comic characters. By the turn of the decade, the neorealist film, like the neorealist novel, was wearing thin. The directors were discouraged and without money; De Sica—one of Italy's most talented actors—was obliged to lead a double life, as he played (opposite some sultry popular actress) in the light, quick-selling films that would earn him the funds to go on with further productions of his own. The 1950's were to be lean years in the Italian cinema: while one new director of talent—Federico Fellini—won respect abroad with such meticulously honest creations as *La Strada* and *Cabiria,* most of those responsible for the Italian film renaissance fell out of circulation as they waited for better times.

3. FROM FANTASY TO PSYCHOLOGY IN DEPTH

In 1958 there appeared without warning the novel that was to be more discussed than any Italian work of fiction since Manzoni's *The Betrothed* of a century and a quarter earlier—*The Leopard,* by the Sicilian Prince of Lampedusa. The posthumous and unfinished work of a literary amateur, the manuscript of *The Leopard* had passed from publisher to publisher in a protracted search for one willing to take a chance on it. For Lampedusa's novel scarcely promised to be a best-seller: it was low-keyed and stylistically old-fashioned. Yet when it finally appeared, both the Italian critics and the general public were unhesitating in recognizing it as a masterpiece.

The phenomenal success of *The Leopard,* better than any other single work, epitomized the changes in taste and emphasis that the Italian educated public was experiencing in the mid-1950's. Almost everything about it differed from the canons of neorealism. Its provincial background was not merely incidental: it was the very stuff of the novel itself, which would have been meaningless without its Sicilian setting. Where the neorealists' tone had been affirmative, the Prince of Lampedusa's was gently ironical; while they had looked resolutely to the future, the author of *The Leopard* recalled with melancholy a vanished past; as against neorealism's absorption in ideology and external events, Lampedusa was concerned for psychological precision and carefully delineated shades of meaning.

Which is all to say, perhaps, that with *The Leopard,* the Italian novel finally came of age. An anemic and sporadic growth in earlier eras, with no such continuous tradition as had sustained the writing of fiction in France or England, the Italian novel in the immediate postwar years had been characterized more by profusion and intense commitment than by the excellence of its literary craftsmanship.

No individual neorealist novel had won unqualified endorsement in the countries where fiction was a firmly established genre. With the publication of *The Leopard*, all this changed: Italy had at last produced a work of fiction which could stand comparison with the best in Britain or France or the United States.

Giuseppe Tomasi di Lampedusa did not live to see his own triumph. Sick, isolated, and profoundly skeptical, he was in any case too old and discouraged to lead a new literary movement. But there were younger writers who were already breaking away from realism in a quest like Lampedusa's for the hallucinatory memories of a near or a remote past. There was Elsa Morante, the author of *Arthur's Island*, the haunting recollection of a lonely adolescence, and Italo Calvino, whose tales of fantastic figures from earlier centuries put into modern idiom the chivalric tradition of courtly verse. These were more careful novelists than the neorealists: they wrote with less urgency, and with a finer ear for language and emotional nuance. By the mid-1950's, the essential things about the misery of the Italian people had already been said; the dismal record had been spread before the reading public. Now there was time for craftsmanship, for lingering memory, and for an expert probing of human motivation.

The same kind of change occurred in the cinema, when at the end of the 1950's a second wave of film-making put Italy once more in the forefront of experiment. On the one hand the old masters returned to their most congenial theme—the suffering and the dignity of Italians caught in the grip of war: De Sica adapted for the screen *Two Women*, one of the rare novels in which Alberto Moravia had permitted his readers a glimpse of his human sympathies, and he teamed up for the first time with Rossellini—the former as actor, the latter as director—in *General della Rovere*. In each case, an individual figure was now in the foreground, with mass action less prominent than it had been a decade earlier. But these were not the films that puzzled, delighted, or exasperated audiences both at home and abroad. The great innovators were Fellini once more and a new director, Michelangelo Antonioni. Antonioni taxed the patience of the public more than any of his predecessors. Each succeeding production in his trilogy of major films—*L'avventura, La notte, L'eclisse*—stretched more unbearably his audience's powers of attention and understanding. For Antonioni attempted the all but impossible task of displaying in full dimension his characters' boredom and inconsequential behavior and inability to communicate with each other. Hence his slow pace and his obsessive tempos. With Antonioni, the Italian cinema reached an ultimate in psychological understanding from which the next point of departure was difficult to perceive.

In Fellini's work also, individual psychology or the emotions of a limited number of characters predominated, as opposed to the immediate postwar concern for ideology and social problems. Here the change in cinematic emphasis paralleled the shift that was simultaneously taking place in the writing of fiction. Similarly, what was fantastic or nostalgic in the novel of the 1950's was echoed in Fellini's most unorthodox production, which bore the cryptic title *8 1/2*. A film within a film, conceived on more than one level of understanding, *8 1/2* was its director's personal summing-up, his apologia for the craft his own endeavors had so notably enhanced.

Yet it was *8 1/2*'s predecessor, *La dolce vita*—longer, less individual, and wider in its social dimension—which had first catapulted Fellini to international fame and become the most discussed Italian film of all time. During the early months of 1960, it frequently seemed that Italians were incapable of talking about anything else. But what they found in *La dolce vita* varied with the prejudices or previous experience they brought to it. Some merely admired its virtuosity of technique. Others focused on a single character as epitomizing one or another aspect of contemporary Italian society. Its defenders—even certain Jesuit critics—explained its importance as a twentieth-century morality play and underlined its indictment of Rome's aesthetic cliques and café society. The majority restricted themselves to conventional (and possibly hypocritical) shock at its sexual frankness.

In any event, *La dolce vita* fused the neorealists' social anger and the more recent absorption with psychology in depth. In this sense, it capped nearly two decades of cinematic experiment. Moreover, like so many of its predecessors and successors, *La dolce vita* could not be shown at all until it had run the gauntlet of a peculiarly vexatious form of censorship. In the 1950's and early 1960's, Italy was technically living under a regime in which both the press and the entertainment industry enjoyed full freedom of expression. In practice, however, the situation was considerably less permissive. Under the terms of loosely-worded enactments authorizing the banning of films offensive to public decency, patriotism, or "family order," any motion picture that was in the least unorthodox might incur the wrath of some zealous public official. Such condemnations were far from automatic: they varied from city to city, depending on the local balance of political forces or the whim of the police and magistracy. Thus the launching of a new film might require a series of scattered court battles before its nationwide showing was insured. In the end, nearly every motion picture of importance emerged victorious—perhaps after some trivial deletions of offending scenes. But the toll in delay, expense, and frayed nerves added not a little to the desperate strain—immortalized in *8 1/2*—undergone by the Italian film director who refused to compromise his aesthetic standards.

The *reductio ad absurdum* of such official capriciousness came in 1961 with the banning of the anti-war film *Non uccidere* ("Thou shalt not kill"). The mayor of Florence, Giorgio La Pira—a saintly and totally independent figure, whose eccentric understanding of Christian Democracy had long annoyed the ruling party—decided that it deserved to be shown nonetheless. So he arranged for a special screening in one of the public buildings belonging to the Florentine municipality. The result was a tragicomic battle in which the unworldly mayor proved himself far more astute than his adversaries had supposed:

It seems that the whole long course of the negotiations which . . . held at bay the prefect . . . the chief of police, the prime minister, the minister of the interior . . . were punctuated by a continuous series of small dodges and ruses on the part of the saintly mayor, who reduced his . . . opponents to fainting fits by citing St. Paul, the Gospels, Thomas a Kempis' *Imitation of Christ,* and other edifying pages of the fathers and doctors of the Church. . .

Apparently enjoying himself tremendously, "La Pira fluttered gaily from the Ten Commandments . . . to the articles of the Constitution" in his effort to convince the Prime Minister—who was, of course, his fellow Christian Democrat—of the "mystic goodness" of the film showing he had planned.

In the end—not unpredictably—the mayor of Florence won his bureaucratic battle. The episode had brought into clear focus the

stupidity and inconsistency of administrative action against offending films, while drawing attention once again to the anomaly of
having such a drama played out within the confines of the same
political party. The caustic comment of a Radical critic epitomized
the danger for democratic principles:

It is sad [to note] . . . that in order to oppose thickheaded ministers . . .
obtuse censors, timid prefects, and zealous chiefs of police, one must be a
little bit crazy in a saintly way, to the point that merely a correct understanding of the Constitution must be considered in Italy as something
of a miracle . . . *

Such were the hazards that Italy's creative writers and artists were
still encountering two decades after the fall of Fascism. Vexations
like these were not remotely comparable to the persecution that free
speech had suffered under Mussolini. But they violated Italy's new
republican constitution and were unworthy of a governing party
that prided itself on its unyielding defense of democracy. A narrow
and uncomprehending attitude on the part of officialdom, an aesthetically slack and conformist temper among the bulk of the population—these were the limitations that still discouraged or held in
check the Italian cultural renaissance. Not the least among the urgent
tasks facing the new Socialist ministers as they entered the government at the end of 1963 was to ensure a more liberal interpretation
of the constitutional guarantees of free expression.

Nor, in a wider sense, was the battle for a full and realistic
confrontation of Italy's miseries yet won as the country entered the
second half of the 1960's. The aesthetic emphasis might have shifted
—the younger writers and film directors might insist far more than
in the recent past on refinements of technique and sensibility. But
there was no sharp break between generations: most of the aesthetic
innovators regarded themselves as socially engaged and the cham-
pions of the disinherited. In this sense, the postwar cultural renaissance had a single major theme; even dream and fantasy—as in
Calvino's novels or Fellini's films—were not so much an escape as
a way to a clearer understanding of reality. The dominant tone
remained, as before, a protest against despair—a characteristically
Italian affirmation of the value of living itself, and a refusal to give
up one's sense of humor in the face of misfortune.

* "Il frutto del miracolo," *Il Mondo,* November 28, 1961, p. 2.

12

Italy in the Western Community

1. A EUROPEAN FOREIGN POLICY

IT WAS A TRIBUTE to the vision and determination of the statesmen who conducted Italy's foreign relations in the immediate postwar years that from the wreckage they had inherited they succeeded in constructing a policy which won their country an impressive array of friends and a minimum of enemies. This achievement was the work of the two men who with one short interruption between them filled the office of foreign minister from the end of 1944 to mid-1953, Prime Minister De Gasperi and Count Carlo Sforza. It was De Gasperi who took up the unrewarding task of reintegrating Italy in the Western community of nations while the war was still in progress, and of conducting the peace negotiations with the victorious powers. And after the retirement of Sforza from the foreign ministry in 1951, the Christian Democratic leader again assumed the added responsibility for foreign affairs. In this second period of office, however, he simply followed the lines of policy marked out by his predecessor. For it was Sforza who was primarily responsible for developing a concept of Italy's international role that was European in scope.

Count Sforza was a great Italian patriot. Beyond that he was a good European and a citizen of the world. An aristocrat and a democrat with equal conviction, Sforza combined a sovereign self-confidence and hauteur with an ease and familiarity of manner and a negligence in speech and dress. He was at once charming and tactless—his outspokenness was proverbial—and he inspired both strong personal devotion and strong dislike. In post-Fascist Italy, despite his record as the leading figure in the emigration, he never became truly popular: he had no solid constituency behind him.

Yet De Gasperi saw that Sforza could bring to the government an indefinable quality of *grandezza* that it otherwise almost totally lacked. From 1920 to 1921 Sforza as foreign minister had tried to stem the rising flood of nationalist agitation by pursuing a policy of modest goals and international understanding. A quarter century later he resumed the same task, and with more lasting results. From his appointment as foreign minister in 1947 to his death in 1952, Sforza consistently urged on his timorous colleagues a bold and imaginative concept of European federation. For his long residence abroad had given him more than a familiarity with and affection for foreign nations, particularly for France and the United States. It had inspired in him a passionate devotion to the ideal of European unity. And in this respect at least Sforza had behind him a distinguished and influential segment of Italian public opinion.

Out of an unpromising situation, De Gasperi and Sforza undertook to win for Italy a place of respect in a European community newly conscious of its common interests. Their first achievement was restoring good relations with France. Here there was much to hinder the work of understanding: the French could not quickly forget the "stab in the back" of 1940, and many Italians resented the loss of the few square miles of Alpine valley that the peace treaty had assigned to the French. But the common interests and traditions of the two nations, sedulously stressed by the foreign ministers of both powers, proved strong enough to overcome prejudice on either side. In February 1948, Italy and France agreed to work out a customs union to come into effect gradually over the next two years.

The Franco-Italian customs union soon ran into nearly insuperable technical difficulties. But it served as a rehearsal for more substantial achievements to come. In the same year, the Western European economic cooperation under the Marshall Plan began. And the decade that followed brought the treaties that bound together the six nations of the narrower Western European alliance in the European Coal and Steel Community (Schuman Plan) of 1951, Euratom of 1956, and the Common Market of 1957. In these negotiations—and in the advisory deliberations of the Council of Europe that accompanied them—Italy almost invariably took the lead. Sforza and De Gasperi consistently pressed for a bolder initiative and a more rapid timetable. In addition, Italy played an indispensable role as balance and buffer between France and Germany. One reason why the French and Germans were willing to work together so soon after the end of the war was the presence of the Italians to reassure them both. For if Italy had developed strong ties to France, she also had evident bonds of sympathy with a Germany that, like herself, was a former fascist power, ruled by a Christian Democratic government, and similarly striving for full acceptance among the Western democratic nations.

The original architects of Italy's postwar foreign policy, then, did their best to strengthen the political and economic links that joined the nations of the West. This policy reflected a sure understanding of Italian needs and interests. Sforza and De Gasperi saw that in a game of independent prestige politics, Italy could never rank higher than fourth among the powers of Western Europe: this was the reckless sort of competition that had led Mussolini to disaster. It was better to accept a more modest role, and by taking the lead in renouncing the formal paraphernalia of sovereignty, to persuade the larger powers similarly to limit their possibilities of pursuing independent adventures. Such was the wisdom that nearly a century of hesitation and experiment in Italian foreign policy had taught.

Unfortunately, De Gasperi's successors were not always so prudent. Beginning with the Pella government of 1953, the country's foreign ministers periodically succumbed to the temptation to launch a policy that would make more noise on the international stage. As prime minister, Pella tried to exploit the Trieste issue to win nationalist support; in his subsequent tenure of the foreign ministry, he indulged in similar appeals to old-fashioned national sentiment. The same was true of Gaetano Martino—the Liberals' choice for the foreign office in periods of coalition government. The rationale for such behavior was flimsy in the extreme: with the Italian electorate steadily moving away from the rightist parties, there was less and less reason to appease the traditionalist constituency. The basic explanation lay rather in one of the lingering anachronisms of Italian popular psychology.

The penchant for the *bel gesto,* for cutting a fine figure in foreign policy, betrayed itself in all sorts of symptomatic actions that non-

Italians were inclined to dismiss as insignificant, mistaken, or possibly even comic.* Italy's press and foreign ministry kept stressing the "presence" or "voice" of their country in international bodies where in fact the Italians had very little to say. The nation's leaders sought to act as mediators whether or not their services were welcome—the extreme instance being President Gronchi's trip to Moscow in the spring of 1960 which most commentators found incompatible with his constitutional role. And Italy's foreign representatives similarly tried to find "free" areas between Soviet and American influence where their own country's prestige could be brought to bear. The opportunity closest to home was of course the Mediterranean and the Arab world. Here many Italians argued that their modest share in earlier colonial adventures and lack of racial prejudice particularly fitted them to win the Arabs' sympathy as British and French influence receded. This contention was perfectly realistic when it came to Enrico Mattei's revolutionary oil contracts, which in fact gave more favored treatment to the Middle Eastern states. On the sentimental level, however, it lacked substance and merely recalled Mussolini's pro-Islamic posturings.

Such gestures were almost invariably without a sequel. In the decade following De Gasperi's retirement, the Italian search for new initiatives in foreign policy was barren of results. And the more realistic observers of that policy kept reminding the public that most of the time Italy could scarcely expect to make its voice heard, as the world community grew larger and Italy's position in that world was correspondingly reduced. Only as a member of a larger unit could the Italian nation cut a significant figure. Hence all experiments in foreign policy eventually led back to Sforza's and De Gasperi's insistence on the interests of Western Europe as a whole. This was the course that in the long term alone made sense. And it implied a relationship of equality among the six nations of the Common Market. European-minded Italians were virtually unanimous in resisting De Gaulle's pretensions to leadership; they also agreed that democratic Britain belonged in the Common Market and that authoritarian Spain did not.

Within this shared loyalty to the European idea, two contrasting interpretations struggled for a hearing. The more conservative

* Norman Kogan, *The Politics of Italian Foreign Policy* (New York, 1963), p. 145.

interpretation—and the one that predominated throughout the post-De Gasperi decade—stressed dependence on the United States and the Western alliance as Italy's shield against leftist subversion at home. The alternative line of argument contended that the leftist menace was a bogey inherited from the past, that in the late 1950's and early 1960's there was not the remotest chance of a Soviet invasion welcomed by Italian Communist embraces. This second school of thought further held that Italy's main focus of concern should not be foreign policy at all, but her demographic and economic needs, that as an underdeveloped nation herself Italy needed freedom from foreign tensions and high military expenditures. Such a point of view—in its narrow definition of the Atlantic alliance—was close to that of the Norwegians and the Danes.

If the more conservative and American-oriented interpretation characterized the Christian Democratic party, the second was espoused by the Italian Socialists after they broke their ties with Communism. In the late 1950's the Socialists grudgingly accepted the Atlantic Pact as a "fact of life": the Soviet repression of the Hungarian revolt in 1956 had convinced them that any unilateral withdrawal from either major power bloc could endanger the peace by upsetting the existing balance. But this acceptance was carefully hedged: the Socialists insisted that the Western alliance be given a "purely defensive interpretation." The corollary was strenuous Socialist opposition to American missile bases in Italy—an opposition that may have contributed to their eventual liquidation—and a similar resistance to the American project of a European multi-lateral nuclear force. On one point in particular the Italian Socialists were immovable: they refused to countenance the proliferation of nuclear weapons, whether in the form of the French independent *force de frappe* or as a thinly-disguised grant of such weapons to a resurgent German military establishment.

Such deep-seated differences on foreign policy reinforced the already existing disagreement about economic and social priorities which made the Center-Left coalition so precarious. For the Christian Democrats were prepared to go along with the American nuclear initiatives that the Socialists found intolerable. These foreign policy cleavages need also to be borne in mind in assessing the most recent vicissitudes of the opening to the Left.

2. THE NEW POLITICAL COURSE

The parliamentary election of 1963 had in effect endorsed the opening to the Left. But it had done it in so bewildering a form—most notably through reinforcing the Communists—that both of the major coalition partners felt aggrieved and rebuked by their constituents. In the post-electoral recriminations, the Christian Democrats talked of a "cleaned-up" Center-Left (which presumably meant dropping the ministers most closely associated with the new course), while the Socialists were even warier than before of compromise with "bourgeois" policies. The first and most apparent conclusion from the nearly universal disappointment was that Fanfani must go. His logical successor was Aldo Moro, the Christian Democratic party secretary and a key participant in the Center-Left policy.

In the early days of June 1963—when the attention of most Italians was rivetted on the protracted death of Pope John—Moro put together a new coalition of Christian Democrats, Republicans, and Social Democrats, with the Socialists once more counted on to supply support from outside the government. Its program and composition were slightly to the right of the defunct Fanfani ministry— an understandable response to the Christian Democrats' conviction that the opening to the Left had lost them votes, but certainly not in line with the general leftward move of the electorate. This was the view of a powerful minority among the Socialists; at the last moment the opposition of Riccardo Lombardi, Nenni's most influential collaborator and heir apparent, brought the artfully contrived combination crashing down.

There was no recourse but the usual stopgap *monocolore*. The election results had ruled out any Christian Democratic trafficking with the Right. They had also made impossible the sort of pseudocaretaker government—such as Pella and Tambroni had headed in the past—that served as a cover for a conservative resurgence. The ministry formed by Giovanni Leone on June 21 (the very day Giovanni Battista Montini was being elevated to the papal throne as Paul VI) was just what it pretended to be, a device for getting through the summer months while giving Italy's political parties a chance to recover from their post-election shock. No more than a routine Christian Democratic politician himself, with the titular distinction of being president of the Chamber, Leone at least remained true to his mandate and kept the conduct of government business at a correspondingly routine level.

As political therapy, the Leone experiment worked. Once the party leaders had regained their equilibrium, they realized that nothing was fundamentally changed—that there was no alternative to the previous coalition. This was the conclusion of the Christian Democratic party meeting in August; indeed, the final motion went beyond the previous opening to the Left in suggesting that the Socialists should be included in the new ministry. Such was also the outcome of the Socialists' deliberations two months later, when a comfortable majority of the congress authorized Nenni to begin negotiations (for the first time in more than sixteen years) for full Socialist participation in the government. The delegates had been sobered by hearing the seventy-two-year-old Nenni recite a record of four decades of lost opportunities, the greater part of which had been his own. Yet the voice which had most impressed the congress was that of Riccardo Lombardi—now back by Nenni's side—who had warned that Italian Socialism could not afford to reject the chance of influencing the economic transformation which the next decade would bring. This was an argument that touched the party's central aspirations and was calculated to win assent on all sides. In comparison, foreign-policy considerations seemed secondary: the Socialist congress neatly side-stepped the issue of the multilateral force by passing to the British Labour party the initiative in opposing it.

With a double party endorsement now behind him, Moro could try once more with better hope of success. In early November, Leone resigned and Moro began to form a coalition ministry; as finally constituted a month later, it included sixteen Christian Democrats, six Socialists, three Social Democrats, and one Republican. Nenni was designated vice-premier and Saragat foreign minister, with Socialists and conservative Christian Democrats canceling each other out in the economic portfolios. Economic issues naturally dominated the new government's reform program: besides the perennial matter of overhauling the tax system and the civil service, Moro made precise commitments in the four areas where the coalition partners could agree that prompt action was urgent—the establishment of regional administration, a radical revision of agrarian tenures, urban planning and housing construction, and the strengthening of public education. The parliamentary vote of confidence went through with ease in mid-December, although about thirty of the Christian Democratic Right threatened to walk out of the Chamber, and a slightly smaller number of the Socialist Left actually did so; the latter were to be heard from again within a very short time.

This painless beginning was deceptive. For one thing, three of the strongest proponents of the opening to the Left remained outside the government—Fanfani, Lombardi, and La Malfa. While Fanfani's absence was understandable, that of Lombardi was more serious, since he was Italian Socialism's leading economic strategist. These two were presumably expressing their doubts of Moro's ability to keep their divergent parties working in harmony. But La Malfa's absence could be attributed only to political ingratitude: the Socialists wanted his ministry, and in the scramble for office La Malfa's long service in the cause of economic planning was forgotten; his colleagues in the diminutive Republican party might also have remembered that their chief reason for continuing to exist was to provide their most talented figure with a secure political base.

Beyond these disappointing omissions, the Moro experiment—the full opening to the Left as opposed to the partial one that Fanfani had inaugurated nearly two years earlier—had come too late. It had come after a decade of political struggle, and by the time it finally arrived, much of the moral impetus behind it had already been expended. Still worse, it came in the full flood of inflation. In the previous two years imports had mounted sharply, and the rival labor federations—for once working in harmony—had lifted the workers' share in the national product by nearly five percentage points. This wage raise was certainly overdue and in itself was not necessarily inflationary. But it had been delayed so long that it impinged on the economy with explosive force and in the absence of official measures for controlling other inflationary pressures such as the boom in real estate.

The new government was aware of the problem it faced. In their initial statement of the coalition's program, the Center-Left partners had agreed on the need of short-term anti-inflation measures sufficient to deal with the current crisis in international payments while not so drastic as to impede the rhythm of Italy's economic development. This carefully-balanced double talk betrayed how fragile the understanding between the parties had been. The deeper divergence could not be papered over: the Christian Democrats put the fight against inflation before everything else; the Socialists refused to sacrifice their reform goals. From the outset, the Moro government labored under an almost insuperable handicap.

Nor was the Prime Minister himself a man to dominate his colleagues, or by overpowering personal force to induce them to settle their differences. He had neither Fanfani's drive and economic expertise nor Nenni's standing as an already half-legendary historical figure. Skeptical, infinitely patient, a southerner with the congenital melancholy of the *Mezzogiorno* joined to an almost Anglo-Saxon impassivity, Moro might be a nearly ideal leader to put a coalition together, but he was less equipped to control his own party's representatives in the ministry when they began to quarrel with the Socialists. By early summer Moro's Christian Democratic colleagues had lost all restraint: the Minister of the Treasury leaked to the press a supposedly confidential letter to the Prime Minister in which he announced that the country was on the verge of bankruptcy; somebody else slipped into the budget a special appropriation for Church schools which even the Socialist under-secretary in the Ministry of Education knew nothing about. This last—a trifling matter in itself—exhausted the Socialists' dwindling reserve of forbearance. They abstained from the vote on the offending provision, and the government was left seven votes short of a majority. Moro resigned: for once a ministry was overthrown in a conventional parliamentary fashion rather than through the backstage intrigues of the Christian Democrats themselves. But the irony of the whole episode was that Italy's economic situation was already improving: the balance of payments crisis had been relieved, and it was recession rather than inflation that was now the danger.

After nearly a month of political maneuvering—and with a nationwide rail strike threatening—in late July Moro reconstituted his government almost exactly as it had been before. He had accomplished this in the face of bitter reproaches from his conservative party colleagues and a further secession of Socialists. Perhaps the ministerial hiatus had brought home to both sides the perils of inter-party warfare. Yet the basic disagreement between them remained unchanged; only the economic outlook had brightened.

This disagreement flared up five months later when with the incapacity of Antonio Segni—President of the Republic since 1962 —it became necessary to elect a new head of state. After nearly two weeks of deadlock and an unprecedented twenty-one ballots, Foreign Minister Saragat was finally chosen. Italians of laical views were naturally jubilant that the presidency, which had been for nearly a decade in Christian Democratic hands, was once again independent of Catholic influence. Proponents of the opening to the Left also felt that the choice of Saragat had strengthened the new political formula. But the disarray within the governing coalition (and within Christian Democracy itself) that the protracted struggle over the presidency had revealed remained unresolved: it was, if anything, intensified by the return to power in early 1965 of the perennially ambitious Fanfani as Saragat's successor in the foreign ministry.

The divergence within the coalition over Church schools, and the even deeper cleavage on how to deal with inflation, are far from sufficient to explain the agonizing difficulty in keeping Christian Democrats and Socialists in tandem. The simple fact is that neither party trusts the other. Such a lack of mutual confidence is nothing new in European politics: it had always characterized the relations between Catholics and Marxists-turned-democrats ever since the two first began working together under the Weimar Republic; sometimes the distrust has been minimal—as in the Netherlands today—sometimes it has flared into open civil war—as in Austria in the 1930's. In Italy things have never gone that far: for nearly a generation the two parties had a common enemy in Fascism. But the fact that under Italian conditions Christian Democracy is necessarily more Catholic and Socialism traditionally more socialist than elsewhere has given a particular local bite to their mutual antagonism.

Italian Christian Democracy stands in a special relation to Catholicism for the obvious reason that Italy is the headquarters of the universal Church whose head is an Italian. Hence it is peculiarly sensitive to directives or hints emanating from the Vatican. This closeness created no serious political problem so long as the party and the Papacy had common interests—however it might infuriate Italian anti-clericals. During the De Gasperi era the two could agree on the overriding importance of the Communist danger; Catholic Action was happy to supply the precinct workers for a party that most of the time remained true to the cause of political and social conservatism. Then in the mid-1950's things began to change: Fanfani scandalized the orthodox by pushing Christian Democracy toward positions that seemed quasi-socialist. A half decade later something even more extraordinary occurred: under Pope John's guidance the Papacy took a great leap leftward—clean over the heads of the Christian Democratic majority—and good Catholics were perplexed by the thought that the crusade against Communism might no longer be a holy war at all. The result was a profound confusion which certainly contributed to Christian Democracy's loss of votes in the election of 1963.

Today the party, while still the welter of factions and interests that it has always been, has two main tendencies struggling for domination—those who want to keep Christian Democracy about as it has been in the past and those who want to make it a vehicle for welfare-state policies within a modern industrial society. The former include what remains of the party Right—now led by Mario Scelba, who has joined so many other Christian Democratic "notables" in an evolution toward conservatism—and, more importantly, a shifting, pragmatic Center that for the present is willing to work with Moro and the party Left. The label under which this group travels changes every few years; of late they have been calling themselves the *Dorotei*. But their underlying purpose remains constant: refusing to draw the consequences from the fact that Christian Democracy is no longer the majority party, they try in every possible way to maintain its hegemony over Italian public life; cooperation with the party reformers and even with the Socialists ranks in their minds as only one more device toward this higher purpose. Meantime their grass-roots support is gradually being eroded: it is composed too heavily of old people, of women, and of earnest adolescents who soon drop out of party activity. This was what Fanfani realized long ago: he saw that it was necessary to raise up a new generation of leadership which would be drawn from and appeal to the junior executives, the technicians, and the skilled workers who were the type-figures in Italy's new industrial society. Yet he never scored more than a half success: for one thing, leaders like himself and Moro remained too much old-fashioned politicians to recast their party utterly. The modernizing faction within Christian Democracy is best represented by younger men whose names are totally unknown to the American newspaper public: strong at party congresses, it becomes progressively weaker as the young reformers try to rise to a seat in parliament and beyond that to a ministerial portfolio.

Italian Socialism is more socialist than in other European countries in the sense that it has not forgotten its pre-First World War origins. Its rank and file and more sectarian leadership remain class-conscious, profoundly anti-war, and millenialist in their hopes for the future. This ideological innocence can be both appealing and exasperating: it was largely responsible for the party's disastrous two decades of cooperation with the Communists. Yet for all his mistakes, Nenni is still one of the most attractive figures on the Italian political landscape—a true popular leader whose honesty of purpose no one can question. Perhaps he alone could have persuaded the ordinary Socialist militant that it was no class treason to go into coalition with Christian Democracy.

But Nenni belongs to another age: he is of Mussolini's generation, as he was in the Duce's Socialist days, Mussolini's friend. It is younger men who will have to drag Italian Socialism, despite its protestations of fidelity to the heroic past, into the late twentieth-century world. It is they who must make the mighty effort to lift the party over fifty years of history from the atmosphere of pre-1914 Marxism into the post-Keynesian universe of input-output analysis. In this respect, Italian Socialism is obliged to make an even greater leap than Christian Democracy. The party militants are aging: they hate ideological change, and they distrust intellectuals. One of the gravest handicaps that Lombardi and his colleagues suffer under as party reformers is that so many of them are intellectuals, in a movement where until very recently such people were regarded as outsiders, and that their ideological origins derive from the wartime Party of Action rather than from Marxism.

Suspicions of this sort had a great deal to do with the walkout of twenty-five Socialist deputies during the voice of confidence on the first Moro government. Subsequently these deputies organized a secessionist party—the PSIUP*—under the leadership of Tullio Vecchietti. Although the secession deprived Italian Socialism of more than a quarter of its deputies, the effect on the rank and file was less serious. Many of the trade union leaders remained with the old party; some of them may have reasoned that their Communist union colleagues wanted them to do so, since the Communist party as a whole was far from happy about a split that merely created new competition on the Left while weakening the philo-Communist minority within the main body of Italian Socialism. Moreover, one of the two chief types among the rare recruits that the new party picked up was of particular concern to Communists on the alert for deviations within their own ranks. They were not worried about the older Marxist sectaries who rallied to Vecchietti. They were alarmed rather by the young men with "Chinese" or Castroist enthusiasms whose protests against "respectability" and compromise with the Italian "establishment" they were already hearing at their own party gatherings.

The secession from Italian Socialism, then, weakened the main party only slightly. On the positive side it made it more homogeneous and increased the likelihood of its reunification with Saragat's Social Democrats, who had lost their *raison d'être* when Nenni completed his evolution toward parliamentary democracy. The importance of the new splinter group—if it has any at all—is its position to the Left of Communism as truer to Marxist doctrine and more genuine in its revolutionary claims. The only ideological standing-ground it can find is as the first European version of a "Chinese" Marxist party. Such an evolution still lies in the future. Its chief role today is to call attention to the curious phenomenon that Italian Communism has become since the death of Stalin.

In searching out the reasons for the Communists' gains in the election of 1963, Italian observers noted that although this had happened throughout the country, it had been most apparent in the two areas where Communism was already especially strong—the industrial Northwest and the "red belt" of the North-Center. To explain the party's victories in the triangle Turin-Genoa-Milan was not particularly difficult: here it sufficed to point to the new

* *Partito Socialista Italiana di Unità Proletaria.*

voters who had poured in from the South. In regions like Tuscany and the Emilia-Romagna, the election returns were more puzzling: the population shifts had been less extensive and social discontents less apparent. The explanation could be found only in terms of Communism itself having been transformed into a kind of "establishment." In the north-central part of the country, the Communists had been powerful for so long that they had become the dominant vested interest: they controlled the cooperative movement, the trade unions, and several important municipalities. Such tasks had given them a sense of public responsibility; as the holders of local power, they even received credit for the prevailing prosperity. In the "red belt," to cast a vote for Communism meant to endorse a going concern.

It is hard to tell how deep this new attitude of respectability goes. Certainly Togliatti and his chief political heirs have done their best to project a "social-democratic image." Some recent statements suggest that they may be ready to make the final jump to democracy in the Western sense and accept the idea of free competition among political parties even under a Communist regime.* They loathe the idea of violent revolution and would not like to risk the secure position they have achieved as a domesticated opposition within Italian society. Nobody can say whether the Communists intend to live up to their democratic professions until they have a chance to put them into effect—and then it may be too late. Meantime Italian Communism's electoral strength and reassuring stance are a constant source of embarrassment to the two chief partners in the Center-Left coalition. How long will it be possible to keep from a share in power a party whose popular appeal is undeniable and whose ideological evolution so satisfactory? By the same token, the Communists' current posture is—or should be—a major foreign policy puzzle for the United States.

3. THE IDEOLOGICAL ALTERNATIVES

The Italian Communists today are back where they have always wanted to be—back to the conditions of 1945 before the cold war opened and Stalin forced them into a position of intransigence. With

---

* See the declaration of the Communist leader Berlinguer in "Domande ai Comunisti," *Il Mondo*, January 28, 1964, p.2. Togliatti died the following summer.

the near-collapse of the rightist parties (which again recalls the immediate postwar situation) and the lack of a conservative alternative to Center-Left government, the only remaining possibility is a Popular Front. This the Italian Communists are well aware of: their current propaganda is largely directed toward stressing its advantages and minimizing its dangers. As little as half a decade ago, a ministerial coalition including the Communists was unthinkable. Today it is only barely imaginable—an outside possibility at the very most. A few years from now, if the cold war continues to subside and the Italian electorate maintains its drift toward the Left, a Popular Front may become a real alternative.

In the past, such a possibility was excluded, among other things, for the simple reason that the United States would not have permitted it. In those days, one had only to see the Sixth Fleet riding at anchor in the bay of Naples to get a direct physical sense of the weight of America's armed presence in Italian affairs. In Italy, as elsewhere in the Mediterranean, the United States had inherited a position of predominance that was originally to have been Great Britain's. During the Second World War, by an unstated but apparently well understood agreement between Roosevelt and Churchill, Italy was treated as a country in which British influence was paramount. And the activities of the chief British representatives there, both civilian and military, strongly suggested that their government intended to prolong its quasi-protectorate into the postwar period. But here, as in Greece, the British proved unable to maintain the position they had won for themselves during the war, and the American government felt obliged to step in to fill the void. Under De Gasperi and his immediate successors, the Italian relationship to the United States was one of mitigated (and comparatively benign) satellitehood.

In Italy, as opposed to France, this dependent status aroused little resentment. The American yoke (if such it could be called) was the lightest that the Italians had borne in their long history of foreign overlordship. Yet when the time came to shake it off, the country was far from unwilling. With the French doing most of the talking, the Italians simply shared in the new independence from the United States that Western European prosperity and the relaxation of cold war tensions brought with them. The change arrived so effortlessly and imperceptibly that neither Italians nor Americans quite realized what had happened. A decade ago it was still possible to imagine our country's armed forces intervening in Italy to cancel the results of a leftist electoral victory. Today it is *this* that has become unthinkable.

It is not beyond the bounds of possibility, then, that sometime in the future the United States might face the unprecedented problem of a Popular Front government in a major Western country. Far more probable, however, would be a quasi-neutralist regime of Socialists and left Christian Democrats for which the Communists would provide the sort of support from outside the government that Nenni's party gave the original opening to the Left. Or, to put the matter in terms of domestic Italian choices, the way to avoid a Popular Front would be through an evolution in the policy of the two present coalition partners that would make Communist participation unnecessary.

Neither Christian Democracy nor Socialism in its current form is very well suited to governing a modern industrial democracy. Each is too burdened with anomalies inherited from the past. But no new political formation is likely to replace them. Like our own parties, the Italian Christian Democrats and Socialists embody such deeply-rooted and even hereditary loyalties that it would be unrealistic to expect them to give way to something else. For all their faults, they are Italian democracy's visible and viable supports, and the real political question is not one of finding a substitute for them but how they can be modernized and adapted to contemporary purposes.

Most obviously, the Christian Democrats need to shed their clerical associations; these do them quite unnecessary damage in arousing mistrust and hostility among most of Italy's intellectual elite. Fortunately the policy of *aggiornamento*—of bringing the Church up to date—sponsored by Popes John and Paul is helping to steer the more old-fashioned Catholics away from clericalism. Likewise the social changes now in process, more particularly the population shifts from country to city and from South to North, are breaking up the fastnesses of Christian Democratic conservatism—and with them the power of local notables over their political fiefs and *clientele*. Viewed from this standpoint, Christian Democracy appears easier to modernize than Socialism: its history is shorter and its ideology less codified. Indeed, the ideological task for Moro and Fanfani and the young party reformers is almost the reverse of the one facing the Socialists—how to bring together the scattered and often contradictory precepts of social Catholicism into a coherent philosophy of the welfare state.

Italian Socialism is already a welfare-state party stressing economic planning rather than nationalization. In realistic terms, Italy's Socialists are not very different from their Social Democratic rivals in their own country or from other Western European parties that call themselves by similar names. But they hate to admit it: as opposed to British Labour's or German Social Democracy's pride in its ideological apostasy, Italian Socialism clings to its great memories and to the class-warfare phraseology of the past. And this injures the party's reputation among the middle-class and uncommitted public in the same fashion in which the Christian Democratic "image" suffers from the charge of clericalism. Italian Socialism needs to reunite with its Social Democratic offshoot; it needs more young people in its ranks; it needs to find a new flexibility in practice while retaining the innocence of aspiration that is so precious an ideological asset; but perhaps more than anything else it needs to convince itself and its constituents that wholesale collectivization is not its goal—that it is concerned rather to use as an instrument for social planning the massive segment of the Italian economy which is already in public hands.

The more alert and purposeful leaders of both Christian Democracy and Socialism can agree on their commitment to planning and the welfare state. This emphasis is only natural in terms of Italy's moral tradition and contemporary needs. The two parties are true to an age-old feeling for common humanity among their countrymen when they give first priority to the relief of poverty; it is when they indulge in sectarian appeals that they betray what is best in the Italian tradition. And in view of Italy's handicapped position within the Western community, the social welfare of its inhabitants quite properly comes before anything else. To such a purpose even Americans must assent when they ask the question (which is posed all too seldom in our deliberations on foreign policy): what is good for the Italian people themselves?

If in the future Italy's leaders put less stress than in the immediate past on foreign and military policy and on the alliance with the United States, this is not necessarily bad for our country. The American government is gradually getting used to the idea that it is perfectly legitimate for the rulers of poor nations to try to keep out of cold war entanglements. And while it may be argued that Italy is only in part an underdeveloped country, it is undeniable that much of its twentieth-century history of misfortune has arisen from involvement in international quarrels that were none of its concern. As a member of the European six-nation community, Italy is in no position to set out on a neutralist course of its own. It is more likely that Western Europe as a whole will move in that direction, with Italy encouraging the process. In all the most relevant respects—cultural, religious, sentimental—the Italians are certain to remain friendly to the United States; it is only the formal ties that may be relaxed.

Italy today is not merely absorbed in becoming a consumer-oriented society resembling our own. Its people are also engaged in an extraordinary spiritual and social adventure, often glimpsed in the past but never coming close to realization—nothing less than reconciling the two great popular faiths, Catholicism and socialism, whose antagonism has immobilized so much of the country's ideal energy. It is far from certain that such an ideological realignment can be accomplished. Yet even its partial fulfillment would give Italians a new hope for the social consensus that has so long eluded them and release from the dead weight of inherited skepticism about the possibility of human improvement.

Appendix I. Charts and Statistics

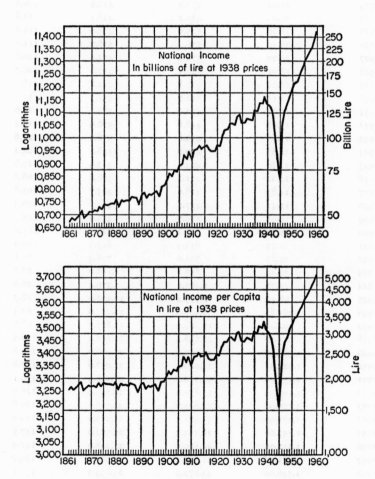

Source: Shepard B. Clough, *The Economic History of Modern Italy* (New York, 1964), p. 367.

MEAN DAILY WAGE

	Mean daily wage (in lire of current value)	Nominal wages	Indices: 1913 = 100 Cost of living	Real wages
1918	6.04	170.6	264.1	64.6
1919	8.84	249.7	268.1	93.1
1920	14.27	403.1	352.3	114.4
1921	18.74	529.4	416.8	127.0
1922	18.13	512.1	414.3	123.6
1923	16.92	478.0	411.9	116.0
1924	17.00	480.2	426.4	112.6
1925	18.96	535.6	479.0	111.8
1926	20.39	576.0	516.7	111.5
1927	20.20	570.6	472.4	120.8
1928	18.71	528.5	437.8	120.7
1929	18.26	515.8	444.8	116.0
1930	18.15	512.7	430.7	119.0
1931	16.74	472.9	389.1	121.6
1932	15.88	448.6	378.9	118.4
1933	15.25	430.8	356.5	120.8
1934	14.86	419.8	338.1	124.2
1935	14.30	404.0	342.9	117.8
1936	14.20	401.1	368.8	108.8
1937	14.83	418.9	403.7	103.8
1938	15.47	437.0	434.7	100.5
1939	16.98	479.7	453.9	105.7
1940	20.22	571.2	529.7	107.8
1941	21.75	614.4	612.9	100.2
1942	24.85	702.0	708.4	99.1
1943	30.40	858.8	1,188.0	72.3
1944	49.77	1,405.9	5,279.4	26.6
1945	98.32	2,777.4	10,398.0	26.7
1946	261.82	7,396.0	12,271.6	60.3
1947	694.00	19,604.5	19,887.5	98.6
1948	943.00	26,638.4	21,056.9	126.5
1949	988.00	27,909.6	21,366.0	130.6
1950	1,028.03	29,040.4	21,078.6	137.8
1951	1,139.10	32,178.0	23,126.0	139.1
1952	1,199.00	33,870.0	24,109.0	140.5
1953	1,225.00	34,604.5	24,578.0	140.8
1954	1,273.00	35,960.5	25,239.0	142.5
1955	1,357.00	38,333.3	25,974.0	147.7
1956	1,422.00	40,169.5	27,238.0	147.5
1957	1,481.00	41,836.2	27,764.0	150.7
1958	1,546.00	43,672.3	29,094.5	150.1
1959	1,576.00	44,519.8	28,972.8	153.1

Source: Cesare Vannutelli, "Occupazione e salari dal 1861 al 1961," *L'economia italiana dal 1861 al 1961* (Milan, 1961), pp. 570–571.

DEMOGRAPHIC BALANCE
(in thousands)

	Population at the beginning of period	Excess of live-births	Migration balance	Population at the end of period
1862–1870	26,328	1,778	— 119	27,987
1871–1880	27,987	2,015	— 462	29,540
1881–1890	29,540	3,201	— 996	31,745
1891–1900	31,745	3,535	—1,545	33,735
1901–1910	33,735	3,894	— 846	36,783
1911–1920	36,783	1,948	—1,165	37,566
1921–1930	37,566	4,517	—1,148	40,935
1931–1940	40,935	4,081	— 882	44,134
1941–1950	44,134	3,567	— 444	47,257
1951–1960	47,257	4,103	— 384	51,152

Source: Clough, *Economic History of Modern Italy*, p. 381.

ITALIAN EMIGRATION
(annual means)

	Expatriated	Repatriated
1861–1870	121,040	—
1871–1880	117,596	81,832
1881–1890	187,920	—
1891–1900	283,473	—
1901–1910	602,669	—
1911–1920	382,807	—
1921–1930	257,844	137,814
1931–1940	70,265	58,986
1941–1950	163,539	63,801
1951–1960	300,651	141,561

Source: Guglielmo Tagliacarne, "La bilancia internazionale dei pagamenti dell' Italia nel primo centenario dell'Unità," *L'economia italiana dal 1861 al 1961*, p. 353.

IRI SECTORAL HOLDING COMPANIES AND THEIR CHIEF SUBSIDIARIES

STET	*FINMARE*	*FINCANTIERI*
STIPEL	ITALIA	ANSALDO
TELVE	LLOYD TRIESTINO	CRDA
TETI	TIRRENIA	NAVALMECCANICA
TIMO	ADRIATICA	OARN
SET		ARS. TRIESTINO
SIT SIEMENS		SEBN
		OCRN DI TARANTO

Urban and interurban telephone services. With 300,000 new subscribers in 1962, the five companies of the STET group have now reached the 3,640,000 mark.

Shipping lines serving Mediterranean ports, North and South America, Africa, the Far East and Oceania. Finmare subsidiaries operate 62 per cent of the nation's passenger and mixed passenger-cargo capacity.

Fincantieri shipyards account for more than 80 per cent of Italian shipbuilding capacity and, apart from ships of all types and sizes, make ships motors, cranes and other engineering products.

FINSIDER	*FINMECCANICA*	*FINELETTRICA*
ITALSIDER	ALFA ROMEO	SIP
DALMINE	ANSALDO	SME
TERNI	S. GIORGIO	TRENTINA
BREDA SIDER.	IMAM AERFER	TERNI
CEMENTIR	FAMIND	UNES
FERROMIN	SALMOIRAGHI	SENN
SANAC	MECFOND	
CMF	OTO MELARA	
SOPREFIN	NUOVA S. GIORGIO	
	DELTA	
	S. EUSTACCHIO	
	SAFOG	
	S. GIORGIO PRA	
	SELENIA	

Production of pig iron, steel, tubes, plates, sections, structural steel, cement, etc. Finsider subsidiaries produce 90 per cent of Italy's pig iron, 56 per cent of its steel and 11 per cent of its cement output.

Motor vehicles and coachwork, aircraft, railway rolling stock, machine tools, electrical machinery and appliances, electronic equipment, optical instruments, etc.

Power generation and distribution. Finelettrica companies produce 26 per cent of the nation's electricity and in 1962 supplied more than 18.1 million Gwh. The 1962 electricity nationalization law has terminated all IRI's technical and financial commitments in this sector.

COMPANIES UNDER DIRECT IRI CONTROL

RAI-TV   ALITALIA   AUTOSTRADE

Radio and television. The company greatly increased its frequency modulation network in 1962 and the second TV channel now reaches 70 per cent of the population through 42 transmitters. The overall number of RAI-TV subscribers had reached about 9 million by the end of 1962; TV subscribers alone increased in 1962 by 600,000 to about 3.4 million.

Alitalia's air fleet operates a network of 156,000 km and serves all continents. In 1962 the company carried some two million passengers—500,000 more than the year before—and inaugurated the following new services: Milan-Genoa - Alghero - Cagliari; Rome-Bari-Tirana; Rome-Leopoldville-Johannesburg; Rome - Teheran - Karachi-Bombay - Bangkok - Hong Kong-Tokio; Rome-Milan-Montreal-Chicago.

Under a 1962 agreement with the government IRI assumed responsibility for the construction and improvement of 2,200 km of toll roads and for their subsequent operation during 30 years. The Rome-Naples leg of the Autostrada del Sole was opened to traffic in 1962 and work continued on the Florence-Rome section. Construction of the Naples-Bari road was begun and improvements carried out on the Florence-Pisa and Milan-Lakes roads.

BANCA COMMERC.   CELDIT   IFAP
CREDITO ITALIANO   SAIVO
BANCO DI ROMA   COTONIERE MERID
BANCO S. SPIRITO   FABBRICONE
         MONTE AMIATA

Banks of the IRI Group in 1962 had a 20 per cent share of all bank deposits in Italy, handled two thirds of all non-government bond issues on the Italian capital market and financed about half of all foreign trade and financial transactions.

A miscellaneous group of companies producing cellulose and paper, glass and refractory materials, cotton and woollen piece goods, mercury, etc.

A staff training company for the IRI Group as a whole, which operates six workers' vocational training centres in different regions of Italy, arranges special courses for foremen and executive staff at intermediate levels, and entertains a Higher Business Administration School for the study of top-level management functions.

Source: *The Economist,* March 28, 1964, p. 1236–1237.

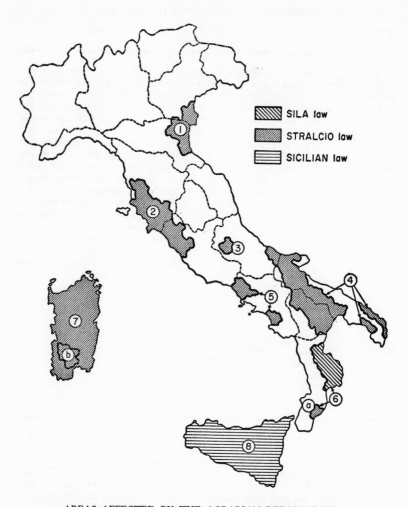

AREAS AFFECTED BY THE AGRARIAN REFORM LAWS

(1) Po delta Board; (2) Maremma Board; (3) Fucino Board; (4) Apulia, Lucania, and Molise Board; (5) ONC—Volturno, Garigliano, Sele; (6) Sila Board; (6a) Caulonia section; (7) ETFAS—The Agrarian Reform Board for Sardinia; (7b) Flumendosa section; (8) ERAS—The Agrarian Reform Board for Sicily.

Source: Clough, *Economic History of Modern Italy,* p. 309.

Source: *The Economist,* March 28, 1964, p. 1244.

Appendix II. Suggested Reading

Literature on Italy in the English language is far less voluminous than one might think. British and American interest in things Italian has concentrated so heavily on art history, cultural appreciation, and earlier epochs like the Renaissance and the Risorgimento, that there has been comparatively little left over for the contemporary scene. Since the Second World War, however, the extraordinary revival of American interest in Italy has produced a number of able studies by American scholars and observers and translations of the work of Italian writers. The British, who have traditionally shown a special sympathy for Italy and Italians, have continued to maintain a high level of writing on these subjects, distinguished particularly for its literary excellence and breadth of view. The books and articles listed below are chiefly of recent vintage; it has seemed best to omit all but a very few of the works published before 1930, most of which are either out of date or written from a point of view that is not especially applicable to Italy's contemporary problems.

1. ITALIAN-AMERICAN RELATIONS

Quite understandably, in view of the scant contacts between Italy and the United States before the First World War, no American scholar has undertaken to trace the whole history of Italian-American relations. The main episodes, however, have been narrated with both verve and scholarly exactitude by Thomas A. Bailey in *A Diplomatic History of the American People* (7th ed.; New York: Appleton-Century-Crofts, 1964). René Albrecht-Carrié's *Italy at the Paris Peace Conference* (New York: Columbia University Press, 1938) covers exhaustively the first serious clash between Italy and the United States, and the activities of Mussolini's over-zealous representatives in our country have been chronicled by Alan Cassels in "Fascism for Export: Italy and the United States in the Twenties," *American Historical Review*, 69:707–712 (April 1964). On the great question that has both linked and divided the two countries—Italian immigration to the United States—there are two excellent books: Oscar Handlin's *The Uprooted* (Boston: Little Brown,

1951) deals on a high plane of generalization with the immigrants' transition from a static peasant community to the crowded slums of the great American cities, while Robert F. Foerster's *The Italian Emigration of Our Times* (Cambridge: Harvard University Press, 1919), written just at the end of the major period of emigration when the American Congress was about to establish the discriminatory quotas, provides an economic and sociological analysis of the whole phenomenon, including Italian settlement in South America and such European countries as France and Switzerland. For a detailed, sympathetic chronicle of the achievements of the Italian-Americans themselves, one may consult the two books by Giovanni Schiavo: *The Italians in America before the Civil War* (New York: Vigo Press, 1934) and *Four Centuries of Italian-American History* (New York: Vigo Press, 1952). Among more specialized works are Andrew F. Rolle's "Italy in California," *The Pacific Spectator,* vol. 9 (Autumn 1955), and Herbert J. Gans's *The Urban Villagers: Group and Class in the Life of Italian Americans* (New York: Free Press of Glencoe, 1962), a study of Boston's West End just before its destruction to make way for urban renewal.

The travels of Americans to Italy in the nineteenth century—and the effect of such contact on American literature and art—are dealt with by Van Wyck Brooks in *The Dream of Arcadia: American Writers and Artists in Italy, 1760–1915* (New York: Dutton, 1958), and by Paul R. Baker in *The Fortunate Pilgrims: Americans in Italy, 1800–1860* (Cambridge: Harvard University Press, 1964).

American relations with Italy during and after the Second World War are considered in a number of works listed under the different headings below. In addition, the brief study by William Reitzel, *The Mediterranean: Its Role in America's Foreign Policy* (New York: Harcourt, Brace, 1948), offers a useful analysis of American strategic interests in the immediate postwar period.

2. THE LAND AND THE PEOPLE

Donald Smith Walker's *A Geography of Italy* (London: Methuen, 1958) provides a satisfactory general introduction. For those who can read Italian, the articles on the various regions of the country in the *Enciclopedia Italiana* (Rome: Istituto Giovanni Treccani, 1929–39) contain a wealth of information and are lavishly illustrated with photographs and maps. This encyclopedia, although produced under Fascism, ranks as the most thorough and elaborate project of its kind undertaken in any country. Supplementary volumes published since the war bring it up to date and correct the comparatively few articles in which Fascist interpretations were permitted to intrude.

For the physical anthropology of the Italian people, the standard handbook is Carleton Stevens Coon's *The Races of Europe* (New York: Macmillan, 1939). Cultural characteristics and the Italian cultural tradition are dealt with in philosophical and extremely condensed form in Leonardo Olschki's *The Genius of Italy* (New York: Oxford University Press, 1949), which without exaggeration may be called the single most rewarding volume on Italy available in English. For those who prefer a more informal approach, Count Carlo Sforza wrote a charming book of essays, *Italy and Italians* (New York: E. P. Dutton, 1949), while Luigi Barzini, in *The Italians: A Full-Length Portrait Featuring their Manners and Morals* (New York: Atheneum, 1964), presents similar material in a skeptical and astringent vein. G. A. Borgese's *Goliath* (New York: Viking Press, 1937), although primarily a study of Fascism, offers an arresting interpretation of the legacy of the Italian past. Novels and reminiscences such as Ignazio Silone's *Fontamara* (New York: Modern Age, 1938) and *Bread and Wine* (New York and London: Harper, 1937), and Carlo Levi's *Christ Stopped at Eboli* (New York: Farrar, Strauss, 1948) illuminate the situation of the southern Italian peasantry more sharply than any economic study. Other contemporary novelists whose work is available in translation, such as Corrado Alvaro, Giuseppe Berto, Alberto Moravia, Vasco Pratolini, and Elio Vittorini, may similarly contribute to the reader's understanding of Italian life, both in the Fascist period and in the postwar era.

3. HISTORICAL BACKGROUND

From the large variety of books on modern Italian history the following may be selected as the most up to date, compact, and generally useful for the nonspecialized reader: Luigi Salvatorelli, *A Concise History of Italy* (New York: Oxford University Press, 1940), a compendious and rather pedestrian survey of three thousand years of Italian development by an eminent Liberal historian; Benedetto Croce, *A History of Italy 1871–1915* (Oxford: The Clarendon Press, 1929), the philosopher-historian's over-serene interpretation of political and cultural life under the united kingdom; Cecil J. S. Sprigge, *The Development of Modern Italy* (New Haven: Yale University Press, 1944), a brilliant little volume by a veteran of a quarter century of distinguished journalism on Italian affairs, who unfortunately has chosen to terminate his account with the advent of Fascism; René Albrecht-Carrié, *Italy from Napoleon to Mussolini* (New York: Columbia University Press, 1950), a less penetrating study than Sprigge's but going through the Second World War; and A. William Salomone, *Italian Democracy in the Making* (Philadelphia:

University of Pennsylvania Press, 1945), a brief, balanced analysis of the Giolittian era. A more recent work, which has outclassed all its predecessors in comprehensiveness, verve of presentation, and range of acquaintance with the latest materials, is Denis Mack Smith's *Italy: A Modern History* (Ann Arbor: University of Michigan Press, 1959), which may be supplemented, from the ideological and intellectual standpoint, by John A. Thayer, *Italy and the Great War: Politics and Culture, 1870–1915* (Madison and Milwaukee: University of Wisconsin Press, 1964).

4. THE FASCIST EXPERIENCE

There is a mass of material on Fascism, most of it, however, so polemical and written so close to the events described as to be of little value today. The following titles represent either post-Fascist reëvaluations or those contemporary works that have best stood the test of time. All of them are to a greater or lesser extent anti-Fascist in tone. While theoretically it would be best to list at least one or two pro-Fascist works, there appear to be none available in English that rise above the level of propaganda.

General Works. Although no comprehensive overall treatment exists, there are two short surveys which are both judicious and up to date: Federico Chabod, *A History of Italan Fascism* (London: Weidenfeld and Nicolson, 1963), translated by Muriel Grindrod, a series of lectures given at the University of Paris in 1950 by Italy's most influential contemporary historian, and S. William Halperin, *Mussolini and Italian Fascism* (Princeton: Van Nostrand, Anvil Books, 1964) a valuable selection of documents plus an introductory text. Among lives of the Duce himself, the best is certainly Ivone Kirkpatrick's *Mussolini: A Study in Power* (New York: Hawthorne Books, 1964), although its discussion of the period after 1929 does not quite live up to the promise of the earlier chapters. One may also mention two small-scale biographies written for the general public: Laura Fermi's perceptive *Mussolini* (Chicago: University of Chicago Press, 1961), which is admittedly "psychological" and selective in treatment, and Christopher Hibbert's more orthodox *Benito Mussolini: A Biography* (London: Longman's, 1962), an ill-balanced work that in several key respects is simply uninformed. To find one's way around the interpretative tangle the Duce left behind him, the reader may turn to Charles F. Delzell's very useful "Benito Mussolini: A Guide to the Biographical Literature," *Journal of Modern History*, 35:339–353 (December 1963).

The Rise of Fascism. Gaudens Megaro, in his *Mussolini in the Making* (Boston and New York: Houghton Mifflin, 1938), has dug up in scholarly and frequently amusing detail the facts on Mussolini's Socialist and antimilitarist past that the Duce so carefully tried to keep concealed. For the period between the end of the First World War and the March on Rome, the classic account is by the former Communist A. Rossi (Angelo Tasca), *The Rise of Italian Fascism 1918–1922* (London: Methuen, 1938), which naturally betrays a primary concern for the fate of the working classes.

Social and Economic Policy. On this, as on the other aspects of Fascist rule, the best general book is still Herman Finer's *Mussolini's Italy* (New York: Holt, 1935). Writing toward the close of the Fascist era, Finer was able to assess the regime in its final form and, without departing from a calm, judicious tone, to render a negative verdict. More polemical, but pungent, witty, and crammed with relevant detail, particularly on the condition of Italian labor, is the book by the distinguished *émigré* scholar Gaetano Salvemini, *Under the Axe of Fascism* (New York: Viking, 1936). A similarly devastating analysis of agrarian policy, from the point of view of a professional economist, may be found in Carl T. Schmidt's *The Plough and the Sword* (New York: Columbia University Press, 1938). For the myth and reality of the corporate state, the basic works, available only in French, are the two volumes by Louis Rosenstock-Franck, *L'économie corporative fasciste en doctrine et en fait* (Paris: Librairie universitaire J. Gamber, 1934) and *Les Étapes de l'économie fasciste italienne* (Paris: Librairie sociale et économique, 1939).

Church and State. On this subject the book by D. A. Binchy, *Church and State in Fascist Italy* (London: Royal Institute of International Affairs, 1941) is nearly everything that could be desired. The work of an Irish scholar, a liberal Catholic with a lofty and tolerant outlook, it is understandably mild in its judgments on papal policy, but critical where criticism seems required. The self-styled "postscript" by Leicester C. Webb, *Church and State in Italy, 1947–1957* (London and New York: Cambridge University Press, 1958), is considerably less inspired. For the relations between Mussolini's regime and the *Popolari,* one may consult Richard A. Webster's *The Cross and the Fasces: Christian Democracy and Fascism in Italy* (Stanford: Stanford University Press, 1960), and the abridged translation by David Moore of A. C. Jemolo's modern classic, *Church and State in Italy 1850–1950* (Oxford: Blackwell, 1960).

The Opposition. W. Hilton-Young's *The Italian Left* (London: Longmans, Green, 1949), besides being a short history of political Socialism in Italy, offers an adequate, if rather fragmentary account of the anti-Fascist emigration and clandestine activity in Italy. A more complete and scholarly historical survey, which has established itself as the standard work in the field, is Charles F. Delzell's *Mussolini's Enemies: The Italian Anti-Fascist Resistance* (Princeton: Princeton University Press, 1961). Hugh Thomas's *The Spanish Civil War* (New York: Harper & Row, 1961) offers a precise, dispassionate evaluation of the role of the Italian anti-Fascist volunteers in the Spanish struggle.

Foreign Policy. The conventional account, written just before the outbreak of the Second World War, is by Maxwell H. H. Macartney and Paul Cremona, *Italy's Foreign and Colonial Policy 1914–1937* (London: Oxford University Press, 1938). The two chapters on Italy by Felix Gilbert and H. Stuart Hughes in the collaborative volume *The Diplomats 1919–1939* (Princeton: Princeton University Press, 1953), edited by Felix Gilbert and Gordon A. Craig, and Gaetano Salvemini's critical assessment of Mussolini's policy in his *Prelude to World War II* (London: Gollancz, 1953) are more interpretive and up to date, since they have been able to take advantage of the wealth of material published since the war. The same is true of Elizabeth Wiskemann's history of the relations between Mussolini and Hitler, *The Rome-Berlin Axis* (New York: Oxford University Press, 1949), which, however, is marred by hasty writing and confusions of style. For a firsthand account of the development of the Duce's policy, one may consult the two volumes of writings by Mussolini's foreign minister, Count Galeazzo Ciano, *The Ciano Diaries 1939–1943*, edited by Hugh Gibson (New York: Doubleday, 1945), and *Ciano's Diplomatic Papers*, edited by Malcolm Muggeridge (London: Odhams Press, 1948); obviously documents such as these cannot always be taken at their face value. For the bitter aftermath of the Duce's glory, including the history of the Republic of Salò, there is F. W. Deakin's exhaustive *The Brutal Friendship: Mussolini, Hitler and the Fall of Italian Fascism* (New York: Harper & Row, 1962), which reads more like a dossier than a finished book, but is irreproachable from the standpoint of scholarship.

5. THE SECOND WORLD WAR

The general histories of the war in Europe published to date, such as Louis L. Snyder's *The War: A Concise History, 1939–1945* (New York: Messner, 1960) and Chester Wilmot's *The Struggle for Europe* (New York: Harper, 1952), deal in rather too summary fashion with Italian participation in the conflict. Wilmot's strategical analyses, however, and in particular his persuasive arguments in support of Churchill's view that the major attack against the Axis should have been directed through the "soft under-belly" of Europe, throw a great deal of light on the conduct of the war in the Mediterranean theater. This theater of operations is the subject of a thorough and objective history by a retired French Admiral, Raymond de Belot, *The Struggle for the Mediterranean 1939-1945* (Princeton: Princeton University Press, 1951), which is focused primarily on navel strategy. Two specialized articles by American scholars illuminate the more controversial aspects of the war in Italy: Howard McGaw Smyth, "The Armistice of Cassibile," *Military Affairs*, 12:12-35 (Spring 1948); and Massimo Salvadori-Paleotti, "The Patriot Movement in Italy," *Foreign Affairs*, 24:539-549 (April 1946). Salvadori, as an Allied liaison officer with the resistance forces in northern Italy, was a participant in some of the events that he describes. For the diplomacy of the conflict, the most comprehensive study is Herbert Feis's *Churchill, Roosevelt, Stalin: The War They Waged and the Peace They Sought* (Princeton: Princeton University Press, 1957), while Norman Kogan's *Italy and the Allies* (Cambridge: Harvard University Press, 1956) deals more particularly with the three-cornered struggle among the British, the Americans, and the Badoglio and Bonomi governments.

From the mass of biographical, autobiographical, and diary material on the war, the following may be recommended as those that best explain the political forces at play in Italy: from the American standpoint, Robert L. Sherwood, *Roosevelt and Hopkins: An Intimate History* (New York: Harper, 1948), Dwight D. Eisenhower, *Crusade in Europe* (New York: Doubleday, 1948), and Mark W. Clark, *Calculated Risk* (New York: Harper, 1950); from the British standpoint, Winston Churchill's magnificent and highly personal history, *The Second World War*, 6 vols. (Boston: Houghton Mifflin, 1948-1953); and from the Italian standpoint, Pietro Badoglio, *Italy in the Second World War* (London: Oxford University Press, 1948). Badoglio's book of reminiscences is largely a personal apologia for his conduct as prime minister following Mussolini's fall, as, to an even greater extent, is the Duce's own account of his political debacle. This extraordinary document, which includes a number of reflections on the history of Fascism in general, has been published in two different tranlations: *The Fall of Mussolini*, edited by Max Ascoli (New York: Farrar, Strauss, 1948), and Benito Mussolini, *Memoirs 1942-1943*, edited by Raymond Klibansky (London: Weidenfeld and Nicolson, 1949), of which the latter is somewhat more complete. The Duce's great philosophical opponent, Benedetto Croce, has published his diary for the year intervening between the fall of Mussolini and the liberation of Rome, during which he was the center of anti-Fascist political activity in Naples: *Croce, the King, and the Allies*

(New York: Norton, 1950), edited by Sylvia Sprigge. A somewhat more specialized, but extremely informative book of reminiscences by an Italian is Admiral Franco Maugeri's *From the Ashes of Disgrace* (New York: Reynal & Hitchcock, 1948), which covers a wide range of wartime activity, including the naval battle off Cape Matapan, escort duty at the side of the fallen Mussolini, and underground work in Rome during the German occupation.

6. POSTWAR POLITICS

There are two general books in English on this subject, Muriel Grindrod's *The Rebuilding of Italy* (London: Royal Institute of International Affairs, 1955), which takes the story only to the mid-1950's, and Giuseppe Mammarella's *Italy after Fascism: A Political History 1943–1963* (Montreal: Mario Casalini, 1964), based on lectures given to American students in Florence. To complete the earlier part of the record, particularly as regards the activities of Italy's two most important political parties, one may turn to the works on Church-state relations by Jemolo and Webb already cited and to the authoritative and judicious collaborative studies published under the auspices of Cornell University's "French-Italian Inquiry": Mario Einaudi, Jean-Marie Domenach, and Aldo Garosci, *Communism in Western Europe* (Ithaca: Cornell University Press, 1951), and Mario Einaudi and François Goguel, *Christian Democracy in Italy and France* (Notre Dame: University of Notre Dame Press, 1952). Subsequent developments may be followed in the chapter on Italian Communism by Giorgio Galli in *Communism in Europe: Continuity, Change, and the Sino-Soviet Dispute,* I (Cambridge: The M.I.T. Press, 1964), edited by William E. Griffith.

The standard handbook on Italy's postwar constitutional and institutional arrangements is *The Government of Republican Italy* (Boston: Houghton Mifflin, 1961) by John Clarke Adams and Paolo Barile. For local government, one may consult Robert C. Fried, *The Italian Prefects: A Study in Administrative Politics* (New Haven: Yale University Press, 1963), which emphasizes the continuity from practice in the Kingdom of Sardinia to the present day. Daniel L. Horowitz has traced the vicissitudes of the organized working class in *The Italian Labor Movement* (Cambridge: Harvard University Press, 1963), which may be supplemented by two studies by Joseph La Palombara: *The Italian Labor Movement: Problems and Prospects* (Ithaca: Cornell University Press, 1957) and *Interest Groups in Italian Politics* (Princeton: Princeton University Press, 1964). In the absence of a general work on diplomacy for the postwar years, Norman Kogan's *The Politics of Italian Foreign Policy* (New York: Praeger, 1963) offers a number of insights on the role of ideologies and pressure groups.

7. ECONOMIC PROBLEMS

The best available introduction is Shepard B. Clough's *The Economic History of Modern Italy* (New York: Columbia University Press, 1964), which, although confusing in organization and approach, offers a wealth of information. One may also consult with profit the statistical volume *A Century of Economic and Social Development in Italy, 1861–1961* (Rome: Istituto Centrale di Statistica, 1961); the *Economic Survey of Europe* issued each year by the United Nations Economic Commission for Europe at Geneva; the special numbers devoted to Italy by the British periodicals *The Statist* and *The Economist* of April 6, 1962, and March 28, 1964, respectively; and *Growth and Structure in the Economy of Modern Italy* (to be published shortly by Harvard University Press) by George H. Hildebrand, whose theoretical sophistication is marred by a strong *laissez-faire* bias.

Italy's role in the process of European economic integration can be followed in two books by William Diebold Jr., *Trade and Payments in Western Europe, 1947–1951* (New York: Harper, 1952) and *The Schuman Plan: A Study in Economic Cooperation, 1950–1959* (New York: Praeger, 1959), and in the collaborative volume edited by Lawrence B. Krause, *The Common Market: Progress and Controversy* (Englewood Cliffs: Prentice-Hall, 1964). Of the many studies dealing with the emerging society of the 1960's, perhaps the most probing are George Lichtheim's *The New Europe: Today—and Tomorrow* (New York: Praeger, 1963) and *A New Europe?* (Boston: Houghton Mifflin, 1964), edited by Stephen Graubard, which includes contributions by several Italian scholars.

As Italy's great problem area, the South has inspired an especially rich economic and social literature. In a class of their own are such works of the social reformer Danilo Dolci as *Report from Palermo* (New York: Orion Press, 1959), which combines moral fervor with social analysis. A more pessimistic view of Sicilian possibilities emerges from Edward C. Banfield's *The Moral Basis of a Backward Society* (Glencoe, Ill.: The Free Press, 1958). On a less polemical level, there is the clear, compact, informative handbook, *The Population Problem of Southern Italy: An Essay in Social Geography* (Syracuse: Syracuse University Press, 1955) by Robert E. Dickinson; the chattier and more informal volume by Margaret Carlyle, *The Awakening of Southern Italy* (London: Oxford University Press, 1962), which presents on-the-spot observations of land reform since 1950; and a theoretical analysis by Hollis B. Chenery, "Development Policies for Southern Italy," *Quarterly Journal of Economics,* vol. 76 (November 1962).

8. CULTURAL LIFE

For a discussion of the major twentieth-century generation of Italian writers and thinkers, one may consult H. Stuart Hughes's *Consciousness and Society: The Reorientation of European Social Thought 1890–1930* (New York: Alfred A. Knopf, 1958); James H. Meisel's *The Myth of the Ruling Class: Gaetano Mosca and the "Elite"* (Ann Arbor: University of Michigan Press, 1958); Cecil J. S. Sprigge's *Benedetto Croce* (New Haven: Yale University Press, 1952), a brief, perceptive study of Italy's great philosopher and historian; and Lander MacClintock's *The Age of Pirandello* (Bloomington: Indiana University Press, 1951), which deals with the whole range of writing for the theater. The closest approximation to a general history of more recent writing is by Sergio Jerry Pacifici: *A Guide to Contemporary Italian Literature* (Cleveland: World Publishing Company, 1962).

On the postwar film renaissance, Vernon Jarratt's pioneer study *The Italian Cinema* (London: The Falcon Press, 1951) may be supplemented by Pierre Leprohon, *Michelangelo Antonioni: An Introduction* (New York: Simon and Schuster, 1963), translated by Scott Sullivan, which includes, in addition to an analysis of individual films, some of Antonioni's own essays and selections from his scenarios. Italy's contemporary achievements in the arts are sympathetically presented by Agnoldomenico Pica, in *Recent Italian Architecture,* and by Marco Valsecchi, in *Young Italian Painters,* both published by the Edizione del Milione in Milan.

9. CURRENT DEVELOPMENTS

To follow the most recent changes in Italian politics and economic life, one must have recourse to newspapers and periodicals. Unfortunately coverage in the American newspaper press, even in such an authoritative journal as *The New York Times,* is by no means complete, and important developments are often reported in only summary fashion. The periodical press, however, is a good deal more satisfactory, and such biweeklies as *The Reporter* and *The New Leader,* and the liberal Catholic weekly *The Commonweal* publish perceptive and well-documented articles on

Italian problems. No American magazine, however, has such complete Italian coverage as the London *Economist,* which makes fairly frequent surveys of Italian policy, and the unpretentious but highly informative monthly, *The World Today,* published by the Royal Institute of International Affairs. For those who read Italian, there is a wealth of useful information and statistics in the monthly publication *Vita italiana: documenti e informazioni,* published by the government Document Center in Rome, and, in less official vein, the the weeklies *Il Mondo* and *L'Espresso* follow political, social, and cultural developments from a center-left standpoint. Among monthly reviews the most notable are *Il Mulino* (Bologna), *Nord e Sud* (Naples), and *Il Ponte* (Florence).

Index

Abruzzi, the, 26
Acerbo Law, 197
Acquarone, Duke, and plot against Mussolini, 116
Action Party (*Partito d'Azione*), 142, 144; formation, 116, 119; absence in Bonomi government, 127; partisan bands of, 130; and Parri's prime ministry, 135; scorned by Togliatti, 138–139; collapse of, 142
Adams, Henry, 5
Aggiornamento, Catholic policy of, 266
Agrarian reform, *see* Land reform
Agrarian tenure, 186–190, 258; in Po valley, 186; *mezzadria*, 187–188; *latifondo*, 188–189; and "Green Plan," 231–232
Albania: invasion of, 10; annexation of, 108; reparations claims of, 148
Alexander, General Sir Harold, 131
Alitalia, 225
Allies: armistice with Italy, 120–123; and Italy's participation, 123–124; and takeover of government, 124–125; liberation of Rome, 126; recognition of CLNAI, 131; military government of, 137, withdrawn, 142; and *1947* Peace Treaty, 148–152
Amalfi, 15
Americans: in Italy in World War II, 11–13; in postwar period, 13. *See also* United States
Ansaldo, 173
Anti-Fascists: Anti-Fascist Concentration, 104, breakup of, 105; in Spanish Civil War, 106, 108; six-party leadership, 119–120; and Bari conference, 125; and Bonomi government, 126–127; partisan bands of, 130; revolutionary hopes of thwarted, 134–140
Antonioni, Michelangelo (director), *L'avventura, La Notte, L'eclisse*, 247–248
Apulia, 26
Arditi, 72
Armistice, with Allies, 120–123
Atlantic Alliance, 3, 255; Italy in, 151
Austria: annexation of, 108; and *1947* Peace Treaty, 149
"Autonomist" electoral list (of Social Democrats), 197–198, 199, 209
Avanti (Socialist journal), 71
"Aventine" secession, 99, 105; failure of, 100, 102

Badoglio, Marshal Pietro: and palace plot against Mussolini, 116, 117; government of, 119–120, 125, 168; and armistice, 120–123; *Italy in the Second World War: Memories and Documents*, 122n; at Brindisi, 124; loss of power, 126
Balbo, Italo, 72
Basilicata, 26
"Battle of the Births," 185
Berlinguer, 264n
Binchy, D. A., 31n
Bissolati-Bergamaschi, Leonida, 71
Blaine, James G., 6
Bolshevik Revolution, and Italian laborers, 58, 59
Bonaparte, Napoleon, 47
Bonomi, Ivanoe, 63, 71, 134; leadership of Mussolini opposition, 116, of post-Mussolini politics, 119; government of, 126–127, 131, 142
Bordiga, Amedeo, 166

Braccianti, 189

Brand, Robert A., 190n

"Brigandage," 38–39, 48

Bruno, Giordano, 45

Bureaucracy: expansion of under Mussolini, 179–180; overstaffed in postwar era, 180

Burns, John Horne, *The Gallery,* 12, 13

Busti, Paolo, and founding of Buffalo, N.Y., 4

Cagoulards, 107

Calabria, 27

Calvino, Italo, 247

Campagna, 25–26

Campania, 26–27

Cassa per il Mezzogiorno (Southern Italy Fund), 193, 195

Castellano, General Giuseppe, 120

Catholic Action, 102, 261; Mussolini's opposition to, 98; support of De Gasperi, 147; conservatism of, 160; in *1953* elections, 198

Catholic Church, 3; role in Italian life, 29–31, 156; and unification, 48–49; in politics, 54, 58; and Popular party, 59; and corporate theory, 75; reconciliation with state, 93–97; opposition to Mussolini, 102; support of De Gasperi, 147; interests promoted by Christian Democracy, 161; in *1953* elections, 198; and "opening to the Left," 217; and education, 235; relationship with Christian Democracy, 260–261; *aggiornamento* policy of, 266. *See also* individual popes

Cavour, Count Camillo Benso di, 47, 51

Center coalition, 197

Center-Left coalition, 255, 256, 264; second try for, 257–259; handicaps of, 259

Cesarini, Marco, quoted, 230

Chamber of Deputies: absolute majority of Christian Democrats in, 147–148; under new constitution, 153–154

Chamber of Fasces and Corporations, 80

Charles Albert, King, 47

Charter of Labor, 79, 88

Christian Democracy: in general politics, 62, 119, 138, 146, 224; formation of, 116, 141; government of, 134, 140–

141; *1946* election victories, 144; *1948* election victories, 151; in new Chamber of Deputies, 154–155; majority party, 147–148, 155; in power, 156–163; anti-clerical opposition to, 158; left-wing of, 159–160; reform debate in, 160; Catholic policies of, 161; spoils system in, 161–162; criticisms of, 162–163; absence of "loyal opposition," 163–164; inroads of MSI in ministry, 165; and corporatism, 171; land reform policies of, 190–195; electoral bonus scheme ("swindle law"), 197; in Center coalition, 197, 199; era of uncertainty, 201–211; under Fanfani, 212, Segni, 213; and "opening to the Left," 215–218, 261; economic Right in, 231, 258; foreign policy of, 251–255; Center-Left coalition of Moro, 256–259; Saragat ministry of, 260; relationship with Catholicism, 260–261; factions in, 261; recent characteristics and future role, 266. *See also* De Gasperi

Church-state relations, under De Gasperi, 156. *See also* Concordat

Churchill, Winston, 127, 265

Ciano, Count Galeazzo, 128; opposition to Mussolini, 117

City-state, prevalence and tradition of, 36

Clark, Eleanor, *Rome and a Villa,* 13

Class: and Mussolini's government, 83–92, persistence of old ruling under, 110–111

Clough, Shepard B., quoted, 227

Colombo, Arturo, 235n

Colonialism: and conquest of Tripoli, 56; and World War I, 56–57; U.N. disposition of former colonies, 150; and overpopulation, 185

Committee of National Liberation for Northern Italy (CLNAI), 131, 132, 136, 140; opposition to Rome government, 135; and Parri government, 136–137

Committees of Liberation (northern Italy), 129, 131, 134; and Parri government, 136–137; dissolution of, 137

Communes, age of, 43

Communism: Pius XI's fear of, 94; Soviet compared to Fascism, 110; anti-

Communism of De Gasperi government, 145; features of Italian, 167, 263–264. *See also* Communist party

Communist party (French), and Popular Front, 105

Communist party (in Italy), 3, 39, 60, 103, 119, 126, 155, 198; opposition to Mussolini, 105–107, 115; coalition with Socialists, 105–106, 107, postwar, 145, 169–170; in Bonomi government, 127; "Garibaldi" bands of, 130, 135; postwar moderation, 137–138; *1946* elections, 144; pro-Catholic vote to renew Concordat, 146; "People's Bloc," 147, 148, 169; and new Chamber of Deputies, 154; and general strike of *1948*, 157; in opposition to Christian Democracy, 163, 166; branches of, 166; intellectuals in, 167; trade union support, 167–169; peasant support, 169; resilience of, 170; appeal of for skilled workers, 183; gains in *1953* elections, 199, in *1958*, 210–211, in *1963*, 218, 220, in North, 230; effects of de-Stalinization controversy on, 207–208; opposition to Tambroni, 214; loss of Socialist alliance, 215; and neorealistic writers, 243–244; recent characteristics of, 263–264; advocacy of Popular Front, 265

Compagna, Francesco, 195n

Concordat of *1929*, 95–97, 99; retention in new constitution, 146, 156

Confagricoltura, opposition to land reform, 191, 192

Confederation of Industrialists, 78, 79

Confederazione generale italiana del lavoro (CGIL): syndicalist origins, 168; Communist dominance in, 168; defections from, 168–169; demonstrations against Tambroni, 214; influence of, 230

Confindustria, 172, 173, 205, 206, 230; failure in *1958* elections, 210; support of Christian Democracy, 212, 213

Confino, 103, 129, 205

Consigli di gestione, 135, 137

Constituent Assembly: selection of deputies, 144; and institutional framework of Italy, 152–158

Constitution (*1948*), 152–156

Constitutional Court: establishment of, 204; problems of, 205

Coon, Carleton Stevens, quoted, 28

Corporate State: institutions of, 74–83; power of, 81–82; sources of, 75–77; postwar persistence, 171–172

Corradini, Enrico, 72

Cottam, Howard R., 190n

Council of Europe, Italian leadership in, 252

Crispi, Francesco, 52, 56

Croce, Benedetto, 55, 73; opposition to Concordat, 97, to Mussolini, 100–101; in Liberal party, 119; and Bari congress, 125; retirement, 143; revolt against cultural leadership of, 238

Croceanism, in post-Fascist era, 238

Cronachi sociali, 159

Cultural "Renaissance": social criticism (post-Crocean), 237–242, conservative concensus of, 237, revolt against Croce's leadership of, 238, Gramsci's leadership of, 238–240, theme of poverty in, 241–242; neorealistic literature, 242–244, cinema, 245–250; psychological literature, 246–247, problems of free expression, 249–250

Currey, Muriel, 122n

Cyrenaica, seizure by Italy, 6

d'Annunzio, Gabriele, 55–56, 57, 77; and Fiume expedition, 71, 76

Dante Alighieri, 5

De Gasperi, Alcide, 62, 102, 140, 175, 176; qualities of, 141; climb to power, 141–142; government of, 142–143; tripartite ministry, 144, 156–157; anti-Communism of, 145–148, 158; in *1948* elections, 147; conservatism of, 159; role of conciliator, 160–161; economic policies, 173–174, 203; and *mezzadria,* 188; land reform policies, 191; fall of, 196–201; foreign policy, 251–253; and U.S. influence, 265

De Gaulle, Charles, 211, 254

De Nicola, Enrico, 125–126, 144, 146; presidency of court, 204, 205

De Sica, Vittorio (director), *Shoe Shine, Bicycle Thief,* 245, *Two Women,* 247; in *General della Rovere,* 247

Delzell, Charles F., 129n

"Democratic Initiative" (of Christian Democracy), 160
Democracy (Italian): collapse of, 8, 59–64; social reasons for, 65; problems of opposition, 164
Democracy of Labor party, 131; formation of, 119; decline of, 135
Depretis, Agostino, 51–52
Di Vittorio, Giuseppe, 106; leadership in CGIL, 168
Dolci, Danilo, 241–242
Dorotei (Christian Democratic Left), 261
Dossetti, Giuseppe, 159

Economic expansion: in recent times, 19, 227–228, nature of, 228; in northern Italy, 221, 223; and Common Market, 222–223; and ENI, 224–225; and IRI, 225–227
Economic planning: Fanfani reforms, 217; and the Common Market, 222–223; and Vanoni Plan, 220.221; unfinished business of, 230–235; in Italian Socialism, 267
Economic recovery: stages of, 174–178; Einaudi's program, 176; and European Recovery Program, 176–177; fiscal reform and bureaucratic problems, 178–180; and standard of living, 181–183; and appeal of Neo-Fascism, 182
Edison Company, 216
Einaudi, Luigi: as Minister of the Budget, 146; recovery program of, 176, 177; first Italian president, 152, 198
Einaudi, Mario, quoted, 189
Eisenhower, General Dwight D., and Italian armistice, 121
Elections: *1948* as conservative victory, 133–134, as Christian Democratic victory, 147–148; of *1946*, 143–144; of *1953*, 198; of *1958*, 205–211, defeat for Right, 210; of *1963*, 217–218, 261
Emigration to New World: effects on agrarian population, 183–184; temporary, 184; limitations on, 184–185
Emilia, 23, 24
Emmanuel, King Victor II, quoted, 40
Enciclopedia Italiana, 73
Ente Nazionale Idrocarburi (ENI), as parastatal enterprise, 224–225
Eritria, 149, 150

Estrema, 54
Ethiopia, 150; reparations claims of, 148
Ethiopian War, 105, 108
Euratom, 252
European Coal and Steel Community (Schuman Plan), 252
European Common Market: Italian membership in, 220, 231, 252, 254; effects of, 222–223
European Recovery Program, 3, 170; collapse of Communist strikes against, 146, 157; and increase of steel output, 176–177. *See also* Marshall Plan
Experimental Center, in Mussolini's regime, 245
"Eyeties," 11

Facta, Luigi, 63–64
Family, as core of Italian life, 32–33
Fanfani, Amintore, 209, 210, 258, 261; spokesman of "Democratic Initiative," 160; prime ministries, 202, 211–212, 213, 214; and "opening to the Left," 215–218; fall of, 256; as Saragat's foreign minister, 260; ideological task of, 267
Farinacci, Roberto, 72
Fasci di Combattimento, organization of, 71
Fascism: Italy as birthplace of, 3; rise of, 61, 62–64; conditions favoring, 65–67; theory and practice of, 68–74; corporatism in, 74–83; and the Church, 94–99; and intellectuals, 101; expediency in, 109–110; end of, 115–118; dissolution under Badoglio, 119; revival in North before liberation, 128; survival under De Gasperi, 162–163; little effect on cultural tradition, 237–238; opposition to in neorealistic literature, 242–243. *See also* Mussolini, Benito; Neo-Fascism
Fascist Public Security Law, 205
Fatti di Luglio, 214
Faulkner, William, influence in Italian literature, 243
Federconsorzi, 230
Federzoni, Luigi, 72
Fellini, Federico (director), 247; *La Strada, Cabiria*, 246, *8 1/2*, *La dolce vita*, 248, 249

FIAT of Turin, 115, 173; wartime strikes at, 115; expansion of, 228

Fincantiere, 225

Finer, Herman, 75

Finmeccanica, 225

Finsider, 225

Fiume, 58; Italian claim to, 7, 71

Florence, 4, 9, 11, 17, 37, 130

Foreign policy (Italian): leadership of, 251–252; goal of European unity, 252, Italian leadership in, 252–253; buffer role between France and Germany, 253; nationalism and *bel gesto* after De Gasperi era 253–254; in Arab world, 254; and U.S., 255; conflicting interpretations, 254–255. *See also* Colonialism

"Forty-Five Days," 118–123, 129, 168

France: in World War I, 7, 8, 10; geography compared to Italy, 14; defeat in World War II, 114; and *1947* Peace Treaty, 149; and Italian immigrants, 185; post-Fascist relations with Italy, 252; Franco-Italian customs union, 252

Free Territory of Trieste, *see* Trieste

Galantuomini, 39

Gambetta, Leon, 211

Gandhi, Mahatma, 242

Garibaldi, Giuseppe, 4, 46, 47

"Garibaldi" bands, 130

Garosci, Aldo, 107n

Genoa, 15, 157; as industrial seaport, 23

Gentile, Giovanni, and fascist ideology, 73

Germany, 9; and Italian armistice, 121, 122

Giolitti, Antonio: defection from Communist party, 208; elected Socialist deputy, 210–211

Giolitti, Giovanni: in Italian politics, 56, 57, 61, 62, 63, 71, 88, 161; influence, 52, 54–55; and use of Fascism, 72

Giolittismo, 52, 67

Guistizia e Libertà, 104, 105, 106, 135; decline of, 107; remnants of form Action Party, 116

Gramsci, Antonio, 103, 166, 167; as leader of post-Crocean social criticism, 238–240

Grand Council of Fascism, 68, 117; trial and execution of anti-Mussolini members, 128

Grandi, Count Dino, 72; opposition to Mussolini, 117

Great Britain: and armistice with Italy, 120–123; mistakes in post-armistice government, 127; influence in Italian affairs, 265

Greece, 42; reparations claims of, 148

"Green Plan," of *1960,* 231–232

Gronchi, Giovanni: election to presidency, 203–204; as president, 211, 212, 213, 224; trip to Moscow, 254

Handlin, Oscar, 8n

Hawthorne, Nathaniel, *Marble Faun,* 5

Hemingway, Ernest, *A Farewell to Arms,* 7; influence in Italian literature, 243

Hersey, John, *A Bell for Adano,* 12

Hitler, Adolph, 67, 70, 99, 107, 109, 110; treatment of Mussolini, 108; and precipitation of World War II, 112; and Italy in World War II, 113

Hull, Cordell, 10

Immigration, Italian, in U.S., 5–6; and quota laws, 8–9; immigrants' role in World War II, 10

Industrialists: support of Mussolini, 77; bargaining with Mussolini, 78; authority under Mussolini, 82–83; and World War II, 112; under Christian Democracy, 172–174; Confederation of Industrialists, 78, 79

Intellectuals: under Mussolini, 90–91, 101–102; in postwar minor parties, 164; in Communist party leadership, 167

International Brigade (in Spanish Civil War), 106

Istituto per la ricostruzione industriale (IRI program), 89, 173, 205, 212, 230, 232; as parastatal enterprise, 225–227

Italian Corps of Liberation, 124

Italian Somaliland, 149, 150

Italians: characteristics of, racial, 28–29, religious, 29–32, values, 32–36, social, 36–41; and sense of history, 42–43; attitudes of toward Fascism, 83, 93, toward World War II, 112–113

Italsider, 226

Italy: role in Western world, 3, in U.S., 4–6; geographical limitations of, 14–16, description of, 16; urban character of, 36–37. *See also* individual topics

James, Henry, 5
James, William, 73
Jefferson, Thomas, 4
Jemolo, Arturo Carlo, 163n; as social critic, 241
Jews, in Italy, 31–32
John XXIII, Pope, 213, 241; and "opening to the Left," 216, 217, 261; *Mater et Magistra,* 217; *Pacem in Terris,* 217; death, 256; *aggiornamento* policy of, 266

Khrushchev, Nikita, de-Stalinization program of, 207
King, Martin Luther, 242
"King's Plot" (against Mussolini), 116, 117–118
Kogan, Norman, 254n
Korean War, 157

La Critica, 101
La Malfa, Ugo, 225, 258; economic planning of, 232–233
La Pira, Giorgio, 249
Labor (Italian): effect of Bolshevik Revolution on, 58; and "occupation of the factories," 61; and goal of class dictatorship, 65–66; and suppression of rights under Mussolini, 78–79, 84, 88; restoration of rights, 119; in postwar era, 133, 135; support of Communism, 167; CGIL, 168–169; postwar corporatism of, 172–173
Lampedusa, Giuseppe Tomasi di, *The Leopard,* 246–247
Land reform: background, 186–190; progress of, 190–195; postwar, 199; Liberal opposition to Christian Democratic, 157–158. *See also* Agrarian tenure
Lateran Treaty, 95
Latifondi, 18, 19, 27, 188–189; reform of, 191, 231
Lauro, Achille, 210; monarchist leader, 199; and Popular Monarchist secession, 206; *qualunquista* (know-nothing) program, 206; appeal in South, 206; opportunism of, 207

League of Nations, economic sanctions against Italy, 81, 108
Leo XIII, Pope, 49; *Rerum Novarum,* 75
Leonardo da Vinci, *Last Supper,* 34
Leone, Giovanni, prime ministry, 256–257
Levi, Carlo, 27, 103; *The Watch,* 39, 140
Liberal party, 54, 207; opposition to Mussolini, 99; revival after Mussolini's fall, 119; decline, 142–143; inclusion in De Gasperi government, 146, departure from, 157–158; following of, 164–165; as mouthpiece of *Confindustria,* 206; gains in *1963* elections, 218
Libya, 149, 150
Liguria, 23
Literature: post-Fascist neorealism, 242–244; psychological, 246–247
Local government, under new constitution, 154–155
Lombardi, Riccardo, 256, 257, 258, 262
Lombardy, 22–23
London, 9
Longfellow, Henry Wadsworth, 5
Longo, Luigi, 106, 135

Madison, James, 4
Mafia, in Sicily, 27, 242
"Mafia" incident (in U.S.), 6
Magalone, Don Luigi, 39
Malagodi, Giovanni Francesco, 206
Malaria: prevalence of, 19–20; effect, 20; control in Sardinia, 186
Manzoni, Alessandro, *The Bethrothed,* 246
March on Rome, 72, 77, 78
Marshall Plan, 177, 226; aid to Italy, 146, 157, 176; Communist strikes against, 168; economic cooperation under, 252
Martino, Gaetano, coalition foreign minister, 253
Marx, Karl, 35, 59, 76; Marxian social criticism in Italy, 239–241
Mattei, Enrico, 254; director of ENI, 224–225
Matteotti, Giacomo, 99; murder of, 107

"Maximalism," as Socialist party policy, 60

Mazzei, Filippo, 4

Mazzini, Giuseppe, 24, 47

Mezzadria (share tenancy), 24, 187–188; in central Italy, 25; spread under Mussolini, 87; Charter of, 87; reform of, 190, 232

Middle class: description, 39–40; role in politics, 49–50, 51; urban, under Mussolini, 90–91; problems in postwar era, 180–181

Milan, 28, 37; headquarters for partisans, 131; population increase, 229

Milan Committee, see Committee of National Liberation for Northern Italy

Monarchists, 198, 201; alliance with Liberals, 143; gains in 1950's, 197, 199–200; factional splits among, 206; support of Segni, 212. See also Popular Monarchists

Monnet, Jean, 177

Monocolore, 202, 212, 256

Montall, Eugenio, 243

Montecatini, chemical monopoly, 173

Montgomery, General Sir Bernard Law, 124

Montini, Giovanni Battista, see Paul VI, Pope

Morante, Elsa, Arthur's Island, 247

Moravia, Alberto: influence on neorealistic literature, 243; The Time of Indifference, 247

Moro, Aldo: and "opening to the Left," 216, 218, 261; and urban development, 234; Center-Left coalition, 256, second try at, 257, handicaps of, 259, failure of, 259; personal characteristics, 259, 262; ideological task of, 267

Mosca, Gaetano, 45, 55, 100

Movimento sociale italiano (MSI): neofascist character, 165; inroads in De Gasperi ministry, 165; anti-Communist appeal, 165–166; disorganization in 1958, 206; Genoa conference, 214

Munich, 28

Mussolini, Arnaldo, 95

Mussolini, Benito: fascist leader, 8, 9, 24, 26, 27, 40, 43, 44, 55, 59, 81, 154, 155; U.S. attitudes toward, 10, 13; fall of, 11, 115–118, 122; anti-Semitic

legislation of, 32, 99; factors in support of, 35; rise to power, 64, 67–68, 72; Il Duce, 69–70; in Socialist party, 70–71; organization of Fasci di Combattimento, 71; and evolution of Fascism, 73–74, 83–88; pragmatism of, 73–74, 84; and corporatism, 74, 76–79; social and economic policies, 84–92, 189; and reconciliation with papacy, 93–97; opposition to Populari, 94, to Catholic Action, 98; author of The Cardinal's Mistress, 95; opposition to, 99–107; Four-Power Pact proposal, 107–108; treatment by Hitler, 108; annexation of Albania, 108; entry into World War II, 109, 112; Memoirs, 110; decline of, 108–111; neo-Fascist Republic, 128–129, 131; death, 132; and emigration restrictions, 185; Acerbo Law, 197

Naples, 11; role in Italian life, 37

Naples, Kingdom of, 36, 48

National Confederation, 78

National Council of Corporations, 80

Nationalist party: formation, 56, 117; merger with Fascist, 68

Nationalization, of electrical industry, 216

Nazi-Soviet pact, 107, 108

Nazism, compared to Italian Fascism, 110

Nenni, Pietro: leader of Socialists, 103, 105, 139, 145, 169–170, 199, 218, 256, 257, 262; "Operation Nenni," 200; and post-de-Stalinization opportunism, 208–209, 210; "autonomous" stand of, 215

Neo-Fascism, 144–145, 198; neo-Fascist Republic, 128–129, 131; De Gasperi's triumph over, 147; in opposition to Christian Democracy, 163; Movimento sociale italiano (MSI), 165–166, appeal of, 182; gains in 1950's, 197, 199; and Tambroni "adventure," 213. See also Uomo qualunque

Neo-Fascist Republic, 128–129, 131, 166

Nervi, Pier Luigi, 236

New Orleans, "Mafia" incident, 6

Nietzsche, Friedrich, 73

Nitti, Francesco Saverio, 63, 103, 146

Non expedit, 49
Non uccidere (movie), banning of, 249–250
Northern Italy: economic expansion in, 221, 223; population shift to, 229–230; Communist gains in, 230, strength in, 263–264

Olivetti company, 226
Olschki, Leonardo, quoted, 13, 34
"Opening to the Left": in Christian Democracy, 211, 213, 215–218, 256, 266; and economic planning, 233; and urban planning, 234; and education, 234–235; and Moro ministry, 257–259
Orlando, Vittorio Emanuele, 94, 140; plot against Mussolini, 116
Osservatore Romano, censure of Fanfani, 213

Pacciardi, Randolfo, 106, 158
Palazzo Chigi agreement, 78
Palazzo Vidoni pact, 78, 79
Palermo, 27
Parastatal enterprise, 222, 223–227; ENI, 224–225; IRI, 225–227
Pareto, Vilfredo, 55, 73
Paris, 9
Parliamentary regime, of Italy, 50–55; *trasformismo* in, 51–52
Parri, Ferruccio, 103, 144, 198; government of, 135–140, 142, 213
Partisans, 134, 175; anti-neo-Fascist activity, 129–132; and Allied take-over, 137
Partito Socialista Italiana di Unità Proletaria (PSIUP), secession from Socialist party, 263
Paul VI, Pope, 256; *aggiornamento* policy, 266
Pavese, Cesare, 243
Peace Conference (Versailles), 7, 94; effect in Italy, 8, 57
Peace Treaty (*1947*), 148–152; punitive quality of, 148
Peasants: role in Italy, 16, 37–38; typical life of, 20–21; poverty of, 21; Southern, 37, 38–39, 48; under Mussolini, 84–88; support of Communism, 169; agitation in Sila, 191, 192. *See also* Agrarian tenure; Land reform; *Latifondi; Mezzadria*

Pella, Giuseppe, 212, 256; prime ministry, 201, 202, 203; nationalistic foreign policy of, 253
Pellagra, disappearance of, 20
"People's bloc," 147, 148, 169
Petrarch, 5
Piedmont, 22–23, 54; as nucleus for unification of Italy, 46–47, 48
Pirelli, rubber monopoly, 173
Pisa, 15
Pius IX, Pope, 48–49
Pius X, Pope, 49
Pius XI, Pope: and Church-state reconciliation, 94; and defense of Catholic Action, 98; opposition to Fascism, 98–99
Pius XII, Pope, 99, 213
Politics (Italian): effect of unification on, 49–50; development of parliamentary, 50–55
Po valley, 15, 17, 23
Pontine plain, reclamation of, 26, 86
Popular Front, 265–266
Popular Monarchists: formation, 206; appeal to South, 206; failure in *1950* elections, 210
Popular party, see *Popolari*
Popolari, 68, 72; Popular party, 59, 61, 98; and failure of democracy, 61–62; opposition to Mussolini, 94, 99, 102; Pius XI's disavowal of, 94; wartime revival as Christian Democrats, 116, 141; pre-Fascist reformism, 159
Population (Italian): homogeneity of, 28; racial diversity in, 28–29; language of, 29; religions of, 29–32; pressures, 183–186, 194; effects of emigration, 183–186; shifts, 226–230
Poujade, Pierre, 206
Pound, Ezra, 9
Poverty, in Southern Italy, 21
Pratolini, Vasco, *A Tale of Poor Lovers,* 244
President (of Italy), functions, 152
Proportional representation, 62
Protestantism, Italian, 31

Qualunquista (know-nothing) program, 206
Quasimodo, Salvatore, 243
Quebec Conference of *1943,* 123

Radical party, 54
Ravagli, Giovanni, quoted, 179
Renaissance, 43
Republic of Salò, *see* Neo-Fascist Republic
Republicans (Italian), 53, 119, 207; opposition to Mussolini, 99; in *1946* elections, 144; inclusion in De Gasperi government, 147; anti-clericalism, 158; following, 165; in Center coalition, 197, 199; in Center-Left coalition, 256, 257
Reynaud, Paul, 211
Rienzo, Cola di, 43
Risorgimento, 4, 44, 67, 104
Rocco, Alfredo, 72
Romagna, the, political traditions of, 24
Rome, 4, 9, 11, 13, 17; historical development, 37, 42–43; liberation of, 126; population increase, 229
Rome-Berlin Axis, establishment of, 108
Rome Committee of Liberation, 126
Roncalli, Angelo Giuseppe, *see* John XXIII, Pope
Roosevelt, President Franklin Delano, 265; quoted, 10; and Italian armistice, 121; and Quebec conference, 123
Rosenstock-Franck, Louis, 75
Rosselli, Carolo, 125, 135; in *confino*, 103–104; in Spanish Civil War, 106; liberal socialism of, 104; organization of *Giustizia e Libertà*, 104; death, 106–107
Rossellini, Roberto (director), *Open City* and *Paisà*, 245, *General della Rovere*, 247
Rossi, Angelo, 61n
Rossi, Ernesto, 180n
Rossi-Doria, Manlio, 194n

St. Francis of Assisi, 30
Salerno, American landings at, 121, 124
Salomone, A. William, 55n
Salvemini, Gaetano, 55, 75
Sansone, Mario, quoted, 237
Santayana, George, 9
Saraceno, Pasquale, economic planning of, 232–233
Saragat, Giuseppe, 103, 200, 210, 211, 218; leadership of Social Democrats, 145, 208–209; prime ministry, 260
Sardinia, 16, 28, 186
Savoy, House of, 47, 152

Savoy-Piedmont, 46
Scelba, Mario: as Minister of Interior, 145, 146, 161; representative of Christian Democratic Center, 160, Right, 261; prime ministry, 202, 203
Schmidt, Carl T., 75
Segni, Antonio, 190, 202; first ministry, 203–205; establishment of Constitutional Court during, 204, economic policies in, 204, 220, 223; second ministry, 212–213; president of Republic, 260
Senate (Italian), 147; under new constitution, 153
Sereni, Emilio, 25n
Sforza, Count Carlo, 103, 158; anti-Fascist spokesman, 125; in Bonomi government, 126; unacceptable to British, 127, 142; in De Gasperi government, 146; shaper of European foreign policy, 251–253; and Franco-Italian customs union, 252
Sicily, 16, 29, 37, 42; distinct character of, 27; Dolci's leadership in, 241–242
Sila, peasant agitation at, 191, 192
Silone, Ignazio, *Fontamara*, 26
Six-party alliance, 119, 136
Social Democrats, 148, 200, 207; splinter from Socialist party, 145, 170; inclusion in De Gasperi government, 147; departure from, 158; lack of appeal, 165; in Center coalition, 197, 199; Nenni's appeals to, 208–209; in Fanfani government, 211, 216; gains in *1963* elections, 218; in Center-Left coalition, 256, 257
Social problems (postwar era): tax evasions, 178–179; overstaffed bureaucracy, 179–180; standard of living, 181; unemployment, 183; population pressure, 183–190, shifts, 229–230; land tenure, 186–190, reform, 190–195; housing, 229
Socialist party, 72, 116, 119, 135, 138, 198; factional character, 35; early organization, 53, 54; and World War I, 58; and collapse of democracy, 59–63; "Maximalism," 60; Mussolini in, 70–71; expulsion of syndicalists, 76–77; opposition to Mussolini, 99, 105, 115; coalition with Communists, 106, 107; absence in Bonomi government,

127; alignment with Communists, 138–139, 169–170; failure of "People's Bloc," 148; in *1946* elections, 144; ineffectiveness in De Gasperi government, 145; secession of Social Democrats, 145; left-wing gains in *1953* elections, 199, in *1958*, 210–211; effects of de-Stalinization, 208; shift from Communist alliance, 215, 216; losses in *1963* elections, 218; foreign policy, 255; in Moro ministry, 257–259; problems in working with Christian Democracy, 260; outdated qualities of, 262; PSIUP secession, 263; recent characteristics and future role, 266–267

Sorel, Georges, 73

South Tyrol, 57

Southern Italy: geography, 18–21, 26–27; population, 29, 39, shift to North, 229; history, 45–46; effect of unification, 46, 47–48; elections in, 52; postarmistice government, 124; support of monarchy, 143; Communism in, 169; *latifondi* in, 188–189; land reform in, 191–195; *Cassa per il Mezzogiorno* (Southern Italy Fund), 193; during Vanoni Plan, 221; industrialization efforts, 221–222, of IRI, 226–227

Soviet Union: claims in *1947* Peace Treaty, 148; support of Yugoslavian claims, 150

Spain, 254

Spanish Civil War, 99, 106, 108, 167

Stalin, Joseph, 70; effects of de-Stalinization, 207–208

Statuto (Piedmontese constitution), 47, 50, 68; similarities in postwar constitution, 152

Stralcio, 192

Sturzo, Don Luigi, 61, 102, 103, 160; reform leadership of, 159

Sullam, Victor B., 190n

Suez Canal, effect on Italy, 15

"Swindle Law," 197–198, 209, 210

Syndicalism, as source for corporate state, 76–77

Tambroni "adventure," 211, 213–214

Tambroni, Fernando, 256; prime minister, 213; neo-fascist support, 213–214

Tax reforms, postwar, 178–179

Tito, Josip Broz: demands for Trieste, 150; break with Cominform, 151–152

To Live in Peace (movie), 12

Togliatti, Palmiro: Communist leader, 126, 137–138, 139, 264; as rival of De Gasperi, 141; and tripartite ministry, 146; shooting of, 157; leadership of, 167; "re-Stalinization" program, 207–208; views of cultural tradition, 237

Trade unions: support of Communism, 167–169; corporatism of, 172; economic position in postwar era, 182–183. *See also* Labor (Italian)

Trasformismo: era of, 51–52, 201, 212; discouragement of in new constitution, 154

Treaty of London, 58

Treaty of Rome (*1957*), 222

Trentino, 62

Trieste, 57, 165, 253; establishment of Free Territory of, 150–151; problems of, 151–152

Tripolitania, Italian seizure of, 6, 56

Truman doctrine, 148

Tunisia, 150

Turati, Filippo, 53, 59, 60, 61, 103, 105

Turin, 178; as Communist stronghold, 166; population increase in, 229

Turkey, 6

Tuscany, 25

Umberto, Prince, 126; "King of the May," 143

Umbria, 25

Ungaretti, Giuseppe, 243

Unification of Italy: role of Piedmont, 46–48; effect on South, 46, 47–48; and Catholic Church, 48–49; effect on Italian politics, 49–50

Unions, absorption of into Fascism, 78

Unità Popolare, see "Autonomist" list

United Nations, General Assembly disposition of Italian colonies, 149–150

United States: American conception of Italy, 3–6, 9, 11; "Mafia" incident, 6, 33; and Italian immigrants, 5–6, quota laws for, 8–9, 184, 186; and

World War II, 9–13; and Italian armistice, 120–123; support of De Gasperi, 145; Italian dependence upon, 157; in *1953* elections, 198; and Italian foreign policy, 255; predominance in Italian affairs, 265–266; future relationship with Italy, 268. *See also* Americans

Uomo qualunque (Common Man Front), 139–140, 143, 165; in *1946* elections, 144; weakening of, 147

Valiani, Leo, 142n
Vanoni, Ezio, 220
Vanoni Plan, 204; goals, 220–221; effect on South, 221
Vecchietti, Tullio, 263
Venetia, 23
Venice, 9, 15, 23, 44
Verdi, Giuseppe, 34
Vichy government, 113
Vico, Giambattista, 45
Victor Emmanuel II, King, 50, 100, 143; weakness of, 110, 111; and wartime plot against Mussolini, 116, 117–118; and "Forty-Five Days," 119; and establishment of royal government of Southern Italy, 124; demand for abdication, 125–126

Vigo, Colonel Francesco, 4
Vittorini, Elio, 243; *In Sicily,* 244
Vöchting, Friedrich, quoted, 18

Wilson, President Woodrow, and Versailles Treaty, 7, 57
"Wind of the North," 134–137
World War I, 5, 67; effect on Italian emigration to U.S., 6–7; and U.S.-Italian alliance, 7; Italian entry into, 56–57
World War II, 44, 107; role of U.S. Italian immigrants, 10; and Americans in Italy, 11–13; Italy's entry into, 108, 112; apathy of Italians in, 112–113, 123; humiliation of Italians in, 114–115; change of sides, 120–123; Italian privations during, 174

Yugoslavia, 7; reparations claims of, 148; border disputes with Italy, 149–152

Zoli, Adoni, 202, 212; caretaker government of, 205